Hubristic Leadership

Sara Miller McCune founded SAGE Publishing in 1965 to support the dissemination of usable knowledge and educate a global community. SAGE publishes more than 1000 journals and over 800 new books each year, spanning a wide range of subject areas. Our growing selection of library products includes archives, data, case studies and video. SAGE remains majority owned by our founder and after her lifetime will become owned by a charitable trust that secures the company's continued independence.

Los Angeles | London | New Delhi | Singapore | Washington DC | Melbourne

Eugene Sadler-Smith

Hubristic
Leadership

With a Foreword by
Lord David Owen

⑤SAGE

Los Angeles | London | New Delhi
Singapore | Washington DC | Melbourne

Los Angeles | London | New Delhi
Singapore | Washington DC | Melbourne

SAGE Publications Ltd
1 Oliver's Yard
55 City Road
London EC1Y 1SP

SAGE Publications Inc.
2455 Teller Road
Thousand Oaks, California 91320

SAGE Publications India Pvt Ltd
B 1/I 1 Mohan Cooperative Industrial Area
Mathura Road
New Delhi 110 044

SAGE Publications Asia-Pacific Pte Ltd
3 Church Street
#10-04 Samsung Hub
Singapore 049483

Editor: Kirsty Smy
Editorial assistant: Jasleen Kaur
Production editor: Sarah Cooke
Copyeditor: Sharon Cawood
Proofreader: Fabienne Pedroletti-Gray
Indexer: Martin Hargreaves
Marketing manager: Alison Borg
Cover design: Francis Kenney
Typeset by: C&M Digitals (P) Ltd, Chennai, India
Printed in the UK

Library of Congress Control Number: 2018941562

British Library Cataloguing in Publication data

A catalogue record for this book is available from the British Library

ISBN 978-1-5264-3116-5
ISBN 978-1-5264-3117-2 (pbk)

At SAGE we take sustainability seriously. Most of our products are printed in the UK using responsibly sourced papers and boards. When we print overseas we ensure sustainable papers are used as measured by the PREPS grading system. We undertake an annual audit to monitor our sustainability.

For Reginald William Sadler-Smith (born: Port Stanley, Falkland Islands, 13th March 1930; died: Halton, Cheshire, 22nd September 2017)

'The only wisdom we can hope to acquire is the wisdom of humility'.

T.S Eliot, Four Quarters, Part II: East Coker

CONTENTS

About the Author   viii

Acknowledgements   ix

Foreword   x

Preface: Introduction and Overview   xi

1   In Perspective   1

2   Mythic and Historical Approaches   19

3   Biological and Neuroscientific Approaches   36

4   The Hubris Syndrome Approach   50

5   A Behavioural Approach   70

6   An Organizational Approach   90

7   A Relational Approach   110

8   Paradox and Processual Approaches   135

9   Avoidance Approaches   156

References   174

Index   198

ABOUT THE AUTHOR

Professor Eugene Sadler-Smith, BSc, PhD, FCIPD, FRSA, FAcSS is Professor of Organizational Behaviour, Surrey Business School, University of Surrey, UK. His main research interests are hubris (in leadership) and intuition (in organizational decision making). His work has been published in international peer-reviewed journals, such as *Academy of Management Executive, Academy of Management Learning and Education, Academy of Management Perspectives, British Journal of Management, British Journal of Psychology, British Journal of Educational Psychology, Business Ethics Quarterly, Creativity Research Journal, Human Relations, International Journal of Management Reviews, Journal of Occupational & Organizational Psychology, Leadership, Journal of Organizational Behaviour, Long Range Planning, Management Learning, Organization Studies, Organizational Dynamics, Organizational Research Methods, Strategic Entrepreneurship Journal,* etc., and professional journals, such as *People Management* and *Work*. His research has featured in *The Times* as well as on BBC Radio 4 and the Insight TV channel *Secrets of the Brain*. He is the author of several books including *Inside Intuition* (Routledge, 2008) and *The Intuitive Mind* (John Wiley & Sons, 2010, shortlisted for CMI Management Book of the Year in 2011, published in four foreign language editions – Japanese, Korean, Portuguese, Russian). He has worked with organizations such as AcademiWales, CIPD, *Forbes* (Korea), Home Office, ICSA, Medact, Metropolitan Police, Surrey Police, Scottish Government, Tesco, The Mind Gym, etc. He was educated at Wade Deacon Grammar School for Boys in Widnes, has a BSc in geography from the University of Leeds and a PhD from the University of Birmingham. Before becoming an academic he worked for British Gas plc from 1987 to 1994.

ACKNOWLEDGEMENTS

I first became interested in hubris through my colleague Dr Graham Robinson; he has not only catalysed my interest in the topic but also been instrumental in shaping my thinking about it. Graham and I have had the privilege of co-supervising the doctoral work of Vita Akstinaite and Tim Wray at Surrey Business School – their intellectual abilities, energy, vitality, curiosity and passion has invigorated and challenged my understanding of hubris.

My sincere thanks also go to: colleagues and organizations with whom it has been my pleasure to share an interest in understanding hubristic leadership and exploring how to contain its potentially destructive consequences, including (but not confined to) Marc Atherton, Sally Bibb, Professor Guy Claxton, Dr Rosemary Field, Professor Peter Garrard, Arie de Geus, John Harris, Heiner Langhein, Geoff Marlow, Bill Tate, Jonathan Wilson, Chris Wiscarson; Professor Nick Bouras of the Daedalus Trust Advisory Group; Professor Richard Roll for kindly reading and commenting on a relevant portion of Chapter 5; the staff and delegates of the AcademiWales winter and summer schools; delegates at the Chartered Institute of Personnel and Development (CIPD) and Institute of Company Secretaries and Administrators (ICSA) events and conferences where I had the privilege to present and work through my ideas; the Maudsley Philosophy Group; *Forbes* Korea for facilitating a meeting of minds at their 'Hubris Forum' in Seoul in the Summer of 2018; and last but far from least, the staff at SAGE, especially Kirsty Smy, Delia Martínez Alfonso, Jasleen Kaur, and Sarah Cooke. I am also very grateful to John I. Taylor, Zenith Electronics LLC., for very helpful comments on relevant sections of Chapter 8.

The Daedalus Trust, Chaired by Lord Owen, has been instrumental in raising hubris awareness in the UK and beyond (www.daedalustrust.com); it has been an honour and a privilege to be involved in its activities. Lord Owen, the Daedalus Trust and Maggie Smart have been unstinting in their support for 'The Hubris Project' at Surrey Business School, and for this I express my most sincere gratitude and appreciation.

Eugene Sadler-Smith, Surrey, September 2018

FOREWORD BY THE
RT HON LORD OWEN CH FRCP

This is a thoughtful yet practical book, a combination which is hard to achieve. The author of *Hubristic Leadership* has a particular quality which makes this possible, he is a rooted individual, firmly moored into personal research and teaching about business. He examines hubris in the round. Its linkage to historical myths, biology, neuroscience and behavior, its impact on organizations, human relations and, above all, what can be done to avoid, curb, contain and control hubris. As he writes it is early days for hubristic leadership research, there is no definitive view on it and any claim to exclusive intellectual authority could be of itself an act of hubris. The search for celebrity status is singled out as a cradle of over-confidence that fans the flames of hubristic leadership. The estimate that in the UK more than half of new business start-ups fail to survive for longer than five years and that a similar figure is found in the US, yet entrepreneurs remain boldly optimistic, seems to be because they trust their abilities first and assume successful outcomes will follow – a hubristic flaw which is not confined to entrepreneurs, leaders in general are equally susceptible. The author ends with the assertion: "Hubris is potent and perilous." He is right and therefore to understand its characteristics, causes and consequences is a duty for anyone in or contemplating a career in business.

September 2018

PREFACE: INTRODUCTION AND OVERVIEW

WISE WARNING

'It is an ancient doctrine that tragedy comes of hubris. In our age, mankind collectively has given itself over to a degree of hubris surpassing everything known in former ages.' (Bertrand Russell, *Portraits from Memory and Other Essays*, 1956)

HUBRIS

Hubris can cause destructive, sometimes tragic, things to happen. This is because hubrists arrive at false ideas about their capabilities. They become deluded by inflated self-evaluation, over-estimate what can go right, under-estimate what can go wrong, and are arrogant and contemptuous towards the advice and criticism of others. Hubristic leadership is fuelled by prior successes and praise, it flourishes where followers collude, conform and comply, and where effective restraining forces and preventive structures are lacking. It also emerges out of complex interactions between people, processes, systems and structures that can cause strengths to morph into weaknesses and bring about unintended negative consequences. Hubristic leadership in business and politics invites nemesis. With hindsight, the pattern of rise and fall often appears self-evident. A question which is sometimes asked – as did Her Majesty the Queen when she visited the London School of Economics just after the financial crash and enquired about the experts' lack of foresight – is why doesn't anyone see it coming?[1] Hubris can lead to bad things happening not because there is a straightforward, linear cause-and-effect relationship between hubris and nemesis, rather hubristic leaders create willingly the conditions out of which unintended negative outcomes can and do emerge.

GOOD LEADERSHIP?

If hubristic leadership is bad leadership, then what does good leadership look like? Here are some pointers and recommendations: (1) have a positive attitude: 'whatever you do have a "lean forward" mindset; don't be afraid to compete; don't be afraid to make a decision. And whatever you do, don't be a bystander. Whatever it is – try. If you lose, pick yourself up, try again and move on'; (2) know what you are doing: 'whatever you do, know your field. Information is knowledge. Knowledge is confidence. And confidence is power. I would add that many times you have to be lucky, but luck, when combined with preparation, only increases your chances for success'; (3) believe in teamwork: 'teamwork is critical for many endeavors. It is not just about you. Successful organizations rely not on stars but on a team and how the team comes together. So, support your family and colleagues. They are your team'; (4) reward good work: 'pay fairly and pay them in stock, so everyone shares in the upside together and expect them to think, act and behave like owners because owners protect the culture'; (5) do the right thing: 'integrity: the good guys do, in fact, win. You grew up in an environment with WorldCom, Tyco and Enron [business scandals]. The world today is desperate for people with integrity. Integrity and quality people carry the day. The key is to always fall back on what's right. When in doubt, do the right thing. This always pays off in the end'.[2] This is sound advice; however readers may be surprised to learn that these are extracts from the Commencement Address given to students by Richard J. Fuld CEO of Lehman Brothers at his alma mater, the University of Colorado Boulder in spring 2006. On 15 September 2008, Lehman Brothers filed for Chapter 11 Bankruptcy. At Lehman Brothers' zenith, Fuld was lauded as a hero; at its nadir he was condemned as a villain.

RICHARD FULD'S RISE

After a false start in a career with the US Air Force, Fuld 'stumbled into international business which got [him] going on a life-long career with Lehman Brothers'[3] where he started out as a trader in 1969. He obtained an MBA from Stern School of Business in 1973. He soon became proficient in fixed-income trading and rose rapidly to become supervisor of both the fixed-income and the equities divisions by the age of 37. Fuld was a 'very smart guy' and one of Wall Street's supreme traders; he was nicknamed the 'Gorilla' and had a toughness that fitted in well with Lehman Brothers' 'cut-throat' culture.[4]

By 1994 Fuld had become CEO, and by 1996 Lehman Brothers' return on equity was up to 14 per cent from a 3 per cent low just after its spin-off from American Express in 1994. He steered the business through the 1997 Asian financial crisis. With the 2003 acquisition of the money management firm Neuberger Berman in a $2.63 billion deal, Fuld had realized his dream of diversifying out of the bond market, putting Lehman Brothers on an equal footing with Morgan Stanley, Merrill Lynch and Goldman Sachs. Fuld's leadership was instrumental in transforming the company. By 2007 Fuld's remuneration package had reached over $22 million. He was named number one CEO in the Brokers and Asset Managers category by *Institutional Investor* magazine, was ranked by *Barron's* amongst the top 30 CEOS, and was, in the words of Fox Business correspondent Charlie Gasparino, nothing less than 'Wall Street Royalty'.[5]

RICHARD FULD'S DEMISE

Lehman Brothers' Achilles heel was its $40 billion, highly illiquid, proprietary real estate business. When the markets began to wobble and the sub-prime crisis materialized, it hit Lehman Brothers badly. The firm needed to shed assets in order to survive. Fuld refused to sell.[6] He was a 'Lehman Lifer' and his persona and identity were wrapped up in a business he had worked in for two decades and led for 14 years. He stuck by Lehman Brothers through thick and thin. He was there in 1969 when Robert Lehman himself passed away, when it merged with Kuhn, Loeb & Co. in 1977, when it was acquired by American Express in 1984 and then spun off by them in 1994, and there for 9/11 and its aftermath. A sale of Lehman Brothers would have taken a large chunk out of a gargantuan but brittle ego: 'As long as I am alive, this firm will never be sold', he said in late 2007, the *Wall Street Journal* reported, 'and if it is sold after I die, I will reach back from the grave and prevent it'.[7] Fuld's hubris allowed his unshakeable loyalty to the firm to spill over into the weaknesses of over-protectiveness and rigid intransigence.

As a person, Fuld was said by many to be aloof, distant and intimidating. His leadership style was a cocktail of indisputable capability and competence mixed with a hard-edged stiffness and bluntness. His brain power was such that he was nicknamed 'The Digital Mind Trader'. In his interactions with staff, a monosyllabic response was the preferred idiom. When times were bad, he said they would get better and when times were good he said the same.[8] He melded his energy, optimism and ambition with aggression, and if anyone was seen to be trying to hurt Lehman Brothers he would react with bloodthirsty rhetoric: 'I'm soft, I'm loveable. But what I really wanna do is I wanna reach in, rip out their [short sellers'] heart and eat it before they die.'[9] Fuld's pride in Lehmans was such that his capabilities and self-confidence spilled over into conceit and over-confidence.

Experts and commentators at the Congressional hearing into the firm's collapse flagged up flawed governance and culture at Lehman Brothers, a situation that was exacerbated by a weak regulatory framework. According to Ben Bernanke, Chairman of the Federal Reserve Bank, Lehman Brothers was able to operate without any robust consolidated supervision and in a situation where no government agency had sufficient authority to rein them in and prevent dangers to the wider financial system.[10] Others at the hearing voiced concerns about the Lehman Brothers' board which was 'too old, had served too long, was too out of touch with massive changes in the industry, had too little of their own net worth at risk, and was too compromised for rigorous independent oversight'.[11] The Congressional hearing also picked up on a flawed strategy. Lehman Brothers was overly aggressive and over-confident in using leverage and debt to finance high-stakes investments. It found itself in this position not by accident but as a result of a high-risk gamble, intentionally and volitionally entered into by its senior leadership team.[12] Lehman Brothers was operating in a weakly regulated environment in an inherently volatile business context and had become organizationally hubristic.

After the crash, Fuld appears to have been in denial, unable to accept that what had happened was actually a 'bankruptcy'. In Fuld's narrative, Lehman Brothers suffered from nothing more than a short-term liquidity freeze and if the Secretary of the Treasury, Hank Paulson, had not chosen to pick 'winners' and 'losers' and, in picking a winner, had bailed out Goldman Sachs and, in picking a loser, let Lehman Brothers go under, he thought they (Lehmans) would still be in business.[13] At the congressional hearing, Fuld blamed the news media, short sellers, the government and the 'run on the bank', but he never really blamed himself.[14] Even if others were at all culpable, in the assessment of many it was Fuld who played the principal part in creating the conditions that invited nemesis.[15] The ultimate hallmark of hubris is a denial of responsibility for what went wrong. For all that, Fuld was not impervious to public perception – shortly after the crisis at a rare social appearance with fellow bankers, he self-mockingly referred to himself as 'the most hated man in America'.[16] Fuld's hubristic rise and demise were complete.

UNDERSTANDING HUBRIS

This book is about understanding the characteristics and causes of hubristic leadership and how to avoid its potentially destructive, and sometimes catastrophic, consequences. It is about trying to understand what went wrong in Lehman Brothers, at Long Term Capital Management, at Royal Bank of Scotland (RBS) and Halifax Bank of Scotland (HBOS), in Deepwater Horizon, in the Iraq invasion in 2003, and many others. The book begins by putting hubristic leadership in perspective (Chapter 1) and then explores hubristic leadership from various angles (Chapters 2–9) (Figure 0.1).

The book's precepts are that it is early days for hubristic leadership research, there is no definitive view on it, and any claim to exclusive intellectual authority on the part of any one academic discipline might be seen as an act of hubris in itself, hence the need for multiple approaches. The main thrust of the book is that the pattern of hubris-inviting-nemesis is archetypal in human affairs and that hubristic leadership appears subtly different depending

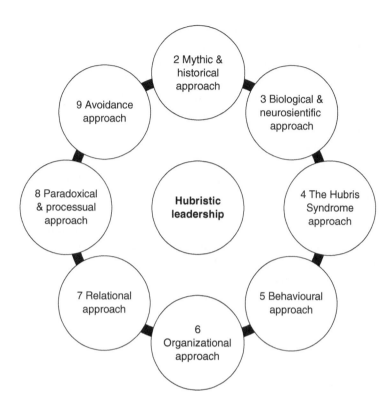

Figure 0.1   Overview of the book: approaches to the study of hubristic leadership

on the lens through which it is viewed. Each of the various approaches offers different insights into what is a perennial and pervasive phenomenon and process. The book's practical concern is how to stop hubris from happening in the first place.

NOTES

1. www.ft.com/content/50007754-ca35-11dd-93e5-000077b07658 (Accessed 12 March 2018).
2. www.colorado.edu/commencement/2006/05/12/richard-fuld-spring-2006 (Accessed 14 April 2016).
3. www.colorado.edu/commencement/2006/02/19/richard-fuld-spring-2006   (Accessed 12 March 2018).
4. www.referenceforbusiness.com/biography/F-L/Fuld-Richard-S-Jr-1946.html (Accessed 15 April 2016).
5. www.youtube.com/watch?v=ShEnNmDShQ8 (Accessed 19 April 2016).
6. www.bloomberg.com/news/articles/2013-09-12/where-is-dick-fuld-now-finding-lehman-brothers-last-ceo (Accessed 17 April 2016).

7. www.bloomberg.com/news/articles/2013-09-12/where-is-dick-fuld-now-finding-lehman-brothers-last-ceo (Accessed 17 April 2016).

8. www.thisismoney.co.uk/money/markets/article-1623226/Profile-Lehman-Bros-boss-Richard-Fuld.html#ixzz43d8Kfl4B (Accessed 17 April 2016).

9. www.youtube.com/watch?v=GZCmWkQuyPc (Accessed 19 April 2016).

10. www.federalreserve.gov/newsevents/testimony/bernanke20100420a.htm (Accessed 12 March 2018).

11. http://abcnews.go.com/Blotter/story?id=5965360&page=1 (Accessed 19 April 2016).

12. http://abcnews.go.com/Blotter/story?id=5965360&page=1 (Accessed 19 April 2016).

13. www.youtube.com/watch?v=ShEnNmDShQ8 (Accessed 19 April 2016).

14. www.nytimes.com/2008/10/07/business/economy/07lehman.html (Accessed 12 March 2018).

15. www.reuters.com/article/us-lehman-backstory/lehman-ceo-fulds-hubris-contributed-to-meltdown-idUSN1341059120080914; https://www.ft.com/content/6168c7f6-828e-11dd-a019-000077b07658 (Accessed 12 March 2018).

16. www.bloomberg.com/news/articles/2013-09-12/where-is-dick-fuld-now-finding-lehman-brothers-last-ceo (Accessed 15 April 2016).

1

IN PERSPECTIVE

WISE WARNING

'Pride goeth before destruction, and a haughty spirit before a fall.' (Book of Proverbs 16:18, King James Version)

Introduction

In recent times, hubris has hardly been out of the headlines. In politics, Donald Trump has become a live, international case study of hubris's role in political leadership ever since his 45-minute presidential candidature speech in 2016 when he made over 250 self-aggrandizing references, including: 'I'm really rich ... I'm proud of my net worth ... I've done an amazing job ... I beat China all the time – all the time'.[1] In business, the new boss of the taxi-hiring firm Uber, Dara Khosrowshahi, speaking at the World Economic Forum in Davos in 2017, blamed Uber's woes partly on the hubris of his predecessor, the firm's founder Travis Kalanick.[2] In 2018 hubris was implicated by a parliamentary report into the collapse of one of the UK's biggest construction company Carillion, a 'story of recklessness, hubris and greed'. There can be little doubt that hubris is a hazard.

BACKGROUND

But despite its relevance and importance in business and politics, when compared to well-established leadership topics such as ''charisma' and 'narcissism', hubris is still a relatively new and unfamiliar area in leadership and management research.[3] As such, its relationship to other, more well-established topics in leadership needs to be explored. 'Charismatic leadership' and 'narcissistic leadership' are two areas which are closely related to hubristic leadership. One feature that charismatic, narcissistic and hubristic leadership have in common is that they can all be connected, in different ways, to the 'darker' sides of leadership (Figure 1.1).

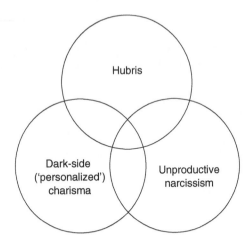

Figure 1.1 Hubris, unproductive narcissism and personalized charisma

Source: based on Padilla et al. (2007)

Leadership's dark side first came to prominence in the 1980s in Jay Conger's foundational *Organizational Dynamics* article where he stated 'Sometimes the dark side of leadership eclipses the bright side – to the detriment of both the leader and the organization' (Conger, 1990: 44). Subsequently, and especially given the dark side's destructive potential, management and leadership scholars have given it greater attention by looking at topics such as 'leadership derailers' (Hogan and Hogan, 2001), 'leadership pathologies' (Kets de Vries, 2003), 'the dark side of transformational leadership' (Tourish, 2013) and 'destructive leadership' (Schyns and Schilling, 2013). Table 1.1 summarizes the similarities and differences between charismatic, narcissistic and hubristic leadership.

Table 1.1 Attributes of charismatic, narcissistic and hubristic leadership

Charismatic Leadership	Narcissistic Leadership	Hubristic Leadership
Greek *khárisma*, meaning 'gift of grace' or 'favour'	Greek *narkissos*; Narcissus, a youth known for his beauty	Greek *hybris*, meaning 'pride, insolence, arrogance'
Idealized vision that is discrepant from status quo which s/he strives to change	Grandiose sense of self-importance	Inflated levels of self-belief and over-confidence
Likeable and honourable 'hero'	Preoccupied with fantasies of unlimited success or power	Strong conviction that they will be proven right and/or prevail
Worthy of identifying with and striving to imitate	Belief in their exceptionality	Overweening (inauthentic) pride

Charismatic Leadership	Narcissistic Leadership	Hubristic Leadership
Uses unconventional means to transcend existing order	Unreasonable sense of expectation and entitlement	Contempt for the advice and criticism of others
Strongly articulates future vision; strong motivation to lead	Exploitative in relationships	Fuelled by contextual stimuli (e.g. recent successes, media praise, celebrity status)
Power based on expertise, respect and admiration. Need for power may distinguish between personalized and socialized charismatic leadership	Lack of empathy; capable of hostility, envy and arrogance	Contingent on the acquisition of significant power; enabled by susceptibility of followers and/or failings of institutional or organizational constraints
Transforms followers to share and participate in the radical change s/he advocates	Fragility of self-esteem, need for inflated self-view to be constantly reinforced	Potentially destructive; causes leaders to over-reach themselves and invite unintended negative consequences
Relationship between leader and followers; enabled or enhanced by leader's personality	Trait-like dimension related positively to extraversion and openness to experience, and negatively to agreeableness	Akin to psychological 'state' brought on by combination of dispositional factors and contextual stimuli
'Intoxicant of followers'	'Intoxicated with self'	'Intoxicated by power and success'

Building on the distinctions offered in Table 1.1, this chapter will compare hubristic leadership with charismatic and narcissistic leadership – particularly their darker sides. Each section starts with a brief outline of charismatic and narcissistic leadership, followed by a discussion of its relationship to hubristic leadership. The chapter will conclude by positioning hubristic leadership as a type of destructive leadership.

CHARISMATIC LEADERSHIP AND HUBRIS

The origins of the study of charismatic leadership can be traced back to the work of the German sociologist Max Weber (1864–1920) who used 'charisma' (from the Greek χάρισμα, khárisma, meaning 'gift of grace' or 'favour') to refer to the authority exercised by a leader over others emanating from her or his exceptional sanctity, heroism or exemplary character (Eisenstadt, 1968; House et al., 1991). In taking up the idea of charisma in business management, Conger and Kanungo (1987: 641) singled out seven key attributes of charismatic leadership, although these vary somewhat between theories (Yukl, 1999; Table 1.2). The processes of charismatic leadership operate through various leader behaviours and motivational mechanisms (for example, expressing confidence in followers, maintenance of hope) which in turn affect followers' self-concept and motivations (for example, heightened self-esteem, social identification, self-expression) and are associated with positive effects on followers' commitment, self-sacrifice, organizational citizenship, etc. (Shamir et al., 1993).

Table 1.2 Attributes and behaviours of charismatic leaders (Conger and Kanungo, 1987)

Charismatic Leaders
Have an idealized vision that is discrepant from the status quo which they strive to change
Are likeable and honourable 'heroes'
Are worthy of identification with and imitation of
Use unconventional means to transcend the existing order
Articulate a future vision and have a strong motivation to lead
Exercise power based on expertise, respect and admiration
Help transform followers so that they are able to share and participate in the radical change they advocate

A general view is that charisma is not a personality trait or type, for example the related concept of 'transformational leadership' only appears to show weak relationships with extraversion (Bono and Judge, 2004). Rather, charismatic leadership is based on a relationship between leader and followers that is 'enabled or enhanced by the leader's personality' (Finkelstein et al., 2009: 71). Like charisma, hubris is likely affected by personality but it is not a personality type or trait as such. Charismatic leadership and hubris are related in several ways: (1) both charismatic leadership and hubris have a dark side; (2) hubris and charisma can co-exist; (3) charisma and hubris are not immutable; (4) charismatic and hubristic leadership are situational; (5) charisma and hubris are potentially destructive and reciprocal.

Charismatic Leadership and Hubris Have a Dark Side

Hubristic leadership is generally associated with undesirable behaviours and destructive outcomes, and it is therefore grouped together with other aspects of leadership's darker side (Tourish, 2013). Charismatic leadership, on the other hand, is paradoxical in the sense of a co-existence of opposites: charisma has both bright and dark sides, and in its darker manifestations it occupies similar space to hubristic leadership. For example, charismatic leadership can be maladaptive when charismatic leaders: (1) pursue personal objectives that fit with their vision at the expense of the interests of others; (2) over-identify with a corporate vision; (3) are manipulative in order to maintain control over their vision; (4) take recklessly over-confident decisions in pursuit of their vision (Shipman and Mumford, 2011).

Researchers have also distinguished between contrasting 'dark' and 'bright' types of charismatic leadership. 'Personalized charismatic leaders' tend to be self-aggrandizing, non-egalitarian and exploitive, whereas 'socialized charismatic leaders' are more collectively oriented, egalitarian and non-exploitive. The former is 'dark' and the latter is 'bright', and they are differentiated by a need for power, Machiavellianism, authoritarianism, self-esteem and locus of control (Bligh et al., 2007; House and Howell, 1992).

As an example of charisma's dark side, in the ENRON scandal much attention was focused on the company's toxic accounting practices, however the dysfunctional effects of the type of charismatic leadership exercised by former ENRON bosses Kenneth Lay (who died in 2006) and Jeffrey Skilling also played a significant role in the company's demise (Table 1.3).

Table 1.3 ENRON and the dark side of charisma (Tourish, 2013; Tourish and Vatcha, 2005)

Dark side of charismatic leadership: Lay and Skilling at ENRON
Having ridden on the crest of a wave (ironically it was lauded as America's 'Most Innovative Company' for six years running, 1995–2000[10]), ENRON collapsed infamously following an accounting scandal in the most spectacular pre-financial crisis business collapse.
Kenneth Lay (chairman) and Jeffery Skilling (CEO) – both of whom were jailed following the collapse for criminal charges including conspiracy, fraud, false statement and insider trading – led what has been described as an almost 'cultish' corporation.
The company made intense 'dramaturgical' effort designed to project an exaggerated and alluring spectacle, for example with allusions to Star Wars and Machiavellian imagery in the ENRON discourse to promote vision, power and achievement. Used as a means to try to convince employees that they belonged to a cause far greater than merely being part of a business or working for a living, and by working for ENRON they could enjoy a much more exalted existence than that of people working for lesser organizations.
At ENRON, leaders' power was taken for granted, employees were unable to offer significant or effective critical voice or resistance to corporate malpractice, the penalties for dissent were severe, whilst the benefits of conformity munificent; the primacy afforded to shareholder value allied to CEO power was the antithesis of a healthy corporate culture.

Hubris and personalized charismatic leadership both occupy the dark side of leadership and as such they have relationships to power; in the case of hubris this manifests as an 'intoxication with power' once it has been achieved, whereas in the case of personalized charisma it is more to do with a need for influence or power (House and Howell, 1992; Owen, 2011a).

Hubris and Charisma Can Co-Exist

Hubris and charisma are not mutually exclusive. The most extreme example of this was Adolf Hitler. According to Ian Kershaw, author of an extensive and authoritative two-volume biography of Hitler subtitled *1889–1936: Hubris* (Kershaw, 1998) and *1936–1945: Nemesis* (Kershaw, 2000), Hitler's power was extraordinary in that it was not derived primarily from position but from the willingness of others – his followers – to see charismatic qualities in him (Kershaw, 1998: xxvi). Hitler's 'charismatic politics of national salvation' (Kershaw, 2000: xxxvi) co-existed with his hubris. In Kershaw's view, Hitler's followers had instilled in him a sense of his own greatness since the early 1920s, which he willingly embraced and which fed his own overweening arrogance and egomania, such that he 'became the foremost believer in his own Führer cult' (Kershaw, 1998: 591). The tipping point between Hitler's hubris and the point where nemesis took over was reached, in Kershaw's estimation, by 1936. The Germany that had envisioned its future in his depraved charisma also 'had shared in his hubris, [and] had also to share in his nemesis' (Kershaw, 2000: 841).

Charisma and Hubris Are Malleable

Charisma is malleable, and as such 'can be gained or lost as conditions change' (Yukl, 1999: 298); likewise with hubris. In the Hubris Syndrome approach to the study of hubristic leadership (see Chapter 4), hubris has been described as an 'illness of position' as much as of the person. As an illness of position, hubris is therefore acquired. It is most often associated with the acquisition of significant power and after a period of sustained success. Hubris also appears to abate once power is lost (Owen and Davidson, 2009).

 The example of the former UK Prime Minister Tony Blair illustrates the transitory nature both of charisma and hubris. Blair's charisma as a political leader was never in doubt, and even amongst his Conservative opponents the majority had to admit that he had the charisma necessary to be a prime minister (Bennister, 2009; Radice, 2010).[4] On the downside, however, he is considered to have become hubristic during his term of office, probably around the time of his involvement in the NATO decision to bomb Kosovo in the 1999 Kosovo War. Things worsened when his hubris intensified around the time of the invasion of Iraq in 2003 (Daddow and Schnapper, 2013; Owen, 2006). Following the Iraq imbroglio and his premature departure from office, attributions to his leadership charisma diminished substantially, to the extent that in the eyes of some he had even attained 'pariah' status.[5] The diminution in his charisma was associated with decisions that resulted in a failure of leadership associated with hubris (Owen, 2008).

Charisma and Hubris Are Situational

When it comes to leadership of any type, context matters and charismatic and hubristic leadership are no exceptions to this (Conger and Kanungo, 1987; Shamir and Howell, 1999; Yukl, 1999). Charismatic leadership is more likely to emerge and be attributed to a leader when the environment is dynamic, uncertain or even critical and perilous, and especially when the challenges faced lend themselves to visionary or ideological inter- pretation (Bryman, 1992; Conger and Kanungo, 1998; Shamir et al., 1993). A corollary of this is that followers and the situation jointly contribute to the emergence of charismatic leadership (Klein and House, 1995; Klimoski, 2012). If a company is headed in the right direction in the right context then a charismatic leader can help it to get there quicker; likewise, if a company is headed in the wrong direction in the wrong context, charismatic leadership can help it to get there quicker too.[6]

In this regard, there are clear parallels with hubristic leadership. In terms of 'destructive leadership theory' (Padilla et al., 2007), hubristic leadership is more likely to emerge when there is a co-existence of a hubristic leader with collusive followers in a conducive context (a so-called 'toxic triangle'), as was the case, for example, in the invasion of Iraq: Bush was a hubristic leader (Owen, 2007), the neoconservatives in the administration (Cheney, Rumsfeld and Wolfowitz) colluded (Beinart, 2010), and 9/11 and the war on terror cre- ated a propitious set of circumstances for the invasion (Smith, 2016). In both charismatic and hubristic leadership, an uncertain and turbulent environment is conducive to their emergence because turbulence amplifies both the threats and the opportunities for each type of leadership to materialize (Yukl, 1999). In such circumstances, a charismatic sav- iour may be sought or a hurbist may be given free rein to do largely as he or she pleases.

Personalized (Dark-side) Charisma and Hubris Are Potentially Destructive and Reciprocal

The dangers of charismatic leadership lie partly in the seductive allure of the term 'charisma'; it is highly leader-centric and legitimizes the concentration of power (for good or ill) in the hands of an individual. The power accorded to charismatic leaders to 'transform' others, or the hubrist's intoxication with power, can result in destruc- tive consequences. Many destructive leaders have a personalized charismatic streak and hubristic inclinations which create the conditions for reckless decision making and invite negative outcomes (Bligh et al., 2007; Deluga, 1997; Padilla et al., 2007). Charisma and hubris contributed jointly to Richard Fuld's failed leadership. Likewise, the charismatic Jürgen Schrempp, as Chief Executive of Daimler, was the princi- pal hubrist behind its failed $36 billion acquisition of Chrysler in 1998.[7] As well as co-existing, charisma and hubris can reciprocate. Charismatic leadership can elicit blind devotion in followers, whilst the mindless adulation of a charismatic leader by followers can induce arrogance, hubris and reckless behaviour (Finkelstein et al., 2009).

NARCISSISTIC LEADERSHIP AND HUBRIS

The cultural origins of narcissism are traceable to Greek myth: the handsome youth Narcissus refused the romantic entreaties of the beautiful nymph Echo, because he deemed her undeserving of his love. Eventually he discovered, in his own reflection, *the* person who was worthy. In Ovid's re-telling of the myth, Narcissus arrived hot and exhausted from the hunt at a 'clear, un-muddied pool of silvery shimmering water'. Thirsty for the water, he started to drink but was overwhelmed by a vision of beauty; he gazed in amazement at his own reflection with its rippling golden curls 'like the locks of a god' and 'fell in love with an empty hope, a shadow mistaken for substance' (2004, *Metamorphóses*, Book 3, line 421).

As with so many of Ovid's morality tales, the outcome for the protagonist was not good. Narcissus' tragic and impossible-to-fulfil self-obsession led to his demise and transformation into the eponymous flower. Like many myths, it is a cautionary tale; in this case, it is a warning against the perils of all-consuming self-love and self-obsession within which lurk the seeds of self-destruction. The myth is as relevant today as it was two millennia ago. Social media offers the modern equivalent of Narcissus's clear, un-muddied pool and is the perfect mirror in which narcissists of all stripes and persuasions in personal, professional and political life can bask in the glory of their reflected self-image as exemplified by Donald Trump's Tweets both before and during his time as president of the United States (Table 1.4).

Table 1.4   Social media as a mirror for modern-day Narcissuses

Trump's Tweets	Time and Date
'Sorry losers and haters, but my I.Q. is one of the highest -and you all know it! Please don't feel so stupid or insecure, it's not your fault.'	1:37pm, 9 May 2013
'I am the BEST builder, just look at what I've built. Hillary can't build. Republican candidates can't build. They don't have a clue!'	12:23pm, 13 May 2015
'Trump is a genius. Rubio and Cruz are not. I want a brilliant mind to run this country.'	4:53am, 27 Feb. 2016
'I started my business with very little and built it into a great company, with some of the best real estate assets in the World. Amazing!'	4:08pm, 27 Feb. 2016
'*Time Magazine* called to say that I was PROBABLY going to be named 'Man (Person) of the Year,' like last year, but I would have to agree to an interview and a major photo shoot. I said probably is no good and took a pass. Thanks anyway!'	2:40pm, 24 Nov. 2017

Personality researchers define narcissism as 'a relatively stable individual difference consisting of grandiosity, self-love and inflated self-views' (Campbell et al., 2011: 269). The origins of its scientific study are traceable to Freud's 1914 essay *On Narcissism*. Out of this came the suggestion that a narcissistic personality type is characterized not only by self-love, self-admiration and self-inflation, but also by a feeling of superiority over others and an expectation of admiration from others. In terms of its relationship to the Big Five personality traits (openness to experience, conscientiousness, extraversion, agreeableness and neuroticism), narcissism is positively related to extraversion and openness to experience and negatively to agreeableness (Paulhus and Williams, 2002). Narcissism has both normal and pathological expressions, ranging from a healthy self-interest which is deemed necessary for normal functioning, to an unhealthy self-preoccupation and self-absorption which can end up being self-destructive (Kets de Vries, 2016; Pincus and Lukowitsky, 2010).

In terms of its 'darker side', narcissism along with psychopathy (high impulsivity, low empathy and anxiety) and Machiavellianism (manipulative personality) is part of the 'dark triad of personality' (Paulhus and Williams, 2002). In its more extreme pathological form, 'Narcissistic Personality Disorder' (NPD), narcissism results in distress or impairment, and whilst its prevalence in the population is comparatively low, the occurrence of narcissistic symptoms (trait narcissism) which are below the level to be classified as a clinical disorder, is likely to be much greater (Campbell et al., 2011). NPD has been operationalized in the American Psychiatric Association's (APA) *Diagnostic and Statistical Manual of Mental Disorders* as a pathological condition characterized by various behaviours and attributes such as grandiosity, exploitativeness, lack of empathy, arrogance and haughtiness.

Narcissism is not uncommon at the top of politics and business, but is by no means exclusively bad. Narcissists hold a potent attraction for others, especially if their narcissism is accompanied by charisma and a grand vision (Deluga, 1997; Rosenthal and Pittinsky, 2006). A study of American presidents from George Washington through to Ronald Reagan found narcissism to be positively associated with various aspects of charisma (e.g. 'iconic', 'energetic', 'determined') as well as with subjectively rated performance on a variety of presidential behaviours (Deluga, 1997).

Narcissists are without doubt a force for change – for good or for ill – in business management. They can lead their organizations to 'unprecedented success or abject failure' (Campbell et al., 2011: 273). 'Productive narcissists' such as George Soros and Jack Welch – embodiments of business success – are arguably narcissistic in the 'right amount' and in the 'right way' (Maccoby, 2000). Larry Ellison was the highly successful, charismatic, and arguably narcissistic, CEO of Oracle about whom a fellow executive quipped famously that 'the only difference between God and Larry is that God doesn't think he's Larry' (Wilson, 2003). CEOs such as Apple's Steve Jobs, Google's Larry Page and former Hewlett Packard CEO Carly Fiorina had more than a trace of narcissism, as well as charisma, and they revelled in the adulation of attentive audiences. In their strong entrepreneurial orientation, leaders such as Jobs, Page and Fiorina gravitated towards bold and sometimes extreme strategic choices by being innovative, proactive and risk taking but were also spontaneous and unpredictable (Chatterjee and Hambrick, 2007; Wales et al., 2013).

But even though narcissists often emerge as highly successful leaders, the fact that they can also display negative attributes and behaviours and can be volatile means that, as with hubrism and personalized charisma, they may ultimately cause harm to themselves, their followers and their organization. Recruiting a narcissist who might turn 'toxic' and bring about a catastrophic downturn can be a serious CEO selection hazard if not handled carefully (Brunell et al., 2008; Nevicka et al., 2011; Wales et al., 2013). Once they are installed in high offices of state or senior management appointments (from which they can be difficult to dislodge), narcissistic leaders can turn toxic and bring about harmful results (Campbell et al., 2011; Maccoby, 2000).

Amongst the unproductive aspects and weaknesses of narcissistic leaders are that they typically are uncomfortable with their own emotions, listen for the kind of information they seek, prefer to indoctrinate others and dominate meetings, and have an intense need to compete (Maccoby, 2000). On the other hand, the productive aspects or strengths of narcissistic leaders are that they can create the future with compelling visions (rather than merely extrapolate or predict the future), and as skilful orators they have an ability to attract, inspire and motivate followers (Maccoby, 2000). Like most leader traits and behaviours, narcissistic leadership cannot be divorced from the context in which it is enacted, nor from the followers with whom it seeks to engage, as when a 'mirror-hungry' narcissistic leader finds an attentive group of 'ideal-hungry' followers and inspires allegiance and loyalty but demands admiration and adulation in return (Padilla et al., 2007; Post, 1986, 1993; Rosenthal and Pittinsky, 2006).

The relationship between narcissism and hubris includes the following points of similarity and difference: (1) narcissism and hubris can co-exist; (2) narcissists and hubrists are over-confident; (3) hubris and narcissism are associated with power; (4) narcissism is more trait-like, whilst hubris is more state-like; (5) narcissistic leadership and hubristic leadership can both be considered as types of destructive leadership.

Narcissism and Hubris Can Co-Exist

The overlap between narcissism and hubris is yet to be determined psychometrically (and to do so we need a valid and reliable 'hubris inventory'), however Donald Trump is a compelling example of the co-existence of narcissism and hubrism. Trump's narcissism was the subject of a letter to *The New York Times* in February 2017 by the eminent psychiatrist Allen Frances (who helped devise the APA's *Diagnostic and Statistical Manual of Mental Disorder IV* criteria for narcissistic personality disorder, NPD). At around the same time, Trump was the subject of an article in *The Atlantic* (January 2017) which speculated on whether his Secretary of Defense, General James 'Mad Dog' Mattis, could protect Trump from hubris[8] (Table 1.5).

Table 1.5 Co-occurrence of narcissism and hubris in Donald Trump (based on letter from Professor Allen Frances to *New York Times*, 2017; Dominic Tierney writing in *The Atlantic* magazine 2017)

A psychiatrist's assessment of Trump's narcissism	A journalist's assessment of Trump's hubrism
'Trump is without doubt a "world-class narcissist" as evinced by his grandiosity, self-absorption and lack of empathy. However, without the associated psychological distress or impairment to himself he does not qualify for a diagnosis of this mental disorder. Trump is not mentally ill in the terms set out in DSM's criteria for NPD, and any attempts to categorize him as such is not only futile, it also demeans and stigmatizes those who truly suffer from mental disorders. Instead of experiencing distress himself, Trump causes severe distress in others and has been rewarded richly for doing so, not least by the honor of being elected to the high office of President of the United States of America.'	'Donald Trump seems almost uniquely likely to succumb to hubris. Not only is he male, American, and a member of the elite (for all his talk of populism), but he also instinctively responds to challenges by coming out swinging. He is prone to arrogant behavior, such as declaring he doesn't need daily intelligence briefings. At different times, Trump has: (1) tweeted a quote from Benito Mussolini, an autocrat known for his self-destructive over-confidence ("It is better to live one day as a lion than 100 years as a sheep"); (2) lauded Saddam Hussein ("you know what he did well? He killed terrorists"). (These remarks were made before the Twitterstorm that has characterized Trump's presidency.)'
Letter from Professor Allen Frances to *The New York Times*, 17 January 2017	Dominic Tierney writing in *The Atlantic* magazine, 14 January 2017

Other commentators have speculated that as a high-profile entertainer who is possessed of a 'stunning blend of ignorance and hubris', Trump accurately mirrored aspects of the 2016 social and political climate.[9]

Narcissists and Hubrists Are Over-Confident

One area of overlap between narcissism and hubrism is over-confidence. Hubris researchers since the 1980s have studied over-confidence and its negative effects on business performance, especially in areas such as mergers and acquisitions. Indeed, the origins of the study of hubris and over-confidence in the management literature can be traced to the 'Hubris Hypothesis' (Roll, 1986) which attempted to explain why CEOs are so confident in over-paying for large corporate acquisitions in spite of the fact that the outcomes of such mergers often fail to deliver the hoped-for results. The reason is that they think their estimation of the value of the acquisition, rather than that of the market's or naysayers' valuations, is accurate. However, this rarely turns out to be the case and, as a large body of Hubris Hypothesis research shows, hubristic CEOs usually end up with a loss-making merger (see Chapter 5).

Likewise, narcissism researchers have looked at the decision-making behaviours of narcissists. It has been found, for example, that in gambling tasks narcissists are over-confident and, as a result, they make risky bets and often end up losing. In spite of this fact, they tend to report that they perform better than others and also would do better than others in similar tasks in the future (Campbell et al., 2004). Even more bizarrely, narcissists are prone to 'over-claiming', for example by asserting knowledge of events and ideas that do not actually exist, such as knowledge of who founded the (fictional) country of 'Anglestan' (Paulhus et al., 2003).

Both narcissistic and hubristic leaders are prone to embracing overly confident and risky decisions which may be appropriate in volatile, uncertain, fast-moving environments (Campbell et al., 2011; Wales et al., 2013), however when these behaviours tip over into over-confidence, impulsivity, sensation seeking and recklessness, they present a serious hazard for organizations.

Hubris and Narcissism Are Associated With Power

Hubris and narcissism are associated with power but in subtly different ways. In the *Diagnostic and Statistical Manual IV*, Criterion 2 for Narcissistic Personality Disorder (NPD) reflects a preoccupation with fantasies of unlimited success or power. Similarly, hubris is known to develop when a leader has been in a position of significant power and has a record of prior successes. A distinction between hubrists and narcissists may lie in their respective power motivations. Narcissism (at least in its maladaptive form) is associated with a preoccupation with, and need for, personal power in order to garner admiration rather than necessarily with a concern for outcomes (Kets de Vries and Miller, 1997). Hubrists, on the other hand, exercise their power in order to accomplish overly ambitious goals rather than necessarily to garner admiration (Brown and Zeigler-Hill, 2004; McClelland and Burnham, 1976; Rosenthal and Pittinsky, 2006). For narcissists, the need for power is motivated by ego enhancement (i.e. their's is a personalized power motivation), whereas for hubrists the exercising of power is motivated by a need for achievement and success (i.e. their's is an achievement-oriented power motivation) (Hayward and Hambrick, 1997; McClelland and Burnham, 1976).

Narcissism Is Trait-Like, Hubris Is More State-Like

Unlike hubris, which is contingent on the acquisition of power, narcissism is believed to emerge 'well before adulthood' and is a relatively stable and enduring trait even when it does not develop into the clinical disorder (Thomaes et al., 2009: 1235). It is associated with parental overvaluation, as in the case of the 'grandiose narcissism' most likely to be encountered in the CEO population, or alternatively parental coldness as in the case of 'vulnerable narcissism' (Campbell et al., 2011; Otway and Vignoles, 2006). Table 1.6 gives a business psychotherapist's perspective on the differences between narcissism and hubrism.

Table 1.6 A business psychotherapist's depiction of narcissism and hubris for *Harvard Business Review*

Narcissism	'Narcissism is a *character* disorder, which means it starts in the teenage years and defines a person's entire *modus operandi*. If, owing to a childhood that left you bereft of good feelings about yourself, you feel a need to preen and self-promote to merely stay afloat psychologically, that problem sticks with you forever. Psychotherapy can dampen a narcissist's tendency to self-aggrandize, but under duress he'll regress and become insufferably self-centred. A narcissist is pretty much a narcissist all the time.'
Hubris	'Hubris is a *reactive* disorder: Either the unfortunate consequence of endless laudatory press clippings leading to supreme over-confidence, or the culmination of a winning streak that causes a person to suffer the transient delusion that he is bullet-proof. Many good people will, under bad circumstances, suffer from hubris – but they tend to recover after toppling from their pedestals shrinks their egos back down to size.'

Source: Berglas (2014) Reproduced by kind permission of *Harvard Business Review*

Whilst hubris is more state-like and narcissism more trait-like, they are further related in that the presence of the symptoms of Narcissistic Personality Disorder before the achievement of power or their subclinical presence (i.e. where it is not severe enough to present definitive/readily observable symptoms) may predispose a leader to becoming hubristic (Ghaemi et al., 2016; Owen and Davidson, 2009). The relationships between charisma and hubris, and narcissism and hubris are summarized in Table 1.7.

DESTRUCTIVE LEADERSHIP

Destructive leadership is systematic and repeated volitional behaviours by a leader that can harm or intends to harm the organization and/or her or his followers (Einarsen

Table 1.7   Relationships between hubris and charisma, and hubris and narcissism

Charisma and Hubris	Narcissism and Hubris
Charismatic leadership also has a dark side	Narcissism and hubris can co-exist
Hubris and charisma can co-exist	Narcissists and hubrists are over-confident
Charisma and hubris are malleable	Hubris and narcissism are associated with power
Charismatic and hubristic leadership are situational	Narcissism exists on a continuum and is trait-like, whilst hubris is state-like
Charisma ('dark side') and hubris are potentially destructive and reciprocal	Narcissistic leadership and hubristic leadership are both types of destructive leadership

Source: By permission of Harvard Business Review

et al., 2007; Krasikova et al., 2013). Destructive leadership is a broad top-level category in which other more narrowly defined categories of destructive leadership can be formed, for example 'destructive decision-making' manifesting in the tendency of some CEOs 'to make high profile but ill-advised acquisitions that lose money' (Craig and Kaiser, 2012: 443). In terms of the five distinctive features of destructive leadership identified by 'dark side' leadership researchers (Padilla et al., 2007), hubristic leadership can be considered a type of destructive leadership (Table 1.8).

Table 1.8   Hubristic leadership as a type of destructive leadership (based on Padilla et al., 2007)

Dimensions of Destructive Leadership (Padilla et al 2007)	Hubristic Leadership as Destructive Leadership
There are good and bad results in most leadership situations; no requirement that destructive leadership is absolutely, exclusively or entirely destructive	Hubristic leadership is not exclusively intentionally destructive; some of the attributes of hubris (e.g. confidence, pride, determination, ambition) are core requirements for successful leadership when not practised to excess
Involves dominating, coercing and manipulating followers and situations, rather than influencing, persuading and gaining followers' commitment	Hubristic leadership often involves dominance and coercion and manipulation of circumstances to attain a leader's goals and ambitions more than influencing and persuading to secure followers' commitment
Has a selfish orientation which focuses more on the leader's needs than those of the wider group	Hubristic leadership focuses on a leader's goals, priorities and needs through a self-serving use of power, rather than a selfless orientation towards the priorities and needs of the wider social group
Produces outcomes that compromise the quality of life for constituents	Process of hubristic leadership brings about outcomes, which may be unintentional, that are detrimental both to the individual and the wider organization

Dimensions of Destructive Leadership (Padilla et al 2007)	Hubristic Leadership as Destructive Leadership
Destructive outcomes are not attributable exclusively to a destructive leader; such outcomes are also the products of interactions between leaders, followers and the environment in which leadership is situated and enacted	Destructive outcomes associated with hubris are not exclusive products of individual leaders, they are a product of interactions between hubristic leadership, susceptible followers and a conducive context

With regard to the fifth dimension of destructive leadership (see Table 1.8), researchers have proposed a 'toxic triangle' model of destructive leadership based on the idea that leadership emanates from leaders' motivation and ability to lead, followers' desire for direction and authority, and circumstances and events that call for a particular style of leadership (Padilla et al., 2007). The toxic triangle has three domains, the interactions between which are associated with harmful outcomes: (1) destructive leaders, with attributes such as charisma, personalized use of power, etc.; (2) followers who can be categorized as 'conformers' (individuals with unmet basic needs, negative self-evaluations, etc.) or ambitious and selfish colluders who share the leader's world views; and (3) conducive environments characterized by instability, perceived threat, particular cultural values, an absence of checks and balances, and institutionalization (Figure 1.2).

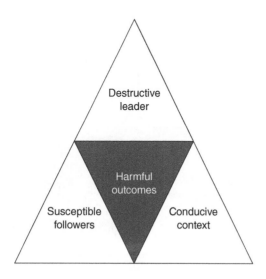

Figure 1.2   Domains of destructive leadership in a toxic triangle framework (Padilla et al. 2007)

Intention and volition are important in framing hubristic leadership as a type of destructive leadership. As far as intentionality goes, hubristic business leaders do not (on the whole) set out to bring about destructive outcomes. For example, Richard Fuld did not seek to contribute significantly to the global financial crisis of 2007/08. In other examples of engineering, financial and managerial recklessness borne of hubris, including the BP Deepwater Horizon oil spill (Ladd, 2012), the Long Term Capital Management bankruptcy (Lowenstein, 2000) and the NASA Challenger and Columbia tragedies (Mason, 2004), no one deliberately courted disaster. Hubristic leaders behave before the fact in ways that were not intended to cause harm, but their actions nonetheless can prepare the way for destructive outcomes.

As far as volition goes, a destructive leadership process arises when a hubristic leader chooses to pursue a goal which can be detrimental to the well-being of the organization or its followers (Krasikova et al., 2013). In such circumstances, hubristic leadership is volitional and potentially destructive only in as far as goals and actions are chosen by the leader from amongst other ultimately more constructive alternatives, often going against authoritative countervailing opinion. The fact that intoxication with power, success and praise leads some leaders to habitually, systematically and repeatedly engage in such behaviours against contrary advice would lead to the expectation that unintended negative consequences in the form of 'nasty surprises' are more likely to accrue in a hubristic leadership process (Figure 1.3).

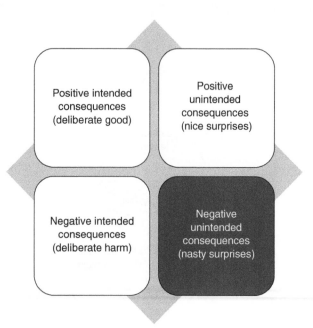

Figure 1.3   Typology of consequences

As technology advances at an increasing rate it is alarming to think that 'nasty surprises' might emanate from non-human agents. In a study of the risks associated with AI and machine learning in the finance industry, the Financial Security Board identified threats from the use of so-called 'opaque' models by multiple agents as a potential hazard (see Chapter 6). AI- and machine learning-based models are so complex as to be difficult to understand and supervise, and are prone to a 'lack of interpretability'. The combination of hard-to-interpret financial models and exuberantly over-confident traders is a potent and perilous mix.

Conclusion

Hubristic leadership is a relatively new and unfamiliar area in leadership studies. It is related to the well-established fields of charismatic leadership and narcissistic leadership. All three can be connected, in different ways, to the 'darker' and more destructive sides of leadership. In terms of their relationship, it is unlikely that pure 'personalized charismatic', 'narcissistic' or 'hubristic' types exist (see Conger and Kanungo, 1998). Dark-side leader behaviours are likely to reflect varying degrees of personalized charisma, narcissism and hubris. If, how or why one aspect dominates at the expense of the others is likely to depend on a complex mix of individual and contextual factors and their interrelationships; this is an important area for further research. When hubristic leaders become intoxicated with power, praise and success, they become over-confident in their own abilities and over-estimate the chances of successful outcomes, and they simultaneously under-estimate what can go wrong and disparage the advice and criticism of others. As a result, they create the conditions that can give rise to damaging, but unintended, consequences. Hubristic leadership also can be considered as a form of destructive leadership that entails behaviours that typically were not intended to cause harm but which nonetheless prepare the way for damaging and sometimes disastrous outcomes.

Further Reading

Hayward, M. (2007). *Ego check: Why executive hubris is wrecking companies and careers and how to avoid the trap.* Chicago: Kaplan.
Robinson, G. (2016). Making sense of hubris. In P. Garrard and G. Robinson (eds) *The intoxication of power: Interdisciplinary insights.* Basingstoke: Palgrave, pp. 1–16.

NOTES

1. www.newyorker.com/news/daily-comment/is-political-hubris-an-illness (Accessed 7 March 2018); http://time.com/3923128/donald-trump-announcement-speech (Accessed 20 April 2017).

2. www.vanityfair.com/news/2018/01/ubers-new-ceo-says-travis-kalanick-was-guilty-of-hubris (Accessed 7 March 2018).

3. A recent search of a database of scholarly publications revealed 218 articles on 'charisma and leadership' published since 2000 and 74 on 'narcissism and leadership', compared to 23 articles on 'hubris and leadership' (November 2017).

4. www.theguardian.com/politics/2005/apr/28/polls.labour (Accessed 7 March 2018).

5. www.telegraph.co.uk/news/politics/tony-blair/10698247/Pity-Tony-Blair-disowned-even-by-his-heir.html (Accessed 22 February 2018).

6. www.ft.com/content/789c0fd2-a1dd-11e2-ad0c-00144feabdc0 (Accessed 7 March 2018).

7. www.ft.com/content/789c0fd2-a1dd-11e2-ad0c-00144feabdc0 (Accessed 7 March 2018).

8. www.theatlantic.com/international/archive/2017/01/trump-mattis-hubris/513206 (Accessed 22 February 2018).

9. www.thetimes.co.uk/article/trumps-hubris-is-such-that-he-could-go-nuclear-to-prove-how-tough-he-is-ldwx0rlfv#; www.nytimes.com/2017/02/14/opinion/an-eminent-psychiatrist-demurs-on-trumps-mental-state.html?_r=0. http://time.com/4654406/america-trump-con-man (Accessed 5 June 2017).

10. http://money.cnn.com/2006/05/29/news/enron_guiltyest (Accessed 20 November 2017).

2
MYTHIC AND HISTORICAL APPROACHES

WISE WARNING

'And then he caught sight of the wings in the water. Dædalus cursed the skill of his hands and buried his dear son's corpse in a grave.' (Ovid, 2004, *Metamorphóses*, Book 8, Lines 233–5)

Introduction

Hubris is a pervasive and inescapable phenomenon in human affairs. We make sense of it through our myths, histories and archetypes. The common theme is that of stories – both real and imagined episodes and narratives – which have at their core a pattern which implicates hubristic excess and retributive justice in the form of nemesis.

Mythic and historical narratives usually include major characters, heroes and villains, mortals and immortals, a plot or story line, and an outcome. A moral or practical implication is either implied or explicitly stated in their recounting and retelling. In western society, including European and North American business schools, their origins are typically Classical Greece and Rome and European and US history and culture. For example, writers on leadership have used Greek myth in general (Schedlitzki et al., 2015) as well as specific narratives about the Ancient Persian King Xerxes (Kets de Vries, 1993), Admiral Lord Nelson (Jones and Gosling, 2011) and Napoleon Bonaparte (Kroll et al., 2000), amongst others.

BACKGROUND

Myths and stories give business and management educators an almost unlimited resource and reflective toolkit for teaching and learning about leadership. They can be used to experience and explore emotions, self-awareness, identity, sense-giving, sense-making, virtue, reflexivity and practical wisdom (Boje, 1991, 1995, 2011; Brown et al., 2009; Gabriel, 2000; Gabriel and Connell, 2010; Gray, 2007; Taylor et al., 2002). Myths and stories are a powerful means of encoding, storing and retrieving knowledge. Given that narratives are open to manipulation by the teller and misinterpretation by the listener, the use of myths and stories in management and leadership also has an important ethical dimension (Auvinen et al., 2013). The potential that myth and history hold for educators is largely inexhaustible because they offer different lessons depending on the context, and each new cohort or generation learns them anew.

The pattern in hubris myths and historical narratives is that of rise and fall, often accompanied by tragedy or even-handed punishment (Swap et al., 2001). The archetype used ordinarily to make sense of such patterns is 'hubris-followed-by-nemesis', as in the Book of Proverbs (Chapter 16, Verse 18): 'Pride cometh before destruction and a haughty spirit before a fall.' Perhaps one reason why hubris is so alluring is because the notion of human excess precipitating a fall is intrinsically captivating (Poole, 2005). It is captured in the Judeo-Christian tradition in 'falling from grace', and in colloquialisms such as 'comeuppance', 'just deserts', 'what goes around comes around', 'you sow as you reap', 'being taken down a peg or two' and 'karma'. The popular and business press and social media are replete with stories, seemingly on a daily basis, of the rise and demise of celebrities and business people, with the accent on demise. When we recognize hubris in a CEO or political leader, we interpret it in terms of the rise-and-fall pattern institutionalized in the myths and stories that we have been familiarized with. We watch each Tweet or indiscretion with morbid fascination and wait with bated breath to see if the gods are ready yet to deliver retribution on the perpetrator.

HUBRIS AND MYTH

In ancient Greece, various acts and dispositions constituted hubris. They ranged from 'thinking big' as a result of over-confidence in one's success, power and good fortune, to humiliating a defeated enemy (as in Achilles' humiliation of Hector's corpse: 'I have dragged Hector's corpse here for the dogs to eat raw', *The Iliad*, Book 23, Line 24) (Cairns, 1996: 11). *Hybris* from which the word 'hubris' is derived was the goddess or personified spirit (*daimōn*) of reckless pride, presumption, arrogance and insolence. Two hubristic high flyers in Greek myth who fell foul (literally and metaphorically) of over-ambition and over-confidence were Phaeton and Icarus (as retold in Ovid's *Metamorphóses*, 2004, Books 2 and 8 respectively) (Tables 2.2 and 2.3).

Narratives have the power to communicate important messages in emotionally charged and compelling ways. Myths are a special type of emotionally charged narrative: they are not mere 'passing enjoyment' but express something that is important and serious – even sacred – and which has immediate cultural relevance (Graf, 2006). Myths concern human experiences which are neither true nor plausible but, paradoxically, have an immedi-ate interpersonal, social or cultural relevance. They compel us – often through a tragic narrative and aesthetic – to take note, and have an emotive, explanatory and educative potential both in personal and professional life. Myths are an effective yet non-coercive way to inform and regulate moral behaviour. In the process of 'restorying' myths, tacit plotlines can be made explicit and this process can catalyse critical self-reflection and a re-appraisal of taken-for-granted assumptions (Schedlitzki et al., 2015: 412).

In common with myths more generally, the Greek myths are rooted in an invisible, more powerful reality (the world of 'the gods') and are often concerned with issues of death and fear of extinction. They are not stories told for their own sake or for amuse-ment (although they are compellingly entertaining), rather they seek to edify and inform us as to how we should or should not behave (Armstrong, 2005). The Greek myths are as relevant to hazards of hubris today as they were two-and-a-half millennia ago (Table 2.1).

Table 2.1 Characteristics of Greek myths relevant to hubristic leadership

Emotionally charged narrative
Explain and make sense of current events in terms of past events and supernatural phenomena
Express something of immediate cultural relevance
Not mere passing enjoyment
Pattern of rise and fall
Assumes a 'cosmic' or natural order which humans should be wary of transgressing
Even-handed punishment by the gods for contraventions of 'cosmic order'
Non-coercive way to inform and regulate moral behaviour

The Greek myths Ovid retold are chosen for and gain authority and traction through their aesthetic values; they serve an aetiological function, that is they explain, and by explaining, organize current social phenomena in terms of events in the distant past. They also legitimate social facts and in so doing fulfil a cognitive need in the immediate present (Graf, 2006). Ovid's myths often concern natural phenomena (animals, plants, rock formations, constellations, etc.) and the metamorphoses of humans into stags, birds, flowers, trees, comets, stars, etc. (Wise, 1977). Ovid's consummate skill as a poet is that he uses myth to 'effortlessly elucidate' complex social, emotional and moral situations (Graf, 2006: 119). Throughout his retellings, Ovid is keen to point out the power of divine influence on human life and that 'it was the gods who did all this' (Graf, 2006: 120). The punishment meted out – often by forfeiture of the protagonist's life, as in Phaethon's and Icarus' deaths by fire and water respectively – is a divine influence, if not direct interven-tion, as a result of humans daring to 'think big' and go beyond their station (Cairns, 1996; Pavlock, 1998).

The Phaethon/Phoebus and Daedalus/Icarus episodes in the *Metamorphóses* communicate tacit and explicit themes around power, success, ambition and wisdom, and forfeiture, punishment and demise (see Tables 2.2 and 2.3). And whilst the Daedalus/Icarus episode is well used in chronicling the perils of hubris (some might say over-used), the Phaethon/Phoebus episode is less well known but each can be used to offer subtly different cautionary narratives around the themes of unbridled ambition and the perils of rampant over-confidence.

Table 2.2   Hubris and unbridled ambition

Phaethon and Phoebus, and the peril of unbridled ambition (*Metamorphóses*, Book 2)
Phaethon, according to his mother Clymene, was son of the sun god Phoebus. He bragged about who his father was but nobody would believe him, so Clymene urged him to set the record straight by getting the truth from Phoebus for himself and prove his detractors wrong once and for all.
He travelled to the east, across Ethiopia and then India, arriving at his father's palace at dawn. On seeing Phaethon, the great god Phoebus whose gaze 'misses nothing', exclaimed 'Phaethon, my son!'.
As proof that he was his father, Phoebus gave Phaethon the chance to ask for anything he liked with the promise that, as his son, he should have whatever he wanted. Much to Phoebus' dismay Phaethon asked to be able to drive the chariot of the sun across the sky for a day. Phoebus warned him that no mortal could ever hope to manage the chariot and its horses since not even a god could survive riding in it for a day.
Phaethon in his youthful obstinacy and recklessness was light-headed with ambition and rejected the pleas of his father to choose something different and wiser. And having made a promise, Phoebus could not refuse his son's insistence. Phaethon took to the sky in the chariot pulled by the horses of the sun. Tragically, his father's worst fears materialized. Phaethon quickly lost control of the horses who swept so low that they caused the clouds to boil and the earth to burn.
To save the Earth from further calamity Zeus drove a thunderbolt into Phaethon which killed him instantly and caused him to fall 'through the sky in a long trail blazing away like a comet which sometimes appears in a clear sky, never to land on earth, but looking as if it is falling' (Book 2, Lines 319–23).

Note: The myth is also re-told more succinctly than in Ovid, and in a more contemporary idiom, by the poet Ted Hughes in his *Tales from Ovid* (Faber, 1997).

Table 2.3   Hubris and rampant over-confidence

Icarus and Dædalus, and the perils of rampant over-confidence (*Metamorphóses*, Book 8)
In Ovid's re-telling, the father (Dædalus, the master craftsman) and his son (Icarus) had been exiled to Crete and held against their will with all routes of escape by land and sea blocked by the island's monarch Minos (for whom, incidentally, Daedalus had built the labyrinth to contain the Minotaur). However, although Minos may have been the 'lord of the world' he was not the lord of the sky. Through Dædalus' ingenuity and craftsmanship he and his son were able to acquire the God-like power of flight and were thus able to attempt an escape. Daedalus meticulously fashioned wings from feathers bound together with twine and wax so as to imitate birds' wings. However, before they took flight Dædalus entreated his son not to fly too high in case the wings be scorched by the sun's rays which would cause the wax to melt. Watchers on the land stood amazed as the two took

Icarus and Dædalus, and the perils of rampant over-confidence (*Metamorphóses*, Book 8)

to the air thinking they must be gods, not men, to be able to soar through the sky, however: all this adventurous flying went to Icarus' head ... he'd fallen in love with the sky, and soared higher and higher. The scorching rays of the sun grew closer and softened the fragrant wax which fastened his plumage. The wax dissolved; and ... Icarus flapped his naked arms deprived of the wings which had caught the air that was buoying them upwards.

As a result, Icarus plunged to his self-inflicted doom in the Icárian Sea. 'And then he [Dædalus] caught sight of the wings in the water. Dædalus cursed the skill of his hands and buried his dear son's corpse in a grave.' (*Metamorphóses*, Book 8, lines 221–30).

Phaethon and Phoebus: in understanding hubristic leadership, the narrative is moralistic in that irresponsible over-ambition and flagrant disregard of authoritative warnings go to the head of a hubrist (Phaethon) who is seduced by opportunity and simultaneously under-estimates the scale of the task he has taken on; in so doing, the hubrist commits serious and fatal errors of risk management which invite disastrous consequences.

Daedalus/Icarus episode: this is the most well-known myth to counsel against reckless over-confidence. For hubristic leadership, the narrative – like that of Phaethon – is moralistic in that power, and the capabilities it confers, eventually delude the hubrist who misperceives, misinterprets and misjudges the realities of the situation. By committing fatal errors of judgement in over-estimating their ability to control events through the use of their innovative technology (wings of wax and feathers), the protagonists invite, and therefore must take responsibility for, disastrous consequences.

One of the principles of hubris in Classical mythology is that of a 'cosmic order'. The corollary of this is that hubris on the part of mortals invites punishment for transgressions of that order: mortals are born mortals, and, with a few exceptions, so it must always remain. Indeed, the code is so strict that even minor deities are not allowed to compete with major deities (Hansen, 2004). Mortals are expected most certainly to understand their position in the pecking order of the universe. Any who have the temerity to transgress this rule by acting as though they were equal or superior to the deities will naturally, and inevitably, incur divine wrath. The myths of Phaethon and Icarus are cautionary narratives which are told with the purpose in the mind of the narrator of dissuading the hearer from over-ambitious and over-confident behaviours that invite, and therefore risk bringing about, unintended negative consequences (Hansen, 2004).

A further relevant, but sometimes overlooked, aspect of the Icarus myth is that Daedalus exhorted his son not only to avoid flying too high but also to avoid flying too low ('if you fly too low the water will clog your wings', in other words to 'keep to the middle way', Ovid, *Metamorphóses*, Book 8, Line 203). This theme is also to be found in the Phaethon myth where Phoebus urges his son to follow the middle way: 'Venture to climb too high and you'll burn the ceiling of heaven, the earth if you sink too low; for safety remain in the middle' (Book 2, Lines 136–9). Hubris researchers see parallels in this with CEOs who need to 'fly at the right height' and strike the right balance between confidence and over-confidence, ambition and over-ambition and authentic pride and hubristic pride (Petit and Bollaert, 2012: 268); points to the paradox of hubris (Chapter 8). The balancing of hubris and humility resonates with the 'ground rules' of the world's most successful investor, Warren Buffett of Berkshire Hathaway (Table 2.4).

Table 2.4   Balancing hubris and humility

Warren Buffett's ground rule for balancing hubris and humility
'Successful investing requires you to do your own thinking and train yourself to be comfortable going against the crowd. You could say that good results come from a properly calibrated balance of *hubris* and *humility* – hubris enough to think you can have insights that are superior to the collective wisdom of the market, humility enough to know the limits of your abilities and being willing to change course when errors are recognized. You'll have to evaluate facts and circumstances, apply logic and reason to form a hypothesis, and then act when the facts line up, irrespective of whether the crowd agrees or disagrees with your conclusions.' Throughout his career, Buffett has found success by daring to be different and rarely being wrong.

Source: Miller (2016: 170, emphases added). By permission of Harper Collins

The capital sin of hubris was fundamentally a lack of balance and represented the antithesis of two qualities greatly prized by the ancient Greeks – *aidos* (Αἰδώς, humble reverence for law) and *sophrosyne* (σωφροσύνη, self-restraint and a sense of proper limits) (Sheard et al., 2012; Wassermann, 1953). Hubris is bad because it is a disturbance of equilibrium which can lead to unintended negative consequences, for example as when taking to excess the factors which drive success, which then become sources of decline (Miller, 1990). Balancing tensions, steering a course between excess and deficiency and maintaining a well-calibrated equilibrium are vital in navigating the paradox of hubris and instrumental in avoiding the potentially destructive consequences associated with hubristic leadership.

No account of hubris, it seems, could be complete without the Dædalus–Icarus episode (e.g. Hayward, 2007; Miller, 1990). This has prompted some to argue that there has been an over-reliance on Icarus as an analogy for executive hubris, and on myth in general, and that this has somehow hindered progress by, for example, militating against precise psychological definitions of the construct (Bollaert and Petit, 2010). The detractors see cause for optimism in research in clinical psychology and psychiatry (see Chapter 4), which not only offers a more precise definition of hubris but also conceptualizes it in terms of 14 symptoms which together constitute what has been hypothesized as an acquired personality change, 'Hubris Syndrome', which can affect persons in positions of authority and power (Bollaert and Petit, 2010). However, leadership educators should be wary of abandoning myth. The narratives which myths embody are not only an important communicative tool for learning, they are also a powerful means for catalysing personal change and transformation (Kaye, 1995; Schedlitzki et al., 2015).

HYBRIS AND HUBRIS

As noted above, 'hubris' is derived from the Greek *hybris* (ὕβρις). In the original Classical Greek formulation, it was concerned with issues of honour and shame, and refers both to a behaviour and a disposition. Someone who actually commits an act of intentional insult which deliberately inflicts shame and dishonour on others is guilty of hybris, as is someone who has merely the disposition to commit an act which perpetrates this dishonour on a victim (Fisher, 1976). 'Hybrism' in the law was inflicting dishonour on another person or deity. In Aristotle's *Rhetoric*, hybris (framed as an 'insolence') requires the initiation of a harmful act from which the person committing the act or disposed towards it (i.e. the 'hybrist' or hubrist) gets pleasure. The pleasure comes from the hybrist's thought of his own superiority and enjoyment from the dishonouring of another person (Cairns, 1996). Aristotle describes hybris as 'doing and saying things that cause shame to the victim simply for the pleasure involved' and notes that the 'cause of the pleasure thus enjoyed by the hybrist is that he thinks himself greatly superior to others when ill-treating them' (*Rhetoric*, Book 2, Chapter 2: 82).

In the Classical formulation, hybris was always voluntary, it was produced by excesses (for example, of youth or wealth), often involved a victim and was indisputably bad (MacDowell, 1976). The rich people of ancient Athens were thought to be especially prone to hybris because of the security from harm which they thought their wealth gave them. Their good fortune made them over-confident, so much so that they felt that they were the most important people in existence, and if anyone objected to their bad behaviour they could simply buy off officials through compensation or bribery (Fisher, 1976).

Hybris is a disposition or behaviour that is insulting and disrespectful, it brings about damage, is a characteristic of the young because of their recklessness and of the rich because of the power of their wealth, and gives the hybrist a false idea of their own worth and misplaced confidence in their successes and good fortune (Cairns, 1996). A hybrist indulges her or his desire to be thought superior to others. But this behaviour is likely to bring them into danger either because those they mistreat may retaliate or, by over-estimating their own powers, they under-estimate the powers of those they dishonour or the perilousness of the circumstances in which they choose to go above their station (Fisher, 1976). It is essentially a self-aggrandizing 'thinking big' which infringes the honour of others because it is a state of mind that is necessarily comparative and diminishing of the other disrespectfully (Cairns, 1996: 32). It is hardly surprising therefore that a dominant theme in Greek tragedy is the punishment of hybris (Lattimore, 1964).

Although not equivalent to modern usage of the term 'hubris', there are insights to be gleaned from Classical hybris which are relevant to leaders in modern organizations. First, hubris may be thought of as a disposition as well as an action, hence it is possible to be a hubristic leader or at least a hubristically inclined leader, by simply thinking hubristic thoughts as well as, of course, carrying them through into an action – on both counts hubris is to be discouraged. Second, hubristic behaviours show disrespect and disregard for others; this manifests in hubristic leadership as contempt and involves the diminishing of others and the denigration of their talents and contribution. Third, hubris entails a taking for granted of good fortune and success and a corresponding down-playing of the role that context, chance and other people may have played in successful business outcomes.

HUBRIS IN HISTORY

Hubristic leadership is prominent in human history, especially in relation to armed conflict which will be the main focus of this section. Hubris and war seem to go together. In some accounts, the Classical goddess Hybris was married to war. When the gods were getting married, Polemos (war) was the last of the bachelors and Hybris became his wife because she was the only one left without a husband. Polemos loved Hybris so much that they went everywhere together. The moral of this fable is: 'do not ever allow Hybris to come upon the nations or cities of mankind, smiling fondly at the crowds, because Polemos will be coming up right behind her.'[1]

In looking at hubris from a historical standpoint, there are few decisions more consequential than those taken by political or military leaders in choosing whether and how to engage in armed conflict with other nations. The plot lines from the history of armed conflict are sometimes used as narrative examples of the perils of hubristic leadership, especially when it co-occurs with the dark side of charisma (for example, Kets de Vries, 1993; Kroll et al., 2000; Ladkin, 2006). Hubristic political and military leaders are open to being seduced by their own confidence and ambition, such that they risk significantly over-estimating the chances of success and seriously under-estimating what can go wrong, thereby inviting negative consequences. Even though in the business arena the collateral consequences of hubristic leadership can be highly damaging for organizations, the fallout from hubris in armed conflict can be catastrophic.

Xerxes Crossing the Hellespont (480 BC)

One of the earliest fictionalized accounts of hubristic leadership in armed conflict can be found in Aeschylus' play *The Persians* (472 BC), a Greek tragedy which drew on historical events that were also documented by Herodotus in the *History of the Persian Wars*, namely the defeat of the Persians by a coalition of Greek city states under Themistocles in the Straits of Salamis eight years earlier. In Aeschylus' drama, the Persian ruler Xerxes was 'Asia's warlike lord' who 'glittered like a god in his radiant state' as the embodiment of Persia's 'resistless might'. He was driven to invade Greece to exact revenge for the humiliating defeat of his father, Darius, at the Battle of Marathon in 490 BC. Xerxes was bent on a mission of unconditional conquest of the Greeks. He assembled, with an unparalleled grandiosity of ambition, an army of unprecedented size – 360,000 soldiers and 750 ships, and set out to cross the Hellespont, a narrow body of water which bounded Europe and Asia. Xerxes' ambition in itself blatantly dishonoured the gods, and his attacking of the Hellespont and other Greek holy places was a sign of this misdemeanour (Papadimitropoulos, 2008). The story is summarized in Table 2.5.

Table 2.5   Xerxes and the crossing of the Hellespont

The hubris of Xerxes in crossing the Hellespont
Xerxes, 4th 'King of Kings' of the Achaemenid dynasty of Persia (519 BC–466 BC), was driven to invade Greece to extract revenge for the humiliating defeat of his father, Darius, at the Battle of Marathon in 490 BC. Xerxes was bent on a mission of unconditional conquest of the Greeks. He assembled, with an unparalleled grandiosity of ambition, an army of unprecedented size – 360,000 soldiers and 750 ships and set out to cross the Hellespont, a narrow body of water which bounded Europe and Asia.
After the Persians' first attempt at crossing was thwarted by stormy weather, Xerxes 'straightway gave orders that the Hellespont should receive three hundred lashes' by way of punishment for its insolence in defying him (Herodotus, 7.49).
His chief adviser Artabanus counselled him to 'imagine all possible calamities' (the Persian army could be cut off if the bridge over the Hellespont is destroyed, hastily planned schemes fail, and Zeus punishes the too mighty) in warning the headstrong Xerxes against being 'insensibly allured onwards' (Herodotus, 7.49).
'Sated with success', Xerxes was dismissive both of wise warnings and ominous portents along the way (e.g. 'A mare brought forth a hare. Hereby it was shown plainly enough, that Xerxes would lead forth his host against Greece with mighty pomp and splendour, but, in order to reach again the spot from which he set out, would have to run for his life' (Herodotus, 7.57).
Oblivious to the likelihood of failure, he strode forward as 'Zeus in the likeness of a Persian man with the name of Xerxes' (Herodotus, 7.56).[2] Intoxicated by hubristic over-confidence in his assembled military might and puffed up by a record of previous victories that rendered him 'equal to god', Xerxes' avaricious ambitions allied to a reckless determination to win and a fatal under-estimation of the Greeks under the command of the wily Themistocles, caused him to commit a series of strategic blunders.
He and his army suffered a crushing defeat by the Greek navy in the Straits of Salamis which forced a subsequent humiliating retreat (Thucydides, 1.73–74).

It was hubris that seduced Xerxes into transgressing the divine decree, and as punishment the gods unleashed nemesis. In crossing the natural boundary of the Hellespont from Asia to Greece – and insensible both to wise advice and portents of doom along the way – he assaulted the honour of the gods against the express ordinance of Zeus (Papadimitropoulos, 2008). In such circumstances, Nemesis, the goddess of retribution, was always quick to act and 'fortune's fateful hand' prepared to 'pour on him the vengeance of the sky' (*The Persians*). The destructive outcome of Xerxes' tragedy is captured in Aeschylus' drama when the ghost of Xerxes' father, Darius, proclaims:

> So now for my whole house a staunchless spring of griefs is opened; and my son in youthful recklessness, not knowing the god's ways, has been the cause of all. He in his mortal folly thought to overpower immortal gods. Was this not some madness that possessed him?

Xerxes returned home in rags, tormented and traumatized by his tragedy. The gods had decreed that the Persians could only attain fame on land and in his rash venture the impetuous Xerxes, whose past successes blinded him to the possibility of defeat, went against all portents and warnings and exceeded his limits, and in such 'cosmic confrontations' (Kets de Vries, 1993: 90) mortals always come off worse.

Lessons for contemporary leadership have been drawn from the example of Xerxes' humiliating defeat and the destructive consequences that followed (Kets de Vries, 1993): (1) hubris is nothing new, it is a recurring theme in leadership because excessive pride and arrogance are part of the human psyche and are associated frequently with the intoxicating effects of power; (2) given the power asymmetries that exist in leadership, it may be tempting for leaders to assume that they can transgress normal constraints on behaviour; (3) followers' idealization and adulation of a highly charismatic leader can blind both parties to the realities of the situation; (4) given the magnitude of risks emanating from the hazards of hubristic leadership, it is necessary to create a countervailing force that militates against regressive and dysfunctional leader–follower relations; and (5) it can be costly to ignore portents, warnings and wise advice (Kets de Vries, 1993).

Napoleon and the March on Moscow (1812)

Over two millennia after Xerxes, Napoleon Bonaparte's decision to invade Russia was a similarly highly destructive and self-defeating act. In 1812, at the height of his powers as Emperor of France, King of Italy and geopolitical and military master of more than half of the Continent, Napoleon set out to vanquish Tsar Alexander 1st of Russia, who represented the final threat to his supremacy on mainland Europe. Napoleon convinced himself that his might and his supremacy were such that he could bring Tsar Alexander and the Russians to heel and subjugate the only nation that would not pay him homage and further build his already vast empire (Kroll et al., 2000).

Napoleon's disposition was, according to Tolstoy, narcissistically inclined already ('insane self-adulation', *War and Peace*, 1st Epilogue, Chapter 3) and his political celebrity and military success were acclaimed widely and praised extravagantly ('he combined all the qualities of the great men of history', *Journal de Paris*, 1807) (Kroll et al., 2000). As well as unremitting praise of followers and flatterers, Napoleon's hubris was fuelled by prior successes – in his military career, he had suffered only three defeats in 35 encounters and most of these were early-career losses or temporary setbacks. Consistent with the hallmarks of hubris, and in common with Xerxes, he showed disdain and disregard for the advice of his experienced commanders as to what he should and should not do (Kroll et al., 2000). Napoleon over-estimated the probabilities of success and under-estimated the chances, as well as the costs, of failure. The story is summarized in Table 2.6.

Table 2.6   Napoleon's march on Moscow

The hubris of Napoleon in the march on Moscow
When Napoleon set out on his campaign in June 1812, never in human history had one commander headed so grand an army. It comprised 611,900 soldiers from 29 different states (including 513,500 infantry and foot artillery and 98,400 cavalry and horse artillery), 1,242 field artillery pieces, 130 siege guns and 32,700 military vehicles drawn by over a third of a million draft animals (Nester, 2013). He forged for himself the largest hammer in military history and set out to knock once-and-for-all the Russian nail.
If the build-up was a logistical triumph, the campaign itself was a military disaster. Soon after crossing the Nieman River into Russian territory, the rot started to set in; the Grande Armée began to melt away because of desertion, disease, starvation and the causalities of battles (Kroll et al., 2000).
Only 12 months later, a miserable remnant of 20,000 personnel out of the almost two thirds of a million who had set out from the same river crossing a year earlier, stumbled home (Nester, 2013).

What was it about Napoleon's leadership that led to so destructive an outcome? Military historians have put this most spectacular of failures down to Napoleon's disregard for, and angry dismissal of, the advice of his experienced senior staff who warned him as to the folly of his venture. He was doggedly and irrationally determined to bring to heel and humiliate Tsar Alexander who had the temerity to defy him and offend his ego. He refused to entertain any doubts that it was he, Napoleon, who was in the right and would prevail irrespective of the odds stacked against him. He assumed that the tried-and-tested formula of hard-hitting attacks that had worked well in the past could defeat Russia on home soil (Nester, 2013). Napoleon's commitment to the venture escalated to a point at which the situation was overtaken by the magnitude of what had been set in train – in his own words, 'motion alone keeps it together. One may advance at the head of it, but not stop to go back' (Nester, 2013: 363).

A number of lessons for contemporary leadership can be inferred from the example of Napoleon's ignominious failure in attempting to subdue Russia (Kroll et al., 2000): (1) be wary of undertaking extravagant ventures on the presumption that a hubristic leader rather than the market, or objective failure rates, or the naysayers, know best – the chances are that markets, failure rates and naysayers know something worth knowing; (2) do not assume that what worked well in the past will work in the future on the presumption that what is unknowable will conform to the predictable patterns of history; (3) leaders should avoid getting so puffed up by the praise of acolytes and sycophants, or so immersed in the venture, as to become blinded by ambition and insensible to the warning signs of impending failure; and (4) escalation of commitment erode one's capability to control events and lock-in occurs, with little chance of back-tracking in a process that can take on a life of its own.

Hitler and Operation Barbarossa (1941)

By a fluke of history Operation Barbarossa – the axis powers' code name for the invasion of the Soviet Union and Hitler's aim to annihilate Soviet Communism in a 'war of extermination' (Ferguson, 2012: 442) – began on 22 June 1941 almost to the day of Napoleon setting out on his ill-fated campaign to invade Russia in June 1812. In the estimation of eminent historians, it was at this point that Hitler's 'genius for war' (Horne, 2015: 161) began to let him down in an act that is 'almost universally acknowledged [as] Hitler's fatal mistake' (Ferguson, 2012: 439). Hitler took an 'intuitive' approach to decisions, but his was a malign form of intuition underpinned by an 'ideological dogmatism ... tactical flexibility and opportunism' (Kershaw, 1998: 342) which could not and dare not be combatted by logical argument. He trusted his instincts and intuitions, had absolute confidence and conviction in his aims and displayed contempt for the opinions of others (Dreijmanis, 2005; Myers, 2002). Kershaw's appraisal of the outcome of Operation Barbarossa is summarized in Table 2.7.

Table 2.7   The outcome of Operation Barbarossa

The hubris of Hitler's decision to invade Russia
The weakness of the plan could not be laid at the door of the Italians (for their failure in Greece) or the Yugoslavs (for their 'treachery') as Hitler had sought to do. The calamity of Operation Barbarossa could only be blamed on the flawed nature and crazed ambition of Hitler and Nazi Germany's war aims which were a co-product of: (1) the driving force of Hitler's ideological obsessiveness, megalomania and will power; (2) the lack of resistance he met in the upper echelons of a regime in which the army fully supported him and shared his gross under-estimation of Soviet military power; and (3) a wildly over-ambitious plan for the campaign to be over long before the Russian winter set in.

Source: Kershaw (2000: 368–9)

Hitler, a malevolently 'intuitive genius' of war (Horne, 2015: 161), over-reached himself on three counts: (1) an ambition to invade the immense landmass of Russia itself; (2) an ill-advised commitment to an all-out attack on Moscow (both of these despite the lessons of history and at odds with the advice of commanders on the ground); and (3) in perhaps the supreme hubristic act of self-deceiving over-reach, the unnecessary declaration of war on the USA in December 1941. His self-delusion, hubristic arrogance and conceit eventually destroyed him and the Third Reich (Horne, 2015). As noted by Kershaw in the second part of his biography of Hitler entitled *Nemesis 1936–1945* (the first part being *Hubris 1989–1936*), the size of Hitler's gamble 'implied a willingness to court self-destruction, to invite the nemesis' which was likely to follow hubris on such a scale (2000: xvi).

Leadership scholars have used the case of Hitler's leadership to illustrate the role played by rhetoric, charisma and hubris in pathological aspects of leadership (referred to by Kets de Vries (2005) as 'leadership by terror'). Hitler's leadership of Nazi Germany is an example of the psychological tendencies of followers to regress into a 'powerless identification' with a leader, thereby 'diminishing their own agency' in the face of malevolent charisma, narcissism and hubris (Ladkin, 2006: 167). Moreover, Hitler's orientation to power was a 'personalized power' which emphasized personal identification and a desire to instil devotion, and the results were evident in the reverence with which his followers regarded him (Ladkin, 2006; Robinson and Topping, 2013; Yukl, 2006). In Hitler's leadership, charisma co-existed with hubris, and the followers who shared in the Führer's hubris fed his overweening arrogance and egomania (Kershaw, 1998), and they too courted disaster and shared in his nemesis (Kershaw, 1998, 2000).

Archidamus' Speech to the Spartans

The final illustration of hubris in armed conflict is a counter example, and takes us back to the Ancient Greeks: it is the exhortation of a wise leader against war – as it turned out, it was an appeal which fell on deaf ears and the conflict that followed is argued by some to have heralded the demise of Greek civilization. The context is the Peloponnesian War (431–404 BC) between the two great Greek city states of Athens and Sparta. Athens and Sparta and their various allies were great enemies. An uneasy truce had existed between them for 30 years, but Athens broke the truce which put the Spartans on a war footing. However, even though Sparta had the stronger army, the Athenians had the stronger navy and were also better prepared for war owing to the large 'war chest' they had built

Table 2.8 Archidamus' speech to the Spartans from Thucydides' *The Peloponnesian War*

Archidamus' 'intelligent restraint' speech
When the Spartans had heard the Athenians, the majority tended towards the view that the Athenians were already guilty and there should be war at once, but their King, Archidamus, who had a reputation as a man of intelligence and good sense, came forward and spoke as follows:
'Slowness and delay are nothing to be ashamed of. If you were to go to war unprepared, a hasty start could mean a drawn-out finish [and] this very slowness could be called intelligent restraint. This quality has kept us, uniquely, from arrogance in success [and] we are not seduced by the pleasant flattery of those who urge us to dangerous action against our judgment. Let us not be rushed in the brief space of one day to a decision affecting many lives, much expenditure, many cities, and our own reputation. This is the more important in that they [the Athenians] have said they are willing to go to arbitration, and when such an offer is given it is not lawful to proceed pre-emptively as if guilt were already established.'

Source: Thucydides, *The Peloponnesian War*, Book 1: 39–42 (abridged). By permission of Oxford University Press

up from the regular tributes received from their empire. Further, Athens was well placed to endure a long war. The Spartan king, Archidamus, spoke immediately before the outbreak of hostilities, urging against recklessness in starting war. Archidamus' speech is considered by many to be 'unsurpassed in its political wisdom' (Wassermann, 1953: 193) (Table 2.8).

The war dragged on through 27 long years of constant and brutal conflict, it engulfed the entire Greek world and it left Athens bankrupt, exhausted, demoralized and defeated. Although the Spartans won, the Peloponnesian war was a calamity for the whole region (Hall, 2015). Archidamus' speech is the voice of the 'warner' but one who is not heeded, even when there is still time to ward off disaster (Wassermann, 1953). Archidamus was a great warrior king who had been a leader of fighting men all his life, he was the personification of Spartan valour and viciousness, but he was also the antithesis of hubris. He is more than a wise warner, he is the epitome of the great Greek conservative virtue of *sophrosyne*, the converse of its opposing pole, the vice of *hybris*. Archidamus was the voice of self-control, reason and steadiness in an age of increasing anarchy in political and social life where rashness and ruthlessness were the early warning signs of a disintegrating society (Wassermann, 1953). The words of the wise warner were unheeded by both sides and the outcomes were devastating for the whole of classical Greece, victors (the Spartans) and vanquished (the Athenians) alike. Archidamus' speech is a lesson in intelligent restraint for political and military leaders of any era.

HUBRIS–NEMESIS AS A 'WARNING ARCHETYPE'

These and other cases from military history, as documented in the eminent military historian Sir Alastair Horne's book *Hubris: The Tragedy of War in the 20th Century* (2015), not only foreground the calamitous consequences of hubristic military and political leadership, they are also testament to the powerful role that irony and paradox play in human affairs: success breeds hubris, and hubris is the handmaiden of destruction in the form of nemesis (Engel, 2005). Hybris in classical Greece, and especially in Greek tragedy, is held to be an offence against the gods. It is an enduring fault of tragic heroes, as in Achilles's excessively violent rampages, Ajax's excessive boastings which offended Athena, or Odysseus's smug and audacious sacking of Trojan cities. As a result of the cardinal failure to not recognize and acknowledge their shortcomings – an attitude contrary to the spirit of the Delphic Oracle's most famous pronouncement 'know thyself' (γνῶθι σεαυτόν) – hubrists in any age are destined to risk the probability of divine punishment (Fisher, 1976, 1990; Friedrich, 1991; Papadimitropoulos, 2008).

Although well known, at least in the West, via classical Greek myth and literature, the dynamic between hubris and nemesis pervades other religions and cultures, not only as noted already in Christian thinking ('pride goeth before destruction, and a haughty spirit before a fall', *Book of Proverbs* 16:18, King James Version) but also Confucianism ('Pride bringeth loss; humility increase. This is the way of heaven. He comes to ruin who says that others do not equal him', in *Book of Documents*, Confucius) and Hinduism ('Pride is the gateway to defeat', Cited in Moses, 2007). The embeddedness of hubris–nemesis in myth and historical narratives points to it as a recurrent and pervasive theme in human affairs. Some have taken this to suggest that various configurations of hubris- and nemesis-like ideas in major religions, mythology, history and literature serve as an archetypal warning alerting us to strivings for power and status that are bad for group living. Hubris can infringe on prosocial behaviours and threaten the stability of groups so much so that human beings may be 'predisposed to protect prosocial behaviours and punish that which threatens them' (Trumbull, 2010: 341).

As a warning archetype, the pairing of hubris–nemesis is a simple but potent and persuasive elucidation of the dangers of hubris and a clear warning of the 'irrevocable vengeance of Némesis' (Morford and Lenardon, 1999: 90). Nemesis was the Ancient Greek goddess of vengeance and retribution, daughter of Nyx (night) and Erebus (darkness) (see Table 2.9). She personified the wrath of the gods towards those who behaved hubristically and duly extracted revenge – as in the narratives of Icarus and Phaethon – on any mortal who had the temerity to assume god-like powers. Nemesis was a powerful force who rewarded virtue and punished vice, including the vice of exaggerated pride in one's achievements or good fortune (Daly and Rengel, 2009).

Table 2.9 Nemesis in classical mythology

Nemesis
Nemesis (Νέμεσις) was both a goddess and an abstract concept. She was one of the daughters of Nyx, and beloved by Zeus. As a goddess she was charged with punishing crime, but more often she was a power charged with curbing all excess, such as excessive good fortune or arrogant pride.
Her role illustrates a basic concept in classical Greek thought: people who rise above their station expose themselves to the reprisals of the gods since they risk overthrowing the order of the world and must be punished.
Nemesis has a famous sanctuary at Rhamnus in Attica where a statue of the goddess was carved from a block of Parian marble acquired by the Persians who intended to make a trophy of it after they had captured Athens. Of course, they did not succeed, but in doing so they showed themselves to be too sure of their victory and consequently their attempt was unsuccessful. The Greek irony was complete.

Source: Hansen (2004)

Hubris, and its coupling with nemesis, may embody a primordial image or archetype in the human psyche that recurs constantly across cultural traditions (Abramson, 2007). Some have argued that Némesis personifies, in Freudian terms, a taboo embedded in primitive instinctual fear for unapproachable, demonic powers which evolved into pro-hibiting forces that manifested in rules, customs and traditions (Trumbull, 2010). From a Jungian perspective, hubris – couched in terms of an 'inflated consciousness' that is egocentric to the extent that it is conscious of nothing but its own existence – is incapable of learning from the past, is hypnotized by itself and therefore dooms itself to calamities that strike it 'dead' (Trumbull, 2010). Linking this to the idea of virtue and its opposite, vice, the egoism of inflated consciousness can cause us to overlook our indebtedness to others, over-estimate our own successes and look down on those less successful or fortu-nate than us, and in so doing we dishonour them. It represents a turning towards the vice of hubris and veering away from the virtue of humility.

A RAND Corporation report sponsored by the CIA's Office of Research and Development, took the hubris–nemesis pairing a step further in proposing a so-called 'hubris–nemesis complex' (Ronfeldt, 1994). The complex is exhibited by powerful leaders who believe they are 'god-like' (hubristic), and becomes 'blatant in moments of provocation or crisis' but is muted at other times (Ronfeldt, 1994: 13). Not only are hubrists inclined towards an arrogance in themselves, but in order to maintain their status they also seek through vengeful desire to 'confront, defeat, humiliate and punish rivals' who themselves aspire to hubris (Ronfeldt, 1994: vii). To maintain his power, the hubrist seeks to bring calamity on other hubrists. For example, Fidel Castro was a destructive and hubristic leader himself but Castro also thought and acted like a nemesis of the USA which he accused of being hubristic (Padilla et al., 2007; Ronfeldt, 1994). Leaders such as Castro fit both elements of the complex; they are hubrists but at the same time see themselves as nemesis to another powerful force they accuse of hubris.

The hubris–nemesis complex has strange dynamics that can lead to high-risk, destruc-tive behaviour, and any attempts to deter, compel or negotiate with leaders who show signs of the complex (for example, the RAND report cited Slobodan Milosevic and Saddam Hussein, both now deceased) are likely to be 'ineffectual or disastrously counter-productive' if they are based on approaches better suited to dealing with 'normal leaders' (Ronfeldt, 1994: vii). The report was prescient in that the leaders (Bush supported by Blair) who sought to deliver nemesis upon Saddam Hussein in 2003 with their policy of regime change in Iraq, were themselves demonstrably hubristic (Owen, 2012; Owen and Davidson, 2009). Each, in turn, met their own form of retribution: Saddam Hussein was executed in 2005; Bush was rated as 38th in 'best US president' ratings, and in the UK Chilcot's Iraq Inquiry delivered a nuanced but damning indictment of the part Tony Blair's leadership played in the invasion of Iraq.

Conclusion

The philosopher Mary Midgley argued that the hubris–nemesis pairing can be framed in terms of 'getting what we asked for' on the basis that bad consequences are not just a matter of chance. Acts that are wrong in themselves can be reasonably expected to have adverse effects, and as such their outcomes are a sign of what was wrong with the act in the first place (Midgley, 2004). Hubris on the part of a leader can therefore be expected to bring about negative consequences. For example, leaders' recklessness and pride combined with contempt and arrogance can be expected to put a strain on resources, cultivate disrespect, undermine trust and promote resentment, and in so doing call forth negative outcomes which are not accidental. A hubrist lacks humility and this is the antithesis of a servant leadership style. Destructive consequences follow, not because there is a direct, provable causal link between actions and outcomes, but because there are effects that someone who behaves hubristically invites and also, whether they like it or not, must therefore be committed to accepting.

Further Reading

Horne, A. (2015). *Hubris: The tragedy of war in the twentieth century*. London: Weidenfeld & Nicholson.
Kets de Vries, M. (2016). The Hubris Factor in leadership. In P. Garrard and G. Robinson (eds) *The intoxication of power: Interdisciplinary insights*. Basingstoke: Palgrave, pp. 89–99.

NOTES

1. www.theoi.com/Daimon/Hybris.html; www.theoi.com/Daimon/Polemos.html (Accessed 18 January 2018).
2. http://mcadams.posc.mu.edu/txt/ah/Herodotus/Herodotus7.html (Accessed 7 January 2018).

3
BIOLOGICAL AND NEUROSCIENTIFIC APPROACHES

WISE WARNING

'He in his mortal folly thought to overpower Immortal gods, even Poseidon. Was not this some madness that possessed him?' (Aeschylus, *The Persians*, 472 BC)

Introduction

A well-known aphorism in political leadership, first enunciated by the British politician and historian Lord Acton in a letter to a senior churchman in 1887, is that 'Power tends to corrupt, and absolute power corrupts absolutely'. Hubristic leadership is a manifestation of the corrupting effects of power – confidence and ambition become unchecked; as a result, hubrists habitually see others as being less powerful than themselves, or lacking their potency. This gives them license to pursue their own agenda unconstrained under the illusion of their personal prowess and invincibility. Beguiled by prior success, power and potency, they end up taking risky and reckless actions that not only show disregard and disrespect for others, but also invite negative outcomes.

BACKGROUND

Power and the trappings of success can lead to corruption both in politics and business. If proof were needed, look no further than Denis Kozlowski, former CEO of Tyco International, who was convicted in 2005 of crimes related to his unauthorized receipt of $81 million in bonuses, the purchase of works of art for $15 million, and the payment of an illegal $20 million fee to a former Tyco director. He was sentenced to a minimum jail term of eight years and four months and received a $70 million fine for his role in the Tyco scandal. As CEO of Tyco, Kozlowski was famed for his extravagant lifestyle and 'brazen use of a public company as his personal cash machine'. In reflecting on the power which corrupted him, Kozlowski was asked by a press reporter at his correctional facility why he wanted to buy a Monet *and* a Renoir. He replied: 'It was more about bragging rights than anything else', admitting that the sole purpose was to impress rich and famous visitors to his multimillion-dollar Fifth Avenue apartment.[1] In Kozlowski's own words: 'You become consumed by your own arrogance and you really think you can do anything.'[2] But why does power corrupt so absolutely and why does confidence become so inflated that successful people can be lured into thinking they can, in the words of Tom Wolfe in his *Bonfire of the Vanities*, be 'masters of the Universe'? Why and how, especially under conditions of volatility and uncertainty, is it possible for Keynesian 'animal spirits',[3] especially in financial markets, to drive the decision making of otherwise rational actors to the point of irrational exuberance?

This chapter will look at some possible biological and neuroscientific explanations of what happens when hubris takes hold of the bodies and brains of successful and powerful people. We will explore how recent developments in biological and neuroscientific research help us to understand how highly intelligent and successful professionals can end up abusing their power or taking decisions that can be irrationally exuberant (or irrationally pessimistic). This is important because the fall-out can not only wreck individuals' careers, it can also bankrupt businesses and damage public finances for decades if the taxpayer has to come to the rescue.

OVERVIEW OF NEUROSCIENCE AND ITS METHODS

Cognitive neuroscience is concerned with the scientific study of the biological and neural mechanisms underlying cognition, including perception, attention, memory, language and decision making – sometimes referred to as the 'neural substrates' of mental processes. The closely related areas of social neuroscience and social cognitive neuroscience (SCN) are concerned with brain-based theories of social cognition and social behaviour and the relevant processes that enable people to understand others and themselves and to navigate the social world (Lieberman, 2007; Ward, 2012). The emergent field of 'organizational cognitive neuroscience' (OCN) applies cognitive neuroscience to organizations (Senior et al., 2011) and advances in neuroscience are beginning to trickle into leadership research (Lee et al., 2012). Of the many branches of neuroscience, social cognitive neuroscience, neuroeconomics and organizational cognitive neuroscience are the most applicable to the study of leadership (Senior et al., 2011; Waldman et al., 2011).

Scientists working in neuroscience and its various subfields rely on a variety of methods of investigation which differ according to their levels of precision and their imaging capabilities. The now very familiar 'brain scan' images which provide visual representations of the processing of information by centres in the brain are derived typically from functional Magnetic Resonance Imaging (fMRI). fMRI is a non-invasive method for measuring neuronal activity in the human brain. It uses signals that arise from changes in local control of blood flow and oxygenation (haemodynamics) as a result of alterations in neuronal activity correspondent with brain function (Heeger and Ress, 2002). Although probably the most familiar method, fMRI is just one of various and rapidly evolving techniques used in neuroscientific research that are making their way into management and leadership studies (Table 3.1). Moreover, as well as studies of brain function, research has emerged in the last decade or so that has linked leader and decision-making behaviour directly with the role of hormones in risk taking and risk aversion[4] (Coates and Herbert, 2008; Waldman et al., 2011).

Table 3.1 Overview of current neuroscience methods

Method	Measures
Electroencephalography (EEG)	Changes in electrical activity
Functional magnetic resonance imaging (fMRI)	Changes in cerebral blood flow (haemodynamics)
Transcranial magnetic stimulation (TMS)	Temporary inhibition/stimulation of specific brain areas/functions
Hormones (e.g. testosterone, cortisol)	Hormone concentrations in saliva or blood
Biological implicit measures	Includes skin conductance responses, eye tracking and pupil dilation

Source: Robertson et al. (2017)

Whilst such research necessarily focuses on biological and brain-based aspects of leaders' behaviour, we must also be mindful of the fact that leadership of necessity involves followers, and that the process of leadership involves complex interactions between neural, behavioural, social and contextual variables. It is unsurprising therefore that the application of neuroscience to management and leadership has come in for criticism, for example the reductionism of 'neuro-leadership' (Lindebaum and Zundel, 2013) and the need to be alert to the dangers of 'neuromania' (the modern equivalent of the hemisphere neuro-mythology of the 1970s in management; see Hines, 1987). However, there is also the danger of over-reacting and dismissing out of hand the potential insights that cognitive and social neuroscience can offer leadership studies (Ashkanasy, 2013). The developments in neuroscience in recent decades have been impressive (Lee et al., 2012), and it would be premature to dismiss them summarily or overlook their potential for expanding the scientific understanding of hubristic leadership, especially since leadership development, for example 'neuro-leadership' (Rock, 2008), seems to be running ahead of leadership research in terms of practical application. Management research needs to be ahead of management development in this area.

In what follows we consider some of the neuroscientific and biological research that offers novel insights into the nature and causes of hubristic behaviours. The focal topics are: (1) power, empathy and hubris, given that hubrists become intoxicated by success and power and typically become contemptuous of, and arrogant towards, others; and (2) decision making and risk, given that one of the hallmarks of hubris is over-confidence in decision making, often to the point of irrational exuberance and even recklessness.

POWER, EMPATHY AND HUBRIS

It was Bertrand Russell in 1938 who said that 'the fundamental concept in social science is Power, in the same sense in which Energy is the fundamental concept in physics' (1938: 4). Hubris has been likened to an 'intoxication with power' and power can have important influence over a variety of important psychological and social processes (Garrard and Robinson, 2016). This is important for hubristic leadership because evidence from experimental studies shows how being in power can modulate various social emotions such as empathy, compassion, and so on. For example, in experiments where subjects were allocated to high-power versus low-power groups via priming (they were asked to write about situations where they exerted power or where power was exerted over them respectively), it was found that individuals in the high-power group were significantly worse at recognizing the feelings of others and less likely to take the perspective of others (Vega and Ward, 2016). The so-called 'Cookie Monster study' illustrates a similar effect (Anderson et al., 2012) (Table 3.2).

Table 3.2 The 'Cookie Monster' study (Anderson et al., 2012)

How high-power individuals violate norms governing consumption of resources
Examined whether arbitrarily assigned power would produce socially inappropriate styles of eating. Same-sex groups of three individuals with one randomly chosen individual as leader (the high-power person) were given a group writing task. After 30 minutes, the experimenter arrived with a plate of five cookies (thus allowing each participant to take one cookie, and at least one participant to comfortably take a second cookie, leaving one on the plate). The experimenters were interested in who would take a second cookie. Consistent with their predictions, high-power individuals were more likely to help themselves to a second cookie. High-power individuals were also more likely to show further impoliteness and disrespect for other participants by eating with their mouths open and creating a mess of crumbs on their faces and the table. Male high-power participants were even more disinhibited in this respect than females.

A paradox of hubris is that the traits that contribute to leaders' ascent to positions of power, such as empathy, collaboration, openness, fairness and sharing, somehow seem to fade when certain individuals gain power; they can even morph into more dysfunctional behaviours such as selfishness, inconsideration and acquisitiveness (Keltner, 2017). The resultant abuse of power can end up tarnishing the reputations and achievements of once-admired leaders (Table 3.3).

Table 3.3   Power, hubris and excess at Royal Bank of Scotland

---

The former CEO of the Bank of Scotland, Fred (formerly 'Sir Fred', knighted for his services to banking) Goodwin, led the Royal Bank of Scotland Group to be the biggest and one of the most successful businesses of its kind in the world, with more than 100,000 employees worldwide and a market capitalization worth more than Coca-Cola at its peak. However, intoxicated by power Goodwin became, in the words of one UK national newspaper, an 'ego in orbit'. He over-reached himself in many respects, especially in the disastrous acquisition of the depleted part of the Dutch Bank ABN Amro. The entire business had to be bailed out by the British government in the wake of the 2007/08 financial crisis to the tune of around than £50billion. The trappings of success in the RBS's Edinburgh headquarters (nicknamed 'Fredinburgh') with its deep-pile carpets and art-covered walls, and Goodwin's obsession with the executive car fleet, which had to be a particular blue called 'Pantone 281', came to epitomize the hubristic excesses of its former boss and were perhaps faint warning signs of what was to come.[8]

Intoxication by power prioritizes the emotions, goals and actions of high-power individuals (for example, manifested in lowered empathy) and can lead them to objectifying lower-power members of the group in un-empathetic and socially disruptive ways (Keltner et al., 2010). Once a leader has acquired power, he or she can lose some of the capacities needed to gain it in the first place. This phenomenon is also observed in narcissists who ingratiate themselves effectively with the members of the group, but can end up being rejected by the group if their narcissism leads them to abuse their power (Rosenthal and Pittinsky, 2006). The danger is that success and power, two of the hallmarks of hubris, can amplify egocentricity and self-absorption, conceit and arrogance, all of which contribute to a lack of empathy.

Researchers have speculated that the reduced empathy witnessed both in laboratory experiments and in the real world may be because of lowered 'mirroring' activity (i.e. reciprocal activation akin to a vicarious experience) in the motor cortex of high-power individuals (Galinsky et al., 2006; Hogeveen et al., 2014). The motor system (the part of the central nervous system involved in the generation and control of movements) is not only active when actions are performed but also when they are observed in someone else. This activation, which is automatic during observing someone else, can also influence the recognition and interpretation of others' actions and can directly affect affiliation with the person being interacted with (Iacoboni et al., 2005). Mirroring – beneath the level of conscious awareness and beyond conscious control (Naish and Obhi, 2015) – can trigger the same feelings in the observer as those experienced by the observed person (the neural substrates themselves are so-called 'mirror neurons'). Further, one of the behavioural consequences of mirroring is mimicry which is thought to aid our affiliation with the person we are interacting with. If mirroring is reduced in a powerful individual, it can lead to an empathy deficit and lowered understanding of the less powerful individual (Keltner, 2017) (Table 3.4).

Table 3.4 Why neural mirroring? (Iacoboni, 2009)

Why were mirror neurons selected for in human evolution, and what adaptive advantage did they confer on our ancestors?
Group living requires inter-subjectivity (understanding the minds of others)
Mirror neurons provide a pre-reflective, automatic mechanism for mirroring what is going on in the brains of other people
Mirror neurons offer an explanation for our ability to understand others effortlessly and intuitively
Mirror neurons also account for our tendency to imitate others automatically
Evolutionary processes 'wired' human beings for empathy
Our ability to empathize is a building block of our sociality and morality

Source: Iacoboni (2009: 666–7)

Biological research suggests that mirroring is the cornerstone of empathy and in terms of its neural substrates. Power may impair the neural process of mirroring such that high-power individuals are less able to understand the needs or intentions of others or see the world from the lower-power individuals' point of view (Iacoboni et al., 2005; Obhi et al., 2011). The mirror neuron system is implicated in 'motor resonance', that is the activation of similar brain networks when watching someone else perform an action. In a study of how power changes the way the brain responds to others, neuroscientists examined 'resonant activity' whereby perceiving and interaction partner involuntarily activates the same neural circuits that would underlie their experience. Scientists measure resonance by recording motor-evoked potentials (MEPs) from a specific muscle response, whilst a subject watches another person performing an action.

The effects of power on motor resonance were studied by allocating individuals to low-, neutral- and high-power groups (via priming) before observing the actions of another person. Motor resonance (MEP) was measured using transcranial magnetic stimulation (TMS). The results of this research offer evidence for the hypothesis that power can change the way the brain responds to others. High-power individuals demonstrated lower levels of motor resonance than low-power individuals, which suggests a reduced mirroring of others in the high-power individuals. Decreased motor resonance might be a neural mechanism that underlies power-induced asymmetries in social interactions and reductions in empathy (Hogeveen et al., 2014) (Figure 3.1).

Empathy involves the subjective experience of the other person's actual or inferred emotional state or at least some minimal recognition and understanding of it (Decety and Jackson, 2004). Research also suggests that there is more than one type of empathy which may be underlain by different networks of neural systems: (1) a more self-referent form that involves thinking about the other in terms of one's own thoughts and feeling; and (2) a more authentic form which 'tunes into' others and attempts to understand the world

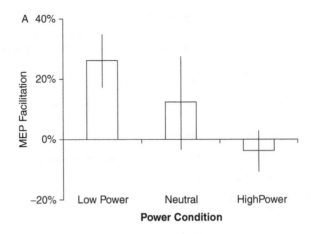

Figure 3.1   Index of motor resonance in low-, neutral-, and high-power groups

Source: Hogeveen et al. (2014). Reproduced by permission of the American Psychological Association

from their perspective (Boyatzis, 2014; Decety and Michalska, 2010). As far as hubristic leaders are concerned, intoxication with power may result in them having lowered empathy for the interests of followers and an elevated concern with their own interests, and any empathy they do espouse may be more self- than other-referent. They end up seeing the world from a single point of view, their own.

Power, and the lack of empathy that it can entail, can also lead to the stereotyping of others. For example, power and the need for control are related to information-seeking behaviour in social groups. Individuals who have low social power are motivated to seek the most diagnostic information about others in the group. On the other hand, those in the group who possess social power are inclined to seek less diagnostic information and thereby become more vulnerable to stereotyping (Fiske, 2009). An implication of this is that powerful leaders may be more likely to make un-nuanced readings of the interests and needs of others in the group and to rely on low-effort approaches to acquiring relevant information about others in the group. Hubrists may become so focused on their own interests that they see little need to integrate relevant information relating to others into their decisions. As well as reducing empathy (which may also be associated with using people as instruments of one's own goals), power can increase levels of hypocrisy, moral exceptionalism, egocentricity and the illusion of control (Robertson, 2013).

SUCCESS, RISK AND HUBRIS

A well-known example of how power and success can influence behaviour and social relations is the so-called 'winner effect' (Robertson, 2012), discovered in animal studies by the biologist Landau in the 1950s. It works as follows: if an individual has a minor contest against a member of their social group which they win (for example, because the opponent is weaker), it causes a slight increase in their chances of winning the next contest against a stronger opponent. Winning aggressive social encounters can enhance the probability of future victories and the phenomenon occurs across species from fish to primates.

This effect is thought to be mediated by post-encounter hormone release (steroid hormones such as testosterone secreted after an aggressive encounter) and can shape social structures and relationships (Fuxjager and Marler, 2009). The winner effect suggests that success may alter brain chemistry, leading to a change in temperament, feelings of greater potency, greater focus, higher confidence and more aggression. In athletic competitions, levels of testosterone rise in athletes preparing for competition, and rise even further in the winning athlete and correspondingly fall in the loser. This testosterone priming of the winner can increase their confidence and risk taking and improve their chances of winning yet again in a positive feedback loop (this is 'the winner effect' in action). However, most winners, no matter how exuberantly confident they are, eventually come up against a stronger opponent and become losers: the cycle of winning is broken (Figure 3.2).

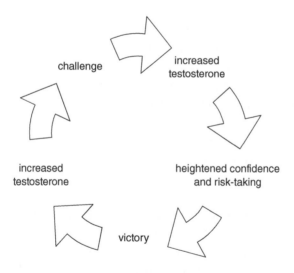

Figure 3.2 The winner effect

Source: Coates et al. (2009). Reproduced by kind permission of The Royal Society of Publishing

On the basis that financial trading is as much about the body as it is about the brain, neuroscientists have studied the role of the endocrine system in financial decision making. For example, a study of testosterone levels amongst traders in the City of London, spread over eight consecutive business days, found that traders had significantly higher testosterone levels on days when they made an above-average profit (Coates and Herbert, 2008). Although it was not possible to determine whether profits raised testosterone levels or vice versa, the researchers did find that on days of high morning testosterone the traders returned an afternoon profit. In both animal and human studies, raised testosterone has been found to increase behaviours that are likely to augment performance in the prospect of positive returns, such as search persistence, appetite for risk and fearlessness (Coates and Herbert, 2008).

If the financial equivalent of the 'winner effect' is taken too far, it could lead to impulsivity, sensation seeking and harmful risk-taking behaviours which could have negative effects on profit and loss accounts, and extend outwards from the individual to the wider market and financial system (Coates and Herbert, 2008). If rising levels of testosterone increase traders' risk appetite in a 'bull' (rising, therefore encouraging buying) market, this could shift risk preferences systematically across the business cycle towards unwarranted risky behaviour and thereby present a de-stabilizing force (Coates et al., 2018). The effect is compounded if, as research suggests, levels of cortisol (a powerful stress hormone) rise in response to volatility and scale back traders' appetite for risk during a 'bear' (falling, and therefore encouraging selling) market. Taken to extremes, this effect could result in investors freezing-up in a state of risk aversion, and in doing so push a bear market into a crash (Coates and Herbert, 2008).

The fact that there is a significant relationship between traders' testosterone levels and financial returns, and between cortisol and financial uncertainty, has implications for financial markets and policy. One effect of hormonal swings could be to substantially exaggerate market moves and contribute to instability, since traders' testosterone levels are likely to rise in a financial bubble, thereby increasing risk taking and exaggerating the market upswing (via irrational exuberance). On the other hand, traders' levels of cortisol are likely to rise in a financial crash, leading to increased risk aversion and exaggerating the market's downswing (via irrational pessimism) (Coates and Herbert, 2008). The implications of traders experiencing hubristic over-confidence in financial markets to the point of irrational exuberance or even recklessness are significant.

Research also points to sex- and age-related differences in hubristic over-confidence. Testosterone surges tend to be higher in males than females (Robertson, 2012) and testosterone declines with age (Coates et al., 2018). Financial 'bubbles' in which hubristic over-confidence comes to the fore in causing a bull market to go too far may be a 'young male' phenomenon (Coates and Herbert, 2008; Coates et al., 2018). A corollary of this is that market stability might be served by having a greater diversity of sexes and ages in trading environments to dampen down market instabilities. These findings have policy implications for the finance industry and for how to manage the destructive effects of hubristic over-confidence to which young male traders may be especially prone (Coates et al., 2018).

Risky behaviours are often undertaken with the anticipation of reward, and financial rewards are especially strong drivers of risk-related behaviours. A general principle is that as rational beings we approach rewards and avoid losses. The signals in the brain's reward system, in the form of chemical messages, are carried by the neurotransmitter dopamine. Dopamine's potency is such that it has been referred to as the brain's 'pleasure chemical' and its presence is related to sensation seeking and risk taking (Peterson, 2007). In terms of their 'routing', the reward system and the loss-avoidance system lie along different neural pathways (Table 3.5).

Table 3.5   Neural pathways for reward and loss-avoidance systems (Peterson, 2007)

Reward approach system	Lies along a dopamine pathway known as the mesolimbic pathway which extends from the base of the brain (the ventral tegmental area, VTA) through mid-brain (the nucleus accumbens, NAcc, in the limbic system) to the frontal lobes (medial prefrontal cortex, MPFC)
Loss-avoidance system	Less defined than the reward system, the loss-avoidance system's activity is mediated by the neurotransmitters serotonin and norepinephrine and it runs through the limbic system, in particular the amygdala and the anterior insula

Risk-seeking choices (such as gambling) are driven by neural mechanisms involving the NAcc (part of the dopamine 'reward' pathway) whilst risk-averse choices (such as buying insurance) are driven by neural mechanisms involving the anterior insula and 'loss' pathway (Kuhnen and Knutson, 2005). A consequence of this is that activating these regions and their associated reward/approach and loss/avoid pathways can lead to a shift in risk preferences. This could explain why casinos surround their guests with pleasurable reward cues such as free food, inexpensive drinks, gifts and potential jackpot prizes. Excessive activation of the reward approach system may lead to risk-driven mistakes which is good news for casino owners and bookmakers (Kuhnen and Knutson, 2005). If hubristic over-confidence is driven by similar neural mechanisms, then the promise of attractive and tangible rewards (for example, excessive bonuses or celebrity status in the business world) may further amplify risk-taking behaviours through neurochemical processes.

The mesolimbic circuit of the reward approach system may also be implicated in excessive risk taking that results from acute mania (a mood disorder characterized by a continuously elevated or euphoric state which causes impairment to social or occupational functioning). In financial behaviour, mania is associated with everything from extravagant shopping sprees to pathological gambling and the excessively risky trading of stocks, sometimes to the point of financial ruin. To make things even worse, treatment is sometimes refused by manic risk takers because of the dampening effect it has on the 'dopamine high' experienced as a result of hypoactivity in the brain's reward circuitry (Peterson, 2007).

GENETIC FACTORS AND RISKY DECISION MAKING

As well as the role of the endocrine system and 'brain circuitry' in risky behaviour, neuroscientists have also explored the role played by genetic factors in financial decision-making behaviour. For example, researchers studied the role played by different variants of the genes associated with the neurotransmitters dopamine and serotonin and how these affected participants' behaviour in a so-called 'framing task' in which they could either choose to receive a certain amount of money or take a gamble (Roiser et al., 2009).

The variants in the genotype (i.e. the different forms of genes, or alleles, present for a particular characteristic) of the serotonin transporter gene 5-HTTLPR[5] are associated with activity of the amygdala (part of the brain's emotional response system). The genotypic variations studied in the research were in terms of the short ('s') and long ('l') variants of 5-HTTLPR, and specifically individuals with the short/short genotype of this gene ('s/s') versus those with the long/long genotype ('l/l') (i.e. the participants selected were 'homozygous' for these alleles).[6] Carriers of the short ('s') allele at this locus are known to exhibit greater amygdala reactivity to emotional stimuli relative to those homozygous for the long ('l') allele (Roiser et al., 2009: 2). The gambling task used by the researchers involved the well-known framing effect, i.e. how the presentation (framing) of a problem affects participants' responses to it (Table 3.6).

Table 3.6 Framing task used in the genetically-mediated bias in decision-making study (Roiser et al., 2009)

Frame	Options for gambling or not with £50
Gain frame	Option A ('keep') was to keep £20 (for certain)
	Option B ('gamble') was to gamble with a 40% chance of keeping the full £50 and a 60% chance of losing everything
Loss frame	Option A was to lose £30 (for certain)
	Option B (the gamble) was as above, i.e. to gamble with a 40% chance of keeping the full £50 and a 60% chance of losing everything

Roiser and colleagues found that a strong bias was evident towards 'keep' (risk aversion) when the decision was framed in terms of gains (the 'gain' frame, i.e. keep £20), and 'gamble' (risk seeking) when the decision was framed in terms of losses (the 'loss frame', i.e. lose £30; the 'framing effect'). Individuals tend to be more risk averse when situations are framed positively, and more risk seeking when they are framed negatively (Tversky and Kahneman, 1981). The novel findings were in terms of the biology of risk-versus-certainty behaviours, i.e. a genetic effect: individuals with the short/short ('s/s') gene variant were significantly more susceptible to the framing effect than were those with the long/long ('l/l') genotype. These findings were thought to be due to the short/short ('s/s') 5-HTTLPR individuals' decisions being biased by automatic negative emotional responses to the framing of the task (which made them more sensitive to losses and risk-averse), and this over-rode analytical decision-making processes (Roiser et al., 2009).

Imaging data acquired at the same time also showed greater amygdala (i.e. emotional) activation in the short/short group, whereas there was increased coupling between the amygdala and the frontal regions of the brain (specifically the anterior cingulate cortex (ACC) which is involved in higher-level cognitive functions and emotional regulation) in the long/long individuals. These findings are consistent with the view that enhanced sensitivity to losses (risk aversion) is driven by automatic negative emotions emanating from the limbic system (of which the amygdala is a part) and that cognitive control emanating from the ACC may be over-riding basic emotional responses in less risk-averse ('l/l') individuals (Rosier et al., 2009).

Other research has extended these findings with studies of the effects of both the 5-HTTLPR gene and DRD4 dopamine receptor gene associated with the processing of risk and reward. Researchers from Northwestern University, Illinois found that individuals carrying one or two copies of the long ('l') allele (i.e. 's/l' or 'l/l' individuals) demonstrated

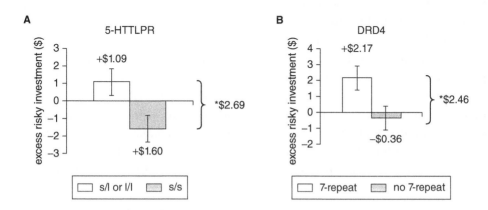

Figure 3.3 Effects of 5-HTTLPR (A) and DRD4 (B) on investment risk

Source: Reproduced from Kuhnen and Chiao (2009) *Genetic Determinants of Financial Risk Taking.* PLOS ONE 4(2): e4362.

significantly greater risk-taking behaviour relative to individuals carrying two copies of the (s') allele (i.e. 's/s'). Specifically, individuals carrying the 5-HTTLPR 's/s' genotype (see above) took 28 per cent less risk than those with short/long or long/long genotypes, whereas those carrying the DRD4 7-repeat[7] allele took 25 per cent more risk (Kuhnen and Chiao, 2009) (Figure 3.3).

These findings suggest that there could be genetic determinants which might account for why some individuals are more risk-averse and under-confident, whilst others are more risk-seeking and over-confident in their financial behaviour (Kuhnen and Chiao, 2009; Rinaldi, 2009; Roiser et al., 2009). Emerging biological evidence indicates a genetic basis for risk-taking behaviours that are consequential for financial outcomes. The relationships between neurology, hormones and genes might help to explain how Keynesian 'animal spirits' can be a major cause of the instabilities that lead to macro-economic fluctuations (Akerlof and Shiller, 2009).

FUTURE RESEARCH

The biology and neuroscience of hubris are in their infancy especially as far as management and leadership are concerned. In moving this area of research forward, several promising avenues of enquiry have been suggested (Waldman et al., 2011) which are relevant also to the study of hubristic leadership: (1) given that leadership involves dynamic processes of mutual influence (for good or ill) within groups of leaders and followers, focusing on individuals can only reveal so much about the important processes, hence theories and methods of neuroscience need to be applied to the study of multiple members of groups and the interactions between them; (2) hubristic leadership involves overly risky and over-confident decision-making processes at the top of organizations, and whilst there are promising early findings in the work on traders, for example, similar approaches need to be applied to the study of risky decision making in other leadership and organizational decision-making contexts; (3) neuroscience is well positioned to offer insights into brain-based differences between those senior leaders who are over-confident, risk-seeking decision makers and therefore may be prone to hubris versus those who are more restrained and risk-averse in their decision making; and (4) if hubristic leadership and its consequences have a moral dimension then recent discoveries regarding the neuroscience of moral judgement which implicate different brain regions in different types of moral assessments might also shed light on the ethical shortcomings associated with hubristic leadership. The application of neuroscience to hubristic leadership also opens up other connections to areas such as behavioural genetics and evolutionary psychology, and given its locus at the intersection of biology, brain and behaviour in social situations, hubristic leadership is likely to benefit most from research that engages in interdisciplinary enquiry (Garrard and Robinson, 2016).

Conclusion

Neuroscience and related sub-fields have made significant steps forward in recent decades in developing our understanding of the biological and neural mechanisms that underlie social behaviours and decision making. However, neuroscience is a comparatively young field and there is a pressing need for replications of many of the findings with work-based samples (Boyatzis, 2014; Cropanzano and Becker, 2013). And even though leadership development practitioners may be running ahead of researchers in applying neuroscience to management and leadership (Butler et al., 2016), the latest discoveries are best treated as exciting and insightful but provisional. Organizations should avoid being beguiled by brain science into encouraging or endorsing significant interventions based on preliminary evidence; more research is required (Cropanzano and Becker, 2013). Future developments in the biology and neuroscience of hubristic leadership promise new and fundamental insights into how and why individuals become intoxicated with power.

Further Reading

Coates, J. (2012). *The hour between dog and wolf: Risk taking, gut feelings and the biology of boom and bust.* London: Fourth Estate.

Garrard, P. (ed.) (2018). *The leadership hubris epidemic: Biological roots and strategies for prevention.* Basingstoke: Palgrave Macmillan.

NOTES

1. Tyco spent millions for the benefit of Kozlowski, its former CEO: www.wsj.com/articles/SB1028674808717845320 (Accessed 20 April 2017); see also Neal (2014: 111).
2. www.businesslive.co.za/bd/opinion/2018-02-02-followers-who-are-not-sheep-are-key-in-preventing-fleecing (Accessed 21 February 2018).
3. See Keynes (1936/2008: 145): 'Most probably our decision to do something positive … can only be taken as a result of animal spirits – an urge to action rather than inaction, and not as the outcome of a weighted average of quantitative benefits'.
4. One of the authors of this study, John Coates, worked for 12 years as a trader for Goldman Sachs in New York's financial district.
5. 5-HydroxyTryptamine (serotonin) Transporter Gene-Linked Polymorphic Region.
6. 'Alternative forms of a given gene are called alleles, and they can be dominant or recessive. When an individual has two of the same allele, whether dominant or recessive, they are homozygous' (Wikipedia entry, Accessed 13 March 2018).
7. Dopamine Receptor D4; specifically those with the 7-repeate allele of this gene were more risk seeking than those without the 7-repeat allele.

4
THE HUBRIS SYNDROME APPROACH

WISE WARNING

'When this check [truth] upon pride is removed, a further step is taken towards a certain kind of madness – the intoxication of power ... to which modern men, whether philosophers or not, are prone. I am persuaded that this intoxication is the greatest danger of our time.' (Bertrand Russell, *A History of Western Philosophy*, [1946] 2009: 652–3)

Introduction

As ongoing events in political and business arenas clearly show, hubris is an ever-present and ongoing danger to civil society and business. Having a hubrist at the helm of a government or business is undoubtedly a hazard – aside from ignoring it, hiding it from view or hoping it will go away, what can institutions and organizations do to reduce the risk of harm? This chapter will explore hubristic leadership from the Hubris Syndrome perspective, i.e. as a condition characterized by a group of maladaptive leadership behaviours which consistently occur together to form an identifiable pattern that is attributable to a common origin or set of factors. Hubris Syndrome has been studied mainly in the context of political leadership; management and leadership researchers have also used it to understand CEO and corporate hubris. The Hubris Syndrome approach bridges the neuroscientific (Chapter 3) and behavioural (Chapter 5) perspectives.

PERSONALITY DISORDERS AND CHANGE IN POLITICAL LEADERSHIP

So-called 'dark-side' personality disorders (Paulhus and Williams, 2002), including narcissistic, antisocial and histrionic personality disorders, Machiavellianism and psychopathy, often co-exist with 'talent, ambition and good social skills' (Hogan and Kaiser, 2005: 176).[1] For example, it was Freud himself who noted that narcissists are especially suited to taking on leadership roles since they can give fresh stimulus to the status quo and thwart stagnation, however their self-obsession can all too often turn pathological (Maccoby, 2000). From a Freudian perspective, certain dysfunctional leader behaviours may be associated with a pathological form of narcissism in which a leader looks back on former successes – as in a kind of 'rear-view mirror' – as a source of self-assurance and affirmation that their future decisions 'must surely be just as successful as those' they made in in the past (Robinson, 2016: 6).

Allied to this, the job of being a senior leader such as a head of government or a CEO is in many respects 'unreal'; presidents and prime ministers are by definition isolated outliers, who may be out of touch with daily life, largely cut off from friends if not family, and subject to flattery and sycophancy or disloyalty and treachery in equal measure. Former UK Prime Minister Tony Blair spoke in his memoir, *A Journey*, about his time in power and of 'my isolation, my precarious grip on power, and – stomach churning thought – my total dependence on things going right, not wrong' (2010: 435). Although CEOs, like prime ministers, rarely garner a great deal of sympathy, leading a business can be a significant physical, mental and emotional burden. A survey of CEOs reported in *Harvard Business Review* found that over half of them experienced feelings of loneliness in their role and almost 70 per cent of first-time CEOs felt that isolation hindered their performance.[2]

On reflection, therefore, it is unsurprising that political leaders and CEOs sometimes succumb to negative moods, personality disorders or changes, and even mental illness, whilst some leaders might even develop into 'functional psychopaths' (Barnard, 2008: 406). Indeed, it may be the case – to paraphrase Dryden – that great leadership and derailed leadership are near allied 'and thin partitions do their bounds divide'.[3] And if it is true, as Henry Kissinger is reputed to have said, that 'power is the ultimate aphrodisiac', we should hardly be surprised if senior political leaders become so intoxicated with power that it has a detrimental effect on their interpersonal relationships and performance.

Mental illnesses and personality disorders of various sorts and severities do not appear to be exceptional amongst leaders at the pinnacle of society. For example, it is estimated that amongst US presidents between 1776 and 1974, 18 out of 37 (49 per cent) met the relevant criteria that suggested psychiatric disorder (depression, 24 per cent, with sufferers including Abraham Lincoln, Woodrow Wilson and Dwight Eisenhower; anxiety, 8 per cent; bipolar disorder, 8 per cent; and alcohol abuse or dependence, 8 per cent, for example Richard M. Nixon). Moreover, in ten cases a disorder became evident during the term of office and is likely to have 'impaired job performance' (Davidson et al., 2006: 47).

British political leaders have not been immune: for example, Churchill experienced periodic depressions, and some psychiatrists also believe that his manic behaviour and crazed exultations may have been indicative of bipolar disorder (Owen and Davidson, 2009). More significantly, various dictators, despots and tyrants are also likely to have suffered from serious mental illnesses, including Benito Mussolini, Mao Zedong and Saddam Hussein, all of whom probably had bipolar disorder[4] (Owen and Davidson, 2009). Allied to this fact is the disquieting observation that the clinical care of heads of government can be 'secretive, chaotic and sub-optimal' (Coles and Coles, 2009: 1407). The gravity of this issue is compounded by the fact that the psychological and mental well-being of political leaders in particular could not be more significant because, especially in times of armed conflict, they hold the lives of the citizens of the state in their hands.

LEADER DERAILMENT IN BUSINESS

Fortunately, senior business leaders do not ordinarily hold the lives of employees in their hands but they undoubtedly have great sway over employees' well-being at work and livelihoods, as well as considerable influence over the interests of other stakeholders and the success or failure of the organizations they lead. Their derailment, like that of heads of government, is a grave and serious matter. And, as in politics, it would be surprising if, in the upper echelons of organizations, issues such as depression, anxiety, stress, alcohol or substance abuse, sleep deprivation or personality disorders were unusual occurrences. Research suggests that CEOs may be depressed by as much as double the rate of the general population and depression may be one of several 'recurring [CEO] pathologies' (Barnard, 2008: 405).[5] Mental health problems in the C-suite present a significant hazard and this is amplified by the fact that leaders' mental health issues or personality disorders may be brushed to one side or become a 'closely-kept and shameful secret' (Barnard, 2008: 418).

Whilst leaders' 'dysfunctional interpersonal dispositions' can exist alongside talent, ambition and skill, they ultimately prevent them from being effective in their role (Hogan and Kaiser, 2005: 176). Specifically, leader incompetence emanating from personality-related issues has been connected by Hogan and colleagues to so-called 'Axis II' personality disorders (i.e. borderline, obsessive-compulsive, avoidant, schizotypal, antisocial and narcissistic personality disorders).[6] For example, 'boldness' may be related to narcissistic personality disorder (is excessively self-confident; exhibits grandiosity and entitlement; is unable to learn from mistakes). The short-term strengths of such a disposition are likely to be courage, confidence and charisma, however the leadership weaknesses which are likely to surface in the longer term include an inability to admit mistakes and a sense of entitlement (Hogan and Kaiser, 2005: 177). Likewise, 'cautiousness' may be related to avoidant personality disorder (being reluctant to take risks as a result of being criticized); the short-term strength of such a disposition for leaders is that he or she is likely to make few mistakes, however a longer-term leadership weakness of being overly cautious could be dysfunctional levels of risk aversion (Hogan and Kaiser, 2005: 177). Other desirable leadership attributes (not linked explicitly to DSM-IV personality disorders), such as taking charge, taking decisions and taking control may, in their most extreme manifestations, even be forms of psychopathic propensities, i.e. 'well packaged forms of coercion, domination and manipulation' (Babiak and Hare, 2006: xi).

If business leaders become derailed, they can end up failing unexpectedly and spectacularly, and inflicting widespread harm (Furnham, 2010; Hogan and Kaiser, 2005). The paradox is that derailment dispositions, for example 'tendencies to blow up, show off, or conform when under pressure' (Hogan and Hogan, 2001: 50), may co-exist alongside strong social skills and other leadership capabilities, and therefore be largely invisible during the selection process for senior leaders or in the earlier stages of their tenure. Indeed, individuals who end up derailed may be highly skilled in making a positive impression in the short run but, once nominated and appointed, their leadership can unravel and they can end up being rejected by followers because of their arrogance, high-handedness or other dysfunctional behaviours (Hogan and Kaiser, 2005) (Table 4.1).

Table 4.1 Relevant Hogan derailment dimensions (Hogan and Hogan, 2001)

Derailment dimension	Strength	Weakness
Excitable	Great charisma and excitement for projects and people	Moodiness, sensitivity to criticism and volatile emotional displays
Bold	Ambitious and self-confident	Self-absorbed, cocky and unwilling to admit mistakes
Mischievous	Charming and friendly	Manipulative, impulsive and taking ill-advised risks

It is often the case that such behaviours emerge eventually in individuals whose personalities predispose them to derailment (Hogan and Kaiser, 2005). The faint signals of a leader's incompetence may be noticed at first by subordinates because 'bad managers let down their guard around their staff' (Hogan and Hogan, 2001: 50). The downside of this is that the early warning signs may escape the attention of those higher up and therefore better positioned to take effective action and to avoid destructive consequences, such as board members or regulators.

Unlike narcissistic personality disorder (NPD), hubris is not formally recognized as a disorder, however hubristic leadership is without doubt a potent derailment factor. As such, it is especially problematic for institutions and organizations because what may at the time of the leader's appointment have been keenly sought-after strengths – such as self-confidence, ambition and pride, and which likely contributed to such individuals 'emerging from the pack to become leaders' (Owen, 2008: 430) – can morph under the influence of power and success into the toxic weaknesses of over-confidence, over-ambition and arrogance. Power and success allied to praise and lack of constraint can catalyse the transformation of leaders' strengths into weaknesses.

HUBRIS SYNDROME

In the Hubris Syndrome approach, hubristic leadership is framed in terms of a group of symptoms that occur consistently together and indicate an abnormality or dysfunctionality (Owen, 2007; Owen and Davidson, 2009). Although research into Hubris Syndrome is so far confined mainly to political leaders, if hubristic leadership is an issue of psychological and mental well-being that can have deleterious effects both for all leaders and followers then there is a need to understand its occurrence and the effects it can have on leaders in all walks of life (Owen, 2011a). Hubris is an occupational hazard for leaders, and when it manifests as a 'sort of mental illness' (Owen, 2007: ix) it can be 'as great a menace to the quality of their leadership as are conventional illnesses' (Owen, 2006: 551).

The idea of 'Hubris Syndrome' was born out of a politician's curiosity into the mental health of political leaders. The originator of the idea is Lord David Owen. The authority and distinctiveness of Owen's contribution stems from the unusual fact that he has occupied positions both as a senior political leader and as a physician specializing in mental health. Indeed, over the generations, many members of his family not only worked in medicine or professions related to medicine but also involved themselves in politics which is perhaps why, in his own words, 'I have found it quite normal that medicine and politics should play the role of natural partners in my life [and] although at times medicine has been crowded out by politics, my love for it has never weakened' (Owen, 2016: xii) (Table 4.2).

Table 4.2   Brief biographical sketch of Lord David Owen, originator with Jonathan Davidson of the Hubris Syndrome concept

Lord David Owen CH PC FRCP: Brief biography
Owen is an independent social democrat in the UK's House of Lords. Prior to this, he held several senior posts in two Labour governments; he served as Navy Minister, Health Minister and Foreign Secretary (1966–92) under Prime Ministers Harold Wilson and James Callaghan. Owen subsequently co-founded and then led the Social Democratic Party (1983–90). On the international stage, Owen served as EU peace negotiator in the former Yugoslavia in 1992–95, working alongside the UN-appointed peace negotiator, US Secretary of State Cyrus Vance (with whom he co-authored the Vance–Owen Peace Plan). However, as well as being a senior politician and statesman, Owen is also a Cambridge-educated physician. He was a neurological and psychiatric registrar from 1964 to 1966 and research fellow in neuroscience in the medical unit from 1966 to 1968 at St Thomas' Hospital in London.[11] Lord Owen was chairman of the Trustees of the Daedalus Trust established to promote the interdisciplinary study of how 'the intoxication of power' in all walks of life can affect personality and decision making.[12]

Placed uniquely as he is to comment on and understand mental health issues as they pertain to heads of government and heads of state, Owen's work in this area has covered both the general mental and physical health of political leaders (*In Sickness and in Power: Illness in Heads of Government during the Last 100 Years*, published 2008) and the particular study of hubris in political leadership (*The Hubris Syndrome: Bush, Blair and the Intoxication of Power*, published 2007). It was he who coined the term 'Hubris Syndrome'

(Owen, 2007) and subsequently elaborated on it systematically in a co-authored arti-cle with Duke University professor of psychiatry and behavioural sciences, Jonathan Davidson (see Owen and Davidson, 2009).

CHARACTERISTICS OF HUBRIS SYNDROME

A syndrome is a condition characterized by a group of symptoms which consistently occur together, rather than separately, and may be attributable to a common origin (Colman, 2001). They form an identifiable pattern that indicates the existence of an abnormality, disorder, disease or mental condition. Owen and colleagues argue that extreme hubristic behaviour constitutes a syndrome, consisting as it does of a cluster of features ('symp-toms') evoked by a specific trigger (substantial power) and characterized by, amongst other things, exuberant self-confidence, recklessness and contempt for others (Garrard et al., 2014; Owen and Davidson, 2009).

Hubris Syndrome is a malaise of leaders who appear to be 'normal' on being appointed or taking office, but who lose capacity and competence as a result of the onset of the syn-drome and for whom nemesis in some guise or other often follows (Owen, 2008). The link to leader derailment was captured by Bertrand Russell in *A History of Western Philosophy*: 'When this check [truth] upon pride is removed, a further step is taken towards a *certain kind of madness* – the intoxication of power ... to which modern men, whether philoso-phers or not, are prone. I am persuaded that this intoxication is the greatest danger of our time' (B. Russell, 1946/2009: 652–3, emphasis added). In aiming to establish connections between power and derailed and destructive leader behaviour that has a 'whiff of mental instability about it', Owen is careful to avoid terms such as 'insanity', 'lunacy', 'madness' or 'psychosis' (G. Russell, 2011), preferring instead to couch it in terms of the intoxicating effects of power on leader personality.

Owen and colleagues have proposed 14 clinical features, or symptoms, of Hubris Syndrome (Owen, 2007, 2008; Owen and Davidson, 2009) (Table 4.3). Several of the symptoms have similarities to those for antisocial, histrionic and narcissistic personality disorders (APD, HPD and NPD), as classified in the American Psychiatric Association's *Diagnostic and Statistical Manual of Mental Disorders*, Version-IV (DSM-IV; the symptoms were formulated before the publication of DSM-V in 2013). Seven of the 14 symptoms of Hubris Syndrome have similarities to the DSM-IV criteria for NPD (HS Criteria 1–4 and 7–9), whilst two of the 14 have similarities to those for APD (HS Criterion 11) and HPD (HS Criterion 14).

Five of the Hubris Syndrome criteria are unique (Criteria 5, 6, 10, 12 and 13), and it may be that these five symptoms give the best clues as to what to look out for when a leader is crossing the line into hubris (Eccles, 2014): (1) an identification with the nation or organization to the extent that the individual regards his/her outlook and interests as identical (Symptom 5); (2) a tendency to speak in the third person or use the royal 'we' (Symptom 6); (3) an unshakeable belief that in that court [i.e. history or God] they will be vindicated (Symptom 10); (4) restlessness, recklessness and impulsiveness (Symptom 12); and (5) a tendency to allow their 'broad vision', about the moral rectitude of a proposed course, to obviate the need to consider practicality (Symptom 13).

Table 4.3   The symptoms of Hubris Syndrome

Proposed criteria for Hubris Syndrome	Correspondence to other personality disorders*
1. A narcissistic propensity to see their world primarily as an arena in which to exercise power and seek glory	NPD 6
2. A predisposition to take actions which seem likely to cast the individual in a good light, i.e. in order to enhance image	NPD 1
3. A disproportionate concern with image and presentation	NPD 3
4. A messianic manner of talking about current activities and a tendency to exaltation	NPD 2
5. An identification with the nation or organization to the extent that the individual regards his/her outlook and interests as identical	Unique
6. A tendency to speak in the third person or use the royal 'we'	Unique
7. Excessive confidence in the individual's own judgement and contempt for the advice or criticism of others	NPD 9
8. Exaggerated self-belief, bordering on a sense of omnipotence, in what they personally can achieve	NPD 1 & 2
9. A belief that rather than being accountable to the mundane court of colleagues or public opinion, the court to which they answer is history or God	NPD 3
10. An unshakable belief that in that court they will be vindicated	Unique
11. Loss of contact with reality; often associated with progressive isolation	APD 3 and 5
12. Restlessness, recklessness and impulsiveness	Unique
13. A tendency to allow their 'broad vision', about the moral rectitude of a proposed course, to obviate the need to consider practicality	Unique
14. Hubristic incompetence, where things go wrong because too much self-confidence has led the leader not to worry about the nuts and bolts of policy	HPD 5

Note: *Correspondence to cluster B personality disorders in DSM-IV (NPD, narcissistic personality disorder; HPD, histrionic personality disorder; APD, anti-social personality disorder).

Source: Owen and Davidson (2009: 1398). By permission of Oxford University Press

Owen and colleagues have proposed that for an affirmative 'diagnosis' of Hubris Syndrome at least three out of the 14 symptoms should be present, including at least one of the unique Hubris Syndrome criteria (i.e. Symptoms 5, 6, 10, 12 or 13). Additionally, there should be no other potential medical or psychiatric explanation (for example, hypomania, bipolar disorder, depression, organic brain disease or injury, drug or alcohol abuse) for the observed abnormal behaviour. This exclusion criterion resulted in some potential candidates for Hubris Syndrome amongst US and UK political leaders being excluded (Garrard et al., 2014). For example, amongst UK prime ministers, although Churchill (1940–45; 1950–55) showed hubristic traits, the fact that he suffered from a major depressive disorder excluded him in Owen and Davidson's categorization of Hubris Syndrome. Likewise, amongst US presidents Theodore Roosevelt (1901–09) and Lyndon B. Johnson (1963–69) both displayed hubristic traits but also suffered from bipolar disorder and therefore were not categorized as displaying the syndrome (Owen and Davidson, 2009: 1399).

Because Hubris Syndrome is linked both with the possession of power and the context in which leaders exercise their power, it is not to be considered a personality disorder as such but rather a 'disorder of the *possession* of power' (Owen and Davidson, 2009: 1397, emphasis added). Power is a prerequisite; Hubris Syndrome grows with power, and when power wanes the syndrome will normally remit (Owen, 2008). Holding substantial power is one of the 'key external factors' for the development of Hubris Syndrome; the others include length of time in power, prior successes, and minimal constraints on the leader's exercising of personal authority (Owen, 2008: 429) (Figure 4.1).

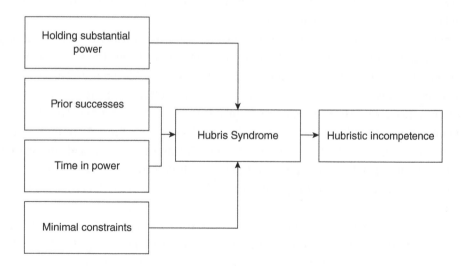

Figure 4.1   Antecedents of Hubris Syndrome

The role of these contextual factors distinguish Hubris Syndrome from other personality disorders and syndromes, such as NPD, that tend to manifest by the late teens and persist over the life span. In this respect, Hubris Syndrome should be seen as 'something that manifests in any leader but only when in power', hence it may be considered 'an illness of the *office* as much as of the person' (Owen, 2011a: xxvii, emphases added). Although Owen's work focuses mainly on politicians, Hubris Syndrome is also pertinent to individuals who hold other powerful professional positions (Russell, 2011).

HUBRIS SYNDROME AMONGST POLITICAL LEADERS

The concept of Hubris Syndrome developed out of Owen combining the mindsets of clinician and politician (Russell, 2011), and it is natural therefore that the focus of attention in Hubris Syndrome research has been the study of political leaders. As noted above, the idea of Hubris Syndrome is part of a wider project by Owen (2011a) to chronicle the effects of illness (both physical and mental) on heads of government. This raises three important issues in relation to the impact of physical and mental illness on decision making at the top of government: (1) the inherent danger in keeping heads of government's illnesses secret; (2) the challenge in democracies or dictatorships of removing heads of government whose competence has been debilitated by illness from positions of power; and (3) the responsibility that illness in heads of government places on their doctors. Similar comments must apply to CEOs.

Owen (2011a) offers several case histories of physical and mental illness amongst heads of state (for example, UK Prime Minister Anthony Eden, US President John F. Kennedy, The Shah of Iran and France's President Francoise Mitterrand). He also identified several heads of state who succumbed to Hubris Syndrome: US President George W. Bush (in office 2000–08), and UK Prime Ministers David Lloyd George (1916–22), Neville Chamberlain (1937–40), Margaret Thatcher (1979–90) and Tony Blair (1997–2007). Owen's research is focused mainly on US and UK leaders. His political life was contemporaneous with Thatcher, Bush and Blair and involved personal encounters with Blair as documented in *The Hubris Syndrome: Bush, Blair and the Intoxication of Power* (Owen, 2008).

It is likely that leaders of other nations, both democratic and dictatorial, suffered from the syndrome (for example, Fidel Castro; see Padilla et al., 2007), but their cases have yet to be documented in any depth. It is also important to bear in mind that relevant exclusion criteria must be applied in any classification. This means that individuals who have incontrovertibly been hubristic in some of their actions are not categorized as having the syndrome because of other factors which may have accounted for their behaviours, for example President Nixon's alcohol abuse disqualified him (see Table 4.4).

Table 4.4   Illnesses related to hubris and Hubris Syndrome amongst US presidents and UK prime ministers in office since 1908 (Owen and Davidson, 2009)

Note: ?= uncertain – probable

Presidents and prime ministers	Related illnesses to hubris	Hubris Syndrome
Presidents		
Theodore Roosevelt (1901–09)	Bipolar disorder	No
Woodrow Wilson (1913–21)	Anxiety disorder; major depressive disorder; personality change due to stroke	?
Franklin D. Roosevelt (1933–45)	None	No
John F. Kennedy (1961–63)	Addison's disease; Amphetamine abuse	No
Lyndon B. Johnson (1963–69)	Bipolar 1 disorder	No
Richard M. Nixon (1969–74)	Alcoholic abuse	?
George W. Bush (2001–09)	History of alcohol-related problems	Yes
Prime Ministers		
Herbert Asquith (1908–16)	Alcohol abuse	No
David Lloyd George (1916–22)	None	Yes
Neville Chamberlain (1937–40)	None	Yes
Winston Churchill (1940–45; 1951–55)	Major depressive disorder: cyclothymic features	No
Anthony Eden (1955–57)	Amphetamine abuse	No
Margaret Thatcher (1979–90)	None	Yes
Tony Blair (1997–2007)	None	Yes

Source: Owen and Davidson (2009: 1398). By permission of Oxford University Press

One UK head of government who was, in Owen's view, indisputably hubristic was the former Prime Minister Tony Blair. Blair came to power in 1997 with a landslide majority and had many notable successes as leader, including the Northern Ireland 'Good Friday Agreement', but was castigated ultimately for his support of George W. Bush's decision to invade Iraq in 2003. During the early days of Blair's premiership, Owen, based on a personal meeting with him in 1998, found him to be 'anything but hubristic'; he was cool and rational with no undue hyperactivity (Owen, 2008: 255).

The signs of Blair's hubris first began to show in relation to NATO's bombing campaign in Kosovo (part of the NATO bombing of the former Yugoslavia in 1999) which was his first major foreign affairs challenge. At this point, according to Owen, Blair's disposition appeared to have changed to one of personal dominance, excessive self-confidence and pride in his own judgements (Owen, 2008; Owen and Davidson, 2009). A member of Bill Clinton's administration is reputed to have remarked that Blair was showing signs of 'grandstanding', overplaying his hand and adopting a Churchillian tone; one US official even remarked that he was 'sprinkling too much adrenalin on his cornflakes' (Owen and Davidson, 2009). Blair's hubristic leadership, like that of George W. Bush (a similarly 'big picture' politician), emerged fully fledged around the time of 9/11. It is also notable that before coming to office Blair, like George W. Bush, had no prior foreign affairs experience. In Owen's estimation, this proved damaging in the final analysis to his premiership (Owen, 2008).

By the time Owen met Blair again in 2002, he had noticed a marked change from the cool rational politician of four years earlier; Blair exuded total confidence in himself and his decisions, was dismissive of the complications of an Iraq invasion and exhibited a restlessness and hyperactivity comporting himself with an almost 'messianic' manner (Owen, 2008: 271). Owen goes on to argue that Blair's over-confidence, over-emotion and contempt for critics manifested as a leadership incompetence which was 'no ordinary incompetence, it was hubristic incompetence' (p. 429). The hallmarks of Blair's hubris are summarized alongside those of another leader judged to have succumbed to Hubris Syndrome, Margaret Thatcher (Table 4.5).

Table 4.5   The hallmarks of hubris in Margaret Thatcher and Tony Blair

Tony Blair (PM, 1997–2007)	Margaret Thatcher (PM, 1979–90)
Zealotry and a lack of nuance and qualification; excessive self-confidence and certainty that reserved decision making to himself and a small inner circle; simplicity, restlessness and inattention to detail; failure to seek or listen to advice and be contemptuous of the views of others, especially if they conflicted with his own; a desire to be at the centre of events, seizing opportunities for eye-catching initiatives; accountability ultimately to god, and post 9/11 waging a battle of good triumphing over evil; restless pursuit of personal legacy up to leaving office in 2007	Warning signs in early 1980s (divisiveness and dismissiveness); confidence boosted by victory in the Falklands war (1982) and 'defeat' of the miners (1985); dispensed with critics and surrounded herself with like-minds; became dangerously confident of her own judgement and contemptuous of other people's; introduction of the universally unpopular poll tax, with the conviction she was right the litmus test of her hubris; use of the royal 'we'; failure to grasp the political reality of German reunification; manic behaviour in the House ('No!, no!, no!' speech)

Source: Burton and McCabe (2009); Owen (2008: 92–96, 262–3); Owen and Davidson (2009)

Prime Minister Thatcher's full-blown hubris became evident in 1990. She returned from a meeting with European leaders and issued statements about what she would not 'put up with' from Europe, was unwilling to compromise and showed scorn and contempt towards senior colleagues, particularly the former Foreign Secretary, the mild-mannered Geoffrey Howe. In the contempt which marked out her hubris, Thatcher devalued and dishonoured Howe and other senior colleagues; unsurprisingly, therefore, Nemesis duly arrived in the unlikely guise of Howe's modestly delivered but devastatingly disparaging resignation speech in the House on 13 November 1990 (Table 4.6). In the end, she was removed not by her 'supine' cabinet but by Conservative MPs who voted in favour of a leadership challenge which she ultimately lost (Owen, 2008: 94–5).[7]

Table 4.6   Extract from Sir Geoffrey Howe's resignation speech delivered to the House of Commons on 13 November 1990

Margaret Thatcher's nemesis: The penultimate paragraph from the resignation speech of Sir Geoffrey Howe (Chancellor of the Exchequer, Leader of the House, Former Foreign Secretary and Deputy Prime Minister, 1979–90)
'In my letter of resignation, which I tendered with the utmost sadness and dismay, I said: "Cabinet Government is all about trying to persuade one another from within". That was my commitment to Government by persuasion – persuading colleagues and the nation. I have tried to do that as Foreign Secretary and since, but I realize now that the task has become futile: trying to stretch the meaning of words beyond what was credible, and trying to pretend that there was a common policy when every step forward risked being subverted by some casual comment or impulsive answer.
'The conflict of loyalty, of loyalty to my right hon. Friend the Prime Minister – and, after all, in two decades together that instinct of loyalty is still very real – and of loyalty to what I perceive to be the true interests of the nation, has become all too great. I no longer believe it possible to resolve that conflict from within this Government. That is why I have resigned. In doing so, I have done what I believe to be right for my party and my country. The time has come for others to consider their own response to the tragic conflict of loyalties with which I have myself wrestled for perhaps too long.'

Source: http://hansard.millbanksystems.com/commons/1990/nov/13/personal-statement (Accessed 25 February 2018)

Blair's hubristic rise and fall was complete in 2007 when he stepped down as prime minister, forced out by his own party, somewhat earlier than he had wished – towards the end of his tenure, when Blair was being subjected to a welter of opprobrium, ever-mounting pressure to resign, and stigmatized by the 'cash-for-peerages' affair. In his autobiography, he commented gnomically that during his last summer as prime minister 'I had my determination to comfort me, and by and large it did (which is what happens to leaders when the final *hubris* overwhelms them)' (Blair, 2010: 600, emphasis added).

HUBRIS SYNDROME AMONGST BUSINESS LEADERS

Even though Hubris Syndrome has been researched mostly in political leadership, there is unrealized potential for its application to the study of hubristic leadership in business organizations (Eccles, 2014). It is undeniable that hubristic leadership at the top of business organizations can have highly damaging effects. The challenges that exist in business in removing senior leaders from positions of power once they become derailed and debilitated by hubris, are of a different category to those in the political arena. In the UK, system cabinet government can serve as a check and balance on hubristic leadership, and the ballot box is an ever-present threat to a leader's power. Hubris at the top of business organizations, on the other hand, places great responsibility on a wider and more diverse constituency of stakeholders, including board members, senior managers and employees more widely, as well as shareholders to recognize hubris and take the necessary preventative or corrective measures, or to avoid appointing a hubrist in the first place.

Owen (2011b) points to the examples of hubristic behaviour in UK banks in the lead up to the financial crisis of 2007/08. He singles out the then Chief Executive of Royal Bank of Scotland (RBS), Fred Goodwin, as an example of the exuberant and excessive self-confidence and contempt for the advice and criticism of others that is one of the hallmarks of the syndrome (Symptom 7). Encouraged by his resounding prior success in the £22 billion hostile takeover of one of the UK's biggest and oldest banks, Nat West, by RBS in 2000[8] Goodwin 'flew too close to the sun' in the disastrous takeover of ABN Amro in 2007, described by some commentators as one of the worst acquisitions ever (Table 4.7).

Table 4.7 Hubris and nemesis at the Royal Bank of Scotland

Knighthood, nemesis and annulment at Royal Bank of Scotland (RBS)
In October 2007, a consortium led by RBS forked out £49 bn for the Dutch bank, a figure estimated to be three times its book value, but by the time the acquisition took place ABN Amro had sold on to Bank of America its most prized asset and encumbered RBS with an underperforming London-based investment banking franchise which had various dubious loans on its books and a handful of smaller Asian operations.[13] This decision was instrumental in RBS's decline and played a significant role in the wider financial crisis, and contributed to the fact that RBS needed a Treasury bailout of RBS in 2008 to stop it going under, which ended up costing the UK taxpayer £45 bn. It proved to be Goodwin's undoing. His tale is one of classic hubristic decline and fall. Goodwin's exalted rise climaxed in his being knighted in 2004 for his services to banking, whilst his nemesis culminated in the honour being annulled by Her Majesty the Queen in 2012 in light of the fact that, in the words of a Cabinet Office spokesman:
The failure of RBS played an important role in the financial crisis of 2008/9 which, together with other macroeconomic factors, triggered the worst recession in the UK since the Second World War and imposed significant direct costs on British taxpayers and businesses. Fred Goodwin was the dominant decision-maker at RBS at the time. In reaching this decision [to annul], it was recognised that widespread concern about Fred Goodwin's decisions meant that the retention of a knighthood for 'services to banking' could not be sustained.[14]
In a 'symbolic moment' in 2018, RBS delivered a profit for the first time in nine years (£752 million).[15]

Hubris is a significant occupational hazard for business leaders. A number of attributes of individuals can protect individuals ('immunity factors') from succumbing to the syndrome in the first place (Garrard, 2018; Otazo, 2018), see Table 4.8.

Table 4.8 Immunity factors against hubris and Hubris Syndrome (Garrard, 2018; Otazo, 2018)

Immunity factor	Description
Modest	Leaders who are likely to retain a personal modesty as they stay in power
Grounded	Leaders who keep, as much as is practical, to their previous lifestyle and eschew the trappings of power and success
Consultative	Leaders who consult carefully even if, as a result of the process of checking, they do not necessarily change their opinion
Respectful	Leaders who accept and respect that institutional or organizational checks and balances should be built-in, acknowledged and respected scrupulously
Open	Leaders who embrace the views of valued confidantes and welcome constructive criticism
Self-deprecating	Leaders who retain a sense of humour about themselves, and are able to exercise self-criticism, self-cynicism and humility

Owen also points to the dangers of collective or cultural, as well as individual, hubris in the business sector and cites the example of British Petroleum. In Owen's view, excessive risk taking under former Chief Executive Lord Browne, who in Owen's assessment 'developed many of the features of Hubris Syndrome during the last few years of his tenure' (Owen, 2011b: 144), led to a 'lack of safety and technical rigour' (2011b: 146). Hubristic over-confidence may well have been a contributing factor in the explosion at the Deepwater Horizon oil well in the Gulf of Mexico in 2010, and subsequent oil spill that is estimated to have cost the company £65 billion.[9]

Collective hubris is a manifestation of the culture of an organization and arises as a result of managers developing shared mindsets and ways of working based on successful performance which are repeated and extended and become self-reinforcing over time to the point of complacency and over-confidence (Shimizu and Hitt, 2004). Moreover, a hubristic culture which takes too much for granted is antithetical to organizational learning (Haleblian and Finkelstein, 1999). A consequence is that hubristic executives, by setting the 'tone from the top', can help to create a hubristic organizational culture which assumes collectively that their organization is unlikely to fail, and this can seduce the business into pushing the boundaries and crossing the Rubicon into dangerous territory.

Creating such a culture can be especially problematic in high-risk endeavours such as oil exploration and production (Ladd, 2012; Sylves and Comfort, 2012) or aeronautics and space (Mason, 2004). The Deepwater Horizon explosion and subsequent oil spill was the result of a relentless pursuit of oil from deeper, more extreme and ever more hazardous locations (Ladd, 2012). Production pressures allied to a culture of over-confidence in human judgement and technological systems and safeguards can seduce decision makers into taking unacceptable risks. For example, at Deepwater, BP was not only highly confident in its sea floor containment-cap technology, it was also experimenting with drilling at a water depth of one mile and then four miles into the sea floor (Sylves and Comfort, 2012: 88; see also Chapter 6).

CRITICISMS OF HUBRIS SYNDROME

In framing hubris as a 'syndrome', Owen and colleagues have given the study of hubristic leadership a rigorous and scientific edge (Bollaert and Petit, 2010). In so doing they have gone some way to rescuing hubris from the imprecisions of hyperbole and rhetoric inherent in popular political discourse (Marquand, 2007). But, nevertheless, as a personality disorder it is rightly accorded a 'tentative' treatment (Coles and Coles, 2009: 1409). Owen himself acknowledges that Hubris Syndrome is not an accepted diagnostic category of mental illness, and that its operationalization requires further refinement and validation before it could be considered for acceptance into the canon of recognized psychiatric conditions in DSM-V or the International Statistical Classification of Diseases 10th Revision (ICD-10) (Owen, 2008; Russell, 2011).

One source of criticism has been its classification. Russell (2011) states that in choosing the term 'Hubris Syndrome', Owen and colleagues have reached a 'cautious compromise' that allows for the identification of abnormal behaviours (operationalized in the 14 symptoms) for diagnosis but without necessarily ascribing a pathological status to the syndrome (p. 143). In Russell's view, Owen has, perhaps wisely, 'hedged his bets' between 'abnormal behaviour' and 'pathology' by avoiding the concept of disease or illness. Indeed, there may also have been some vacillation on how Hubris Syndrome might best be conceptualized – for example, on the one hand, it is something worthy of exploration as a 'medically constituted syndrome' (Owen, 2007: xv), whilst on the other it 'should not be seen as a personality syndrome but as something which manifests in leaders only when in power' (Owen, 2007: 3). Hubris Syndrome researchers appear to have alighted most recently on seeing Hubris Syndrome as an 'acquired personality *trait*', acquired when leaders are in power and abating once power is lost, 'rather than as an acquired personality *disorder*' (Owen, 2016: 23, original emphases).

This is a welcome and positive move for several reasons. Despite the scientific advantages of casting hubris as a psychiatric condition or personality disorder, such an approach could undermine the potential for those closest to the 'sufferer', but who are unlikely to be qualified mental health professionals, to make a diagnosis and initiate corrective actions. Making it a medical condition shifts the burden of proof on to doctors who may be too distant from the leader to recognize the symptoms or too unconnected to the context to take any action (Coles and Coles, 2009). Arguably, it is those closest to hubrists who are best placed to spot the early warning signs and sound the alarm

(Owen, 2007). This latter point is significant. Owen was not only interested in establishing a formal 'diagnosis' but also, and perhaps more importantly, aimed to be able to 'call out' a kind of public cognitive apathy in which followers are often 'slow to acknowledge signs of irrational behaviour in their chosen leaders' (and thereby acknowledge their own poor choice) and are complicit in the hubristic leadership process as colluders or conformers. Such 'calling out' entails constant and ongoing monitoring and critical appraisal to recognize the signs of incipient intoxication of power and take suitable preventative or corrective actions (Osnos, 2017). It also calls for critical reflexivity on the part of senior leaders themselves, and offers opportunities for speaking truth to power ('parrhesia') on the part of followers (Table 4.9).

Table 4.9   Truth telling as parrhesia

Countering hubris through parrhesia
'Parrhesia' (Greek, literally 'saying everything') entails saying what is true. What is spoken is true because the speaker knows it to be true. Moreover, the speaker has the moral qualities required to know the truth and convey such truth to others. The proof of the sincerity of the speaker is is his courage in speaking something dangerous.
The speaker chooses to expose their own life to threat and danger rather than 'reposing in the security of a life where truth goes unspoken' (Foucault, 1983: 3); truth having and truth telling are 'guaranteed by the possession of certain moral qualities' (1983: 2).
In ancient Greek politics, it was the royal advisor's duty to use parrhesia to help the king with his decisions by preventing him from abusing power and becoming hubristic. Parrheisa is a distinctive modality of truth telling, and unlike whistle-blowing where the individual is often protected by law, the truth teller (the 'parrhesiastes') is unprotected, exposed and meets with danger.
A modern-day example of a 'parrhesiastes' ('truth teller') is Grigory Rodchenkov, former director of the Russian anti-doping laboratory who spoke truth to power in 2016 by exposing the extent of a 'state-sponsored' doping programme in Russian athletics. At the time of writing, Rodchenkov was in hiding, presumably in the USA.[16]

Source: Foucault (1983/1999)

One of the challenges for Hubris Syndrome, and the study of hubris more generally, is the perceived overlap with narcissism. In the clinical perspective more generally, comorbidity is not unknown; for example, as Owen and Davidson (2009) note, the comorbidity of narcissistic personality disorder with other personality disorders (such as histrionic) is problematic in that it presents challenges in finding patients who had 'pure' narcissistic personality disorder (NPD) without other co-morbidities. It is likely therefore that individuals who succumb to Hubris Syndrome may display other related tendencies such as narcissism (as in the case of Donald Trump) to an extent. In the formulation of the Hubris Syndrome concept this is to be expected since there is a partial overlap between Hubris Syndrome and NPD, histrionic personality disorder (HPD) and anti-social personality disorder (APD), for example (see Table 4.1), and need not be problematic.

Further research is required to test systematically the veracity of the claim that Hubris Syndrome abates once power is lost. This may prove difficult to assess in practice since high-profile leaders often revert to an inconspicuous private life out of the limelight (Owen and Davidson, 2009). In terms of onset and/or decline, Owen and Davidson have also mooted the idea that Hubris Syndrome may not be an Axis II disorder (in DSM-IV terms), but instead a disorder that has an environmental onset 'akin to a stressful experience' or an adjustment disorder, albeit one that has harmful effects on others but 'ultimately disappears in response to the environmental change' (p. 1404). This might offer one way of accounting for the emergence of Hubris Syndrome, perhaps as an 'adjust-ment disorder' (Owen and Davidson, 2009: 1404), in response to the key external factors identified above, namely: acquisition of significant power; attribution of success to the leader; praise for the leader in the media and other sources; and the lack of environmen-tal constraints on the leader's behaviour. It could also be, perhaps quite understandably, a behavioural response to volatile and stressful situations under the peculiar conditions of significant power. In terms of the challenges faced in the formal operationalization of the syndrome, Russell (2011) recommends some re-casting of the symptoms of Hubris Syndrome in order to make it more palatable for any future judges of the DSM to take account of whether it is to be a candidate for inclusion (see Table 4.10).

Table 4.10 Recommendations for the re-casting of the symptoms of Hubris Syndrome (Russell, 2011)

Aspect	Recommendation
Context	Person developing the disorder should be in a position of power
Behavioural disturbances	Judgement should be based on whether an individual's behaviour is dysfunctional to the extent that it results in unwise and risk-laden decisions; this may manifest as subtle changes perceptible only to those in close contact with the decision maker and the decision-making process
Excessive reactions/stressful events	Individuals' deterioration may be recognizable in excessive reactions to personal and professional events, interpretable as a coping mechanism to threat (for example, impending armed conflict) or hostility (for example, from the media)
Plasticity and personality	Traits which suited a person well in rising to the top may also have a maladaptive influence which contributes to the transformation of a personality trait to a personality disorder to a mental illness (see 'pathoplasticity'[17])

Focusing exclusively on the individual may mean that insufficient account is taken of the political or organizational context in which the syndrome arises. For example, Rogers[10] interprets hubris less as a psychological disorder of the individual and more as a 'distinc-tive patterning of individual and collective behaviour that arises and becomes embedded over time'. In such a view, it is an emergent outcome of the social processes of everyday interactions, for example self-reinforcing behaviours, groupthink, self-delusion and wider collusion (p. 1), and in this view may be considered a relational, organizational or cultural phenomenon as much as a psychological phenomenon (see Chapters 6 and 7).

The situatedness and relationality of hubristic leadership is evident in the case of the 2003 invasion of Iraq. In trying to understand Bush's decision to invade, it is vital to recognize not only Bush's de facto hubris, but also the role played by the complex political agendas of the neo-conservative faction of Bush, Cheney, Rice and Wolfowitz in the Bush administration, with collusion, conformance and compliance, and the conducive context post 9/11 (Wessely, 2006). Likewise, any historian who weighs up Blair's role in the Iraq imbroglio will need to take account not only of his hubristic style of leadership (Owen, 2007, 2008; Owen and Davidson, 2009) but also of a wide range of political, social, economic and cultural factors (Wessely, 2006: 553). Moreover, it was out of the interactions between leaders, colluders, followers and propitious circumstances that destructive but unintended outcomes emanated in this case. For example, the deepening of Shiite–Sunni divisions in Iraq and everything that followed from that were arguably unforeseen and unintended negative consequences of the hubristic leadership which pervaded the Bush administration in the lead-up to the decision to invade in March 2003. The details of this particular case are discussed more fully in Chapter 7.

It may also be the case that a democratic system of government is not the most appropriate context in which to study hubris. In democracies, the checks and balances in constitutional and cabinet government processes, although far from perfect, act to constrain or expunge dysfunctional and maladaptive leaders (as they did with Margaret Thatcher, for example); hence democratically governed societies may not be the ideal location for the emergence of hubristic leadership in its most extreme form (Freedman, 2011). In autocracies and dictatorships on the other hand, hubristic leadership may not only be fostered and have free rein, but also, as suggested by Freedman (2011), be both functional and adaptive, although this is a somewhat controversial position. A corollary of this argument is that for Hubris Syndrome to be researched in its 'purest' form, it might be best studied in autocracies and tyrannies in order that its full-blown manifestations can be scrutinized (Abed, 2011).

Finally, Freedman (2011) has offered a critical appraisal not only of the syndrome, but also of hubris in general, in relation to the important matter of 'judgement'. As he points out, Hubris Syndrome arises when powerful individuals are over-confident both in their ambitions and their capacity to manage affairs, in part because they have lost touch with reality. However, issues of confidence and ambition will invariably and almost by definition, *at the time the decision was taken*, be matters of belief, opinion, judgement, intuition, and so on. The case of Margaret Thatcher is pertinent. In invading the Falkland Islands in 1982 she gambled, and it paid off. She continued to be prime minister for the best part of a decade until she was finally ousted by her own MPs in 1990. Had the Falklands campaign failed, she would no doubt have been accused of recklessness and impulsiveness in 1982 and her premiership would likely have been cut short by a rebellion of her MPs or retributive justice on the part of the electorate.

Conclusion

A fundamental question, as well as a challenge, for Hubris Syndrome and hubris research more generally, is 'How does one judge when self-confidence becomes "excessive", or when actions which in one context might be bold in another appear as restless, reckless and impulsive, or the point at which moral rectitude should give way to practical prudence, or how much concern for image is disproportionate?' (Freedman, 2011: 149). Perhaps, sometimes the mainstream consensus can 'miss the point' and the maverick hubristic outliers occasionally get it right (Freedman, 2011). When destructive consequences ensue, bold risk takers once regarded as heroes are 'seen in retrospect to have suffered from hubris' (Robinson, 2016: 14). Their tragedy is that they behaved before the fact in ways that were not, on the whole, intended to cause harm, but their actions nonetheless prepared the way for and resulted in detrimental outcomes after the fact, and therein lies one of the paradoxes of hubris.

Further Reading

Garrard, P. (2016). On the linguistics of power (and the power of linguistics). In P. Garrard and G. Robinson (eds) *The intoxication of power: Interdisciplinary insights*. Basingstoke: Palgrave, pp. 135–54.
Owen, D. (2008). *In sickness and in power: Illness in heads of government during the last 30 years*. London: Methuen.

NOTES

1. As an aside, maybe a reason for the taboo surrounding, and the disrespect shown to sufferers of, mental illness is because such issues are stigmatized using pejoratives such as 'dark side'.
2. https://hbr.org/2012/02/its-time-to-acknowledge-ceo-lo (Accessed 8 March 2018).
3. John Dryden (1631–1700), Absalom and Achitophel (1681).
4. A class of mood disorders characterized by manic (from the Greek, mania, madness) episodes and, usually, but not necessarily, accompanied by major depressive episodes (*A Dictionary of Psychology* (2001) Oxford: Oxford University Press).

5. www.forbes.com/sites/alicegwalton/2015/01/26/why-the-super-successful-get-depressed/#734964633850 (Accessed 21 September 2017).

6. In DSM IV (1994). DSM V (2013) has moved to a single-axis system and lists personality disorders in the same way as other disorders.

7. http://hansard.millbanksystems.com/commons/1990/nov/13/personal-statement (Accessed 25 February 2018).

8. www.ft.com/content/347318fc-4c3c-11e1-b1b5-00144feabdc0 (Accessed 14 October 2017).

9. www.usatoday.com/story/money/2016/07/14/bp-deepwater-horizon-costs/87087056 (Accessed 14 October 2017).

10. www.chrisrodgers.com/publications/papers-and-articles (Accessed 15 October 2017).

11. www.lorddavidowen.co.uk/biography (Accessed 20 September 2017).

12. www.daedalustrust.com (Accessed 8 March 2018).

13. www.independent.co.uk/news/business/analysis-and-features/was-abn-the-worst-take-over-deal-ever-1451520.html (Accessed 14 October 2017).

14. www.bbc.co.uk/news/uk-politics-16821650 (Accessed 14 October 2017).

15. www.ft.com/content/b275e146-1867-11e8-9376-4a6390addb44 (Accessed 24 February 2018).

16. www.telegraph.co.uk/sport/2018/01/21/doping-whistle-blower-living-fear-cas-begins-hearing-russian (Accessed 13 March 2018).

17. Pathoplasticity, the influence personality style has on mental health disorders, is a burgeoning area of research amongst a variety of highly prevalent psychological disorders, including major depression, anxiety disorders and eating disorders, particularly bulimia nervosa. The principles supporting further development of this theoretical model include an examination of cultural factors on an individual's personality and how these factors might predict and explain a differential response to psychological intervention (Boroughs and O'Cleirigh, 2015).

5
A BEHAVIOURAL
APPROACH

WISE WARNING

'There is a tide in the affairs of men which, taken at the flood, leads on to fortune; omitted, all the voyage of their life is bound in shallows and in miseries.' (Spoken by Brutus in *Julius Caesar*, Act IV, Scene III)

Introduction

This chapter looks at hubristic leadership through a behavioural lens. 'Behavioural science' is an umbrella term for the cross-disciplinary study of how people behave. It uses concepts and methods from fields such as behavioural economics, cognitive and social psychology and, increasingly, neuroscience to understand a diverse range of societal concerns.[1] The relevance of behavioural science research to social policy hit the headlines in 2010 when the UK's Coalition government, led by former Prime Minister David Cameron, set up the world's first government institute dedicated to behavioural science. The Behavioural Insights Team (BIT)[2] based in 10 Downing Street, also known as 'The Nudge Unit',[3] was dedicated to the application of behavioural research to the betterment of society through improved decisions about health, wealth and happiness as well as, in an era of austerity, saving the government money.[4]

BACKGROUND

The significance of the 'nudge' concept, and behavioural science more generally, is such that one of its originators, Professor Richard H. Thaler of the University of Chicago, was awarded the 2017 Nobel Prize for Economics for his contribution to the behavioural sciences.[5] Indeed, Thaler himself pointed towards the significance of hubris-infected behaviours when he highlighted the pervasiveness of undue confidence and optimism in human affairs even when the stakes are high. For example, people generally rate themselves as less likely than others to get fired from their job, get divorced, get sick, or have an accident. If evidence were needed of how unbounded human optimism and confidence can be, look no further than the popularity of national lotteries where in the UK the approximate odds of winning the 'Lotto' jackpot are 1 in 45 million; nonetheless, millions of hyper-optimists are willing to gamble the minimum £2 stake on a weekly basis.[6]

Behavioural science was topical enough to be subjected to the penetrating gaze of Her Majesty the Queen on the occasion of her visit to the London School of Economics (LSE) in November 2008. Her polite but piercing enquiry as to why no one had noticed beforehand that the 2007 financial crisis was on its way, prompted the following formal reply to Buckingham Palace from a group of highly respected members of the British Academy:

> 'most [experts] were convinced that banks knew what they were doing. They believed that the financial wizards had found new and clever ways of managing risks. Indeed, some claimed to have so dispersed them through an array of novel financial instruments that they had virtually removed them. It is difficult to recall a greater example of wishful thinking combined with *hubris*.' (British Academicians' Letter to The Queen, 22 July 2009, emphasis added)

With hindsight, what is perhaps surprising is that behavioural scientists of a variety of persuasions in fact had long known about the downsides of hubristic over-confidence and over-ambition, but many of them chose to overlook the problem. The result was a collective short-sightedness amongst researchers and financiers, the consequences of which have been highly damaging both economically and societally. But hubris has not only plagued decision making in banking and finance; its insidious effects have reached more broadly into leadership in business strategy, entrepreneurship and other aspects of business management, so much so that hubris has been referred to as nothing less than an 'epidemic' (Garrard, 2018).

HUBRIS IN BEHAVIOURAL CORPORATE FINANCE: THE HUBRIS HYPOTHESIS

The best starting point for this survey of the behavioural perspective on hubris is a foundational corporate finance theory formulated almost a quarter of a century before the 2007 financial crisis by Professor Richard Roll of UCLA's Anderson School of Management. Richard Roll's so-called 'Hubris Hypothesis' is important for two reasons: first, he was the earliest researcher to investigate systematically the impact of over-confidence on the value of a firm; second, the Hubris Hypothesis programme of research represents the most extensive body of knowledge in the behavioural sciences on the nature, causes and effects of hubris at the top of business organizations.

It was Roll's work that provided a catalyst for further research which branched out into studies of CEO over-confidence, self-concept and related issues in areas such as strategic management and entrepreneurship. Behavioural researchers more generally have come to treat over-confidence, over-ambition and over-optimism (e.g. unrealistic optimism and unrealistic ambitions) as sources and manifestations of a more general class of cognitive biases and errors in organizational decision-making processes, a number of which stem from inappropriate uses of heuristics and intuitive judgement (Gilovich et al., 2002). Biases of over-confidence, over-ambition and over-optimism, when allied to pride, arrogance and contempt for the advice and criticism of others, constitute hubris, and as we know, hubris is a hazard both for individuals and organizations.

Roll's ground-breaking contribution to hubris research takes as its starting point an assumption that is radically different to that which has been the cornerstone of classical economics. The latter assumes that the environment, combined with the assumption of perfect rationality on the part of the actor, determines economic behaviour; this is an unrealistic position, as pointed out by Simon (1979). Behavioural corporate finance, on the other hand, substitutes traditional economic assumptions of rationality with what was once a radical supposition – but now no longer disputed – that 'some agents are *not* fully rational' (Thaler, 2005: 1, original emphasis). This way of thinking is highly germane to the study of hubristic leadership because it embraces the study of decision makers who have been 'infected' by over-confidence, over-optimism and even recklessness, as well as weak intuitions and other cognitions and behaviours which crowd out rationality and intelligent restraint and give rise to irrational exuberance as a consequence of 'unbridled intuition' (Claxton et al., 2015).

Roll proposed the Hubris Hypothesis in a milestone article – 'The Hubris Hypothesis of Corporate Takeovers' – in the *Journal of Business* that has, at the time of writing, been cited over 4000 times since its publication in 1986. By way of comparison, Nobel Laureate Herbert Simon's seminal *American Economic Review* article on the paradigm-shifting concept of 'bounded rationality' referred to above has been cited an-almost-as-impressive 3000 times.[7] Roll was interested in questions regarding the motivations behind merger and tender offers and whether or not takeovers actually result in an increase in a firm's market value. In essence, the Hubris Hypothesis makes a straightforward claim: firms who are acquiring other businesses ('acquiring firms') simply pay too much for their targets as a result of the hubristically over-confident judgement on the part of acquiring executives that they, not the market, know best what the value of the acquisition to the combined business is likely to be. The hubristic leaders of acquiring firms over-estimate the likelihood that the decisions *they* take will be successful and that it is *they* – and sometimes *they alone* – who can ensure success (Hayward et al., 2006).

Roll's hypothesis predicts – on the basis that hubrists over-pay for their acquisitions – that around the time of the takeover, the combined value of the target and bidder firms falls slightly because, put simply, the value of the bidding firm decreases by more than the value of the target firm increases (see below). The premium that bidding executives are willing to pay for a potential acquisition reflects their hubristic beliefs about how much additional value they believe they can extract from the target firm, and this premium 'underscore[s] acquiring managers' [executives'] convictions that the target's pre-existing stock price inadequately reflects the value of the firm's resources and its prospects, and that in the right hands – *their hands* – more value can be created' (Hayward and Hambrick, 1997: 103–4, emphases added). In this respect, as well as being over-confident, bidding firm managers also appear to be under the 'illusion of control', that is they over-empha-size the extent to which their skills can improve performance whilst under-emphasizing the role of chance and other factors (Langer, 1975; Simon et al., 2000). Bidding firm man-agers not only think they can run the target firm better than the target firm managers, they also believe that they, rather than the market, know the true value of the acquisition[8] (Table 5.1).

Table 5.1   Core features of Roll's Hubris Hypothesis (Roll, 1986)

Bidding executives convince themselves that their estimated value for target firm is correct
Bidding executives assume market does not reflect true economic value of combined firm
Hubris-infected bidders end up paying too much for their acquisitions
Around a takeover, the combined value of bidder and target will fall
Value of the bidding firm should decrease whilst the value of the target firm should increase
Total combined takeover gain to bidding and target firm shareholders ends up non-positive (i.e. zero or negative)

As well as these immediate and short-term effects, there are potential financial and wider consequences further down the line. The premium paid can inversely affect acquirer shareholders' return for several years following the acquisition date, moreover it is not unknown for excessive premiums to have devastating effects – even to the point of bankruptcy – because of the debts incurred in hubristically driven takeovers (Hayward and Hambrick, 1997).

Numerous studies have demonstrated 'hubris effects' consistent, to varying degrees, with Roll's original hypothesis (e.g. Al Rahahleh and Wei, 2012; Antoniou et al., 2008; Ashta and Patil, 2007; Brown and Sharma, 2007; Chen and Wang, 2012; Ismail, 2008; Lin et al., 2008; Majumdar et al., 2010; Pangarkar and Lie, 2004; Sharma and Ho, 2002; Shih and Hsu, 2009). (For a review and assessment of Hubris Hypothesis research, see De Bodt et al., 2014; Picone et al., 2014.) Perhaps Valle's (1998) metaphor of the 'fairytale prince' is apt: hubristic CEOs may pay well over the market value for a target firm in the fixed, but typically false, belief that it is their 'kiss' that will turn a 'toad' into a 'prince'. Regrettably in corporate finance, as in life more generally, the fairytale rarely comes true – acquisitions more often than not result in a decline in the acquirer's longer-term profitability; a hubristic man-ager's kiss turns a toad into a prince only on rare occasions (Valle, 1998).

EXECUTIVE OVER-CONFIDENCE, CELEBRITY AND CONTROL

Confidence is an invaluable executive attribute; it enables executives, and their firms, to do things they would not otherwise have done and to take their firms in new, innovative technological directions (Galasso and Simcoe, 2011; Tang et al., 2015). On the other hand, hubristically over-confident CEOs often make value-destroying investment decisions, even though they do not set out to be destructive and act on an 'honourable stewardship of corporate assets' principle (Roll, 1986: 214). Finance researchers have further developed the Hubris Hypothesis theory by studying the effects of over-optimism (the systematic over-estimation of the probability of good firm performance and under-estimation of bad firm performance) and over-confidence (the distortion of corporate investment decisions such that over-confident managers over-estimate the returns on their investment projects) (Heaton, 2002; Malmendier and Tate, 2005a). Table 5.2 summarizes some of the psychological mechanisms that drive CEO over-optimism and over-confidence.

Table 5.2   Sources of CEO over-confidence

Source of CEO over-confidence	Description
Better-than-average effect	Individuals in general tend to consider themselves 'above average' on positive characteristics, for example most people will rate their driving skills as above average (Alicke et al., 1995)
Attributions of causality	Individuals tend to attribute successful outcomes to their own actions (a 'self-serving attribution') whereas failure is put down to 'bad luck' (Miller and Ross, 1975)
Base-rate neglect	CEOs' inaccurate over-estimations of their abilities may emanate from their comparing themselves to a population average (for example, the 'average manager'), rather than 'average CEO', since in the upper-echelons of organizations there are few other comparators against which CEOs can make accurate self-evaluations (Malmendier and Tate, 2005a)

A further cradle of over-confidence which fans the flames of CEO hubris is the 'celebrity status' that has come to pervade the upper echelons of popular business culture. The fabled CEO superstars – irreplaceable, iconic and heroic leaders such as Jack Welch, Steve Jobs or Jeff Bezos – are now an accepted part of the way business is conducted. Moreover, the trend towards CEO glorification has been fuelled by 'CEO of the Year Awards'.[9] But the consequences for the firm can be far from trifling. The phenomenon of the celebrity CEO can often be a process of dramatic rise and fall that is co-created between the CEO, susceptible followers and the media – and, when hubris becomes involved, the drama can turn into a tragedy (Figure 5.1).

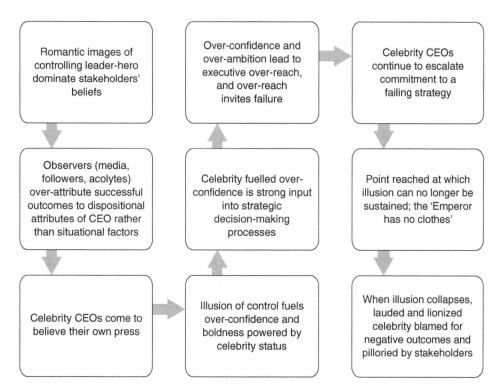

Figure 5.1   The drama and tragedy of CEO celebrity rise and fall (Hayward et al., 2004; Sinha et al., 2012)

Celebrity status has undesirable associations with CEO remuneration and other negative connotations. Researchers found that 'superstar CEO' status (for example, as ratified by major business awards) appears to distort CEO behaviour and can actually be associated with decreases in subsequent firm performance and increased total compensation relative to the next-highest paid executive (Malmendier and Tate, 2009). Award winners not only tend to extract higher compensation from their business in the form of stock and options, they also engage in distractions such as sitting on outside boards as well as petty diversions, for example by writing popular business books or playing more golf, all of which add little benefit to the firm (Malmendier and Tate, 2009). The same study also found that long-term underperformance of superstar CEOs and unrestrained increases in their equity-based compensation were typical of firms with weak corporate governance. The potential consequences for shareholders can be grim, and, for a weakly-governed business, having a 'superstar' at the helm who turns hubristic may end up being more of a curse than a blessing.

Successful executives, like all of us, whether they are celebrities or not, are likely to be labouring under some degree of illusion of control (Langer, 1975). People in general, including executives, prefer to be able to exercise control over events and their environment. Being unable to exercise control can be a source of insecurity and anxiety, whereas being able to exercise control can be a source of security and optimism (Dutton, 1993; Thompson et al., 1998). Even with a random event such as throwing a dice, people like to do it themselves rather than have someone else do it for them. The illusion of control can be especially strong amongst executives who prefer to reject the notion of uncontrollable risk and instead prefer to stick to the view that risky situations are nothing more than another challenge to be overcome (Highhouse, 2001). The problem is likely to be amplified by narcissistic and hubristic executives because they prefer to receive the credit for success even when it can be attributed objectively to other sources or to luck (Hayward and Hambrick, 1997; March and Shapira, 1987).

HUBRIS IN STRATEGIC MANAGEMENT RESEARCH

In further developing the idea of hubristic leadership and addressing some of the short-comings in Roll's original theory, strategic management researchers used a behaviourally rather than financially based definition of hubris. They also used research methods which went beyond the Hubris Hypothesis assumption that a negative market reaction indicates hubris. The definition of executive hubris was sharpened up by adopting a definition from *Webster's Dictionary*: 'exaggerated pride or self-confidence often resulting in retribution' (Hayward and Hambrick, 1997: 106), and the research used decision makers themselves as the unit of analysis rather than the firm. They predicted that hubris would affect two outcome variables: (1) 'acquisition premium' calculated as purchase price minus the pre-takeover (30-days) price, divided by the pre-takeover price; the higher the executive hubris the higher the premiums paid; and (2) cumulative abnormal returns (CAR) (measure of firm performance): an abnormal return to a stock is the portion of the return not anticipated in a model of anticipated, or 'normal', returns which means that a 'positive abnormal return' indicates that the market has upwardly revised its expectations of future returns from the stock and vice versa. The researchers' predictions were that 'acquisitions will tend to destroy value for acquiring firms' shareholders' and the 'greater the CEO's hubris, the worse the subsequent performance of the acquiring firm' will be (Hayward and Hambrick, 1997: 111) – more hubris should mean lower CAR.

In developing a testable research model, three sources of CEO hubris (assembled under the heading of 'The Hubris Factor') and three sources of weak board vigilance were identified (Hayward and Hambrick, 1997: 114). 'Acquisition premium' (see above) was measured in terms of how much above pre-bid market prices CEOs paid for acquisitions (in their data, this averaged 47 per cent but reached as high as 100 per cent) and this was taken to be a direct assessment of how much more valuable hubristic CEOs thought the acquired company would be under their 'exceptional-in-their-own-estimation' leadership.

CEO Hubris (The Hubris Factor) was comprised of recent organizational success, media praise for CEOs, and CEOs' self-importance, and it was predicted to have a detrimental effect on acquiring firms' performance following an acquisition. Acquiring firm performance was measured as stockholder returns for the previous 12 months. Media praise for CEOs was determined by means of a content analysis of national newspaper and magazine articles covering the CEO (in *The New York Times*, *Wall Street Journal*, etc.) published in the three years leading up to the acquisition. CEO relative compensation was used as a measure of CEO self-importance (CEO cash compensation divided by compensation of second-highest paid company officer). The research also looked beyond the individual and argued that the relationship between CEOs' overall hubris and acquisition premiums is likely to be affected by the strength or weakness of the board and its degree of vigilance in either reining in or giving free rein to hubristic CEOs' valuations (Hayward and Hambrick, 1997).

In terms of *weak board vigilance*, the researchers predicted that the effect of CEO hubris would be accentuated by three board-level factors: (1) the consolidation of the board chair and CEO positions, since CEOs who also chair boards are more likely to recommend their personal choices without restraint; on the other hand, if there is a separate board chair, he or she may be in a position to rein in reckless acquisition decisions; (2) a high proportion of insiders on the board could result in board members being unwilling to challenge and therefore more subservient to CEOs, and create the space for unfettered CEO discretion and hubris; and (3) board vigilance is more likely to be weak if outside board members have little financial stake in the company (Table 5.3).

Table 5.3 The Hubris Factor and weak board vigilance (Hayward and Hambrick, 1997)

The Hubris Factor	
Performance	Stockholder returns for previous 12 months
Praise	Content analysis of national newspaper and magazine articles covering the CEO (in *New York Times*, *Wall Street Journal*, etc.)
Pay	CEO self-importance as CEO relative compensation (CEO cash compensation divided by compensation of second-highest paid company officer)
Weak board vigilance	
CEO–chair duality	Consolidation of the board chair and CEO positions
Too many insiders	High proportion of insiders on the board
Outsiders with low stakes	Outside board members have little financial stake in the company

Based on a study of 106 publicly traded transactions of US firms between 1989 and 1992, the researchers found that premiums paid for acquisitions were related positively to the Hubris Factor (i.e. acquiring firms' recent performance, media praise for acquiring firms' CEOs, and CEOs' self-importance). They also found that all three components of the Hubris Factor were associated with negative acquisition outcomes. There were two important further findings: first, the percentage of insider directors on the board heightened the effect of the Hubris Factor on acquisition premiums; second, the consolidation of the CEO and chairman positions amplified the association between the Hubris Factor and acquisition premiums. The behaviour of hubristic CEOs who, in the researchers' estimation, were 'overconfident, very powerful, very greedy' was associated with negative effects on the acquisition process (by over-paying) and on outcomes (Hayward and Hambrick, 1997: 124). This research shows that the Hubris Factor allied to weak board vigilance is likely to be a financially damaging combination for a firm.

Hubris is linked both to risk-taking behaviour and the level of managers' discretion and as such it presents a hazard when: (1) risk taking is encouraged by a conducive business environment; and (2) risk taking is disinhibited by ineffective governance. It is likely that, because of an over-estimation of their own problem-solving abilities and an under-estimation of what could go wrong, hubristic CEOs will interpret risky situations as being less risky than they actually are (Camerer and Lovallo, 1999). When this misjudgement is allied to an under-estimation of the resources required, the firms' resource endowments and the uncertainties faced in carrying decisions forward, then the potential for risky decision making is magnified (Kahneman and Lovallo, 1993; March and Shapira, 1987; Shane and Stuart, 2002). Firms need to be mindful of CEO hubris not only when the Hubris Factor is allied with weak board vigilance, but especially when market conditions are conducive to risk-taking behaviours (Figure 5.2).

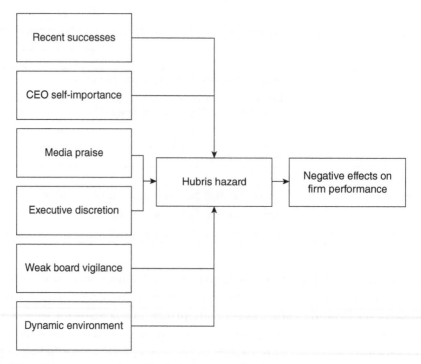

Figure 5.2   The components of the hubris hazard in strategic management

MEASURING EXECUTIVE HUBRIS

As well as investigating relationships between CEO hubris and relevant firm-level outcomes, strategic management researchers have also suggested how to measure CEO hubris as a psychological construct. The umbrella concept of 'core self-evaluation (CSE)' (Judge et al., 1998, 2003) has been proposed as a proxy measure for hubris on the basis that in its extreme form – as 'hyper-CSE' – it aligns closely with what is 'often colloquially called "hubris"' (Hiller and Hambrick, 2005: 297). CSE is a deeply-sourced dispositional trait concerned with how one evaluates oneself. It is the 'common core' of four human qualities or component traits: (1) self-esteem, for example 'I am worthy'; (2) generalized self-efficacy, for example 'I succeed at tasks'; (3) locus of control, for example 'Life's events are within my control'; and (4) emotional stability/neuroticism, for example 'I am free from anxiety/am anxious' (Hiller and Hambrick, 2005: 299) (Table 5.4).

Table 5.4   Core self-evaluation (CSE) component traits and measurement

Core self-evaluation components	Measure (Judge et al., 1997)
Self-esteem, for example 'I am worthy'	10-item 'Self-esteem' scale from Rosenberg (1965)
Generalized self-efficacy, for example 'I succeed at tasks'	10-item scale developed by Judge et al. (1998)
Locus of control, for example 'Life's events are within my control'	'Internality' subscale of Levenson's (1981) Internal, Powerful Others, and Chance (IPC) Scale
Emotional stability/neuroticism, for example 'I am free from anxiety/am anxious'	12-item 'Neuroticism' scale from the NEO-FFI Personality Inventory (Costa and McCrae, 1992)

Researchers have theorized that hyper-CSE is likely to be: (1) related positively to healthy narcissism and negatively to unhealthy reactive narcissism; (2) associated with less comprehensive (i.e. more 'instinctive') decision-making processes, faster strategic decision making and more centralized decision making; and (3) associated with more large-stakes projects undertaken and initiated by the CEO, with more deviation from the central tendencies of the industry, greater persistence in pursuing strategies initiated by the CEO, and more extreme performance (Hiller and Hambrick, 2005).

The researchers have framed core self-evaluation (as opposed to hyper-CSE) as a 'bright side' leadership trait associated with articulating a vision in such a way as to build commitment, being a role model, empowering others and having a realistic sense of their own and their organization's capabilities. In a study of core self-evaluations amongst 75 CEOs of Major League Baseball organizations, positive relationships were found between core self-evaluations and transformational leadership (articulating a compelling vision, fostering goal commitment, and role modelling) (Resick et al., 2009). Given the relationships between CSE and transformational leadership (cf. charismatic leadership), it would be interesting to study the relationship between hyper-CSE and 'personalized' (dark-side) charisma linked to a need for influence or power (Conger and Kanungo, 1998; House and Howell, 1992).

By studying CSE in business venturing environments, researchers also found positive relationships between CEOs' core self-evaluations and their firms' 'entrepreneurial orientation' (i.e. innovativeness, risk-taking propensities, and proactiveness) (Simsek et al., 2010). This suggests that being entrepreneurial entails high self-esteem, self-efficacy, locus of control and emotional stability, however being entrepreneurially successful rather than simply boldly, and perhaps recklessly entrepreneurial is likely to entail exercising these qualities in the right amounts in the right circumstances. An important question for business researchers, as well as a challenge for entrepreneurs and executives, is where does productive CSE stop and unproductive hyper-CSE begin?

More generally, the developments in strategic management research have added considerably to our understanding of concepts related to hubris such as confidence and over-confidence, core self-evaluation and hyper-core self-evaluation, and so on. These are summarized in relation to more fundamental distinctions such as hubris and narcissism in Table 5.5.

Table 5.5 Behavioural constructs in relation to other hubristic leadership concepts

Construct	Description
Hyper-core self-evaluation (CSE)	Excessive levels of self-efficacy, locus of control, emotional stability and self-esteem (Hiller and Hambrick, 2005)
Hubris	A psychological state characterized by over-confident and over-ambitious judgement and decision making, associated with the acquisition of significant power and success, and invulnerable to and contemptuous of the advice and criticism of others (Finkelstein et al., 2009; Sadler-Smith et al., 2016)
Hubris Syndrome	Behavioural transformation of a leader's personality associated with the acquisition of significant power, recognizable in terms of 14 symptoms, five of which are unique to the condition (Owen, 2006; Owen and Davidson, 2009)
Narcissism	Relatively stable individual difference consisting of grandiosity, self-love and inflated self-views; exists on a continuum; narcissists are preoccupied with having their inflated self-view reinforced (Campbell et al., 2011: 269)
Over-confidence	Cognitive bias towards over-estimating the likely positive outcomes of future events (Dowling and Lucey, 2014) based on over-estimation of one's abilities and over-precision in one's beliefs
Pride	Authentic pride: positive emotion felt upon recognizing one's actual contribution to a desirable outcome
	Hubristic pride: negative emotion associated with arrogance, conceit and self-aggrandizement (Bodolica and Spraggon, 2011; Tracy and Robins, 2014).

Researchers have also suggested that pride is related to hubris and have distinguished two facets of pride: 'hubristic pride' and 'authentic pride' (Tracy and Robins, 2014). Authentic pride is a positive emotion felt upon recognizing one's actual contribution to a desirable outcome, whereas hubristic pride, which is the 'dark side' of pride, is associated with arrogance, conceit and self-aggrandizement (Bodolica and Spraggon, 2011; Tracy and Robins, 2014). In a media commentary, Jessica Tracy, Professor of Psychology at the University of British Columbia, has suggested that Donald Trump typifies many of the attributes of hubristic pride (having a grandiose and inflated sense of self, egotism, arrogance, conceitedness, problematic relationships; being disagreeable, anti-social, aggressive and unempathetic):

> Trump fits that model every step of the way. Any time he's challenged, his immediate response is to attack outwards. He's going to show everyone who tries to criticize him that they shouldn't do that because he will retaliate. This is his strategy, this is his way of getting power. And like it or not dominance is an effective way of getting ahead and it's worked quite well for him.[10]

The real estate business in which Trump appears to have excelled is a very different arena to the political sphere. Whilst high levels of self-confidence and ambition in real estate may have produced dividends for him and his business empire, it is not justifiable to assume that real-estate deal- and decision-making skills are transferable to the radically different fields of national and international politics. Domain specificity and lack of transferability of skills are likely to be an additional source of hubristic over-confidence in leaders who switch between significantly different fields.

HUBRIS, GROUPTHINK AND UPPER ECHELONS

Hubris is not solely down to the leader. Hubristic leadership may also arise because of social processes within groups, for example highly cohesive groups might limit their searches for alternatives, become over-confident in their collective judgements and, as a result, 'two heads may not be better than one' (Puncochar and Fox, 2004). Researchers have identified 'groupthink' as a potential source of hubris in business organizations (Kroll et al., 2000).

Groupthink is invoked when strongly cohesive groups (such as top management teams) are insulated from outside influences, have directive leadership, and the group processes produce attitudinal or ideological homogeneity (Janis, 1982). Groupthink provokes an over-estimation of the in-group (as stronger, smarter, superior, etc.) and a consequent under-estimating of the out-group (as weaker, more stupid, inferior, etc.) (Janis and Mann, 1977). Groupthink promotes closed-mindedness and pressures for uniformity and conformity, and could be a significant contributor to organizational hubris (see Chapter 6) through the formation of 'in-groups' as a result of differential social exchanges between leaders and followers (see Chapter 7).

A consequence of this is that overly cohesive and isolated groups can become more prone to sub-optimal decision-making processes because of flawed and/or incomplete information search, inadequate contingency planning and biased assessments of the risks and costs/benefits, as well as the moral implications (such as inadequate consideration of human impacts). One of the problems of prior success – a key factor fuelling hubris – is that it can foster complacency, inattention to detail, routinization and habituation, and breed over-confidence. The upside of failure, on the other hand, is that it can remind managers and leaders of the need for constant vigilance (Starbuck and Milliken, 1988). Ironically, repeated successes can result in errors in decision making being more likely, whilst significant failures can reduce the chances of costly errors if they result in learning. Overly cohesive groups can take decisions that are hubristically insensitive to the likelihood and consequences of failure (Baron, 2009).

Two examples of the consequences of collective, or organizational, hubris are to be found at NASA and the twin space-shuttle disasters of Challenger (in 1986) and Columbia (in 2003) which led to the deaths of 14 astronauts. Researchers have argued that NASA's organizational culture had become 'infested with hubris' (Mason, 2004: 134). Over-confidence influenced the organization's attitudes towards safety, whilst contempt was thought to have been an issue in managers' and executives' attitudes towards knowledge experts (Boin and Schulman, 2008; Garrett, 2004). A hierarchical structure concentrated decision-making power at the top in a culture of self-assurance and a historical context of spectacular prior successes (for example, the Apollo programme which landed the first astronaut on the moon). These factors amounted to a potentially dangerous 'over-confidence trap' in a technical context which was highly complex, inherently unruly and ultimately unpredictable (Mason, 2004). Organizational hubris (see Chapter 6) invited disastrous outcomes that materialized in two catastrophic failures.

Upper echelons theory (UET) is based on bounded rationality (Simon, 1979) and the assumption that in order to understand strategic management it is essential to consider the biases and dispositions of top executives. UET proposes that executives' experiences, values and personalities influence their interpretations of the situations they face and thereby affect the choices they make (Hambrick and Mason, 1984). Counter to the criticism that UET glorifies organizational elites, one of the originators of the theory, Donald Hambrick of Penn State University, made the point that executives are just as prone as other managers to cognitive biases, preening, selfishness, over-ambition and hubris (Hambrick, 2007). By way of illustration, an upper echelons study that explored reasons why directors in the banking industry did not foresee the problems of excessive risk in the lead-up to the financial crisis, found that in high-uncertainty environments experts and males (cf. the 'winner effect') have a higher inclination to under-estimate financial risk than non-experts and women, and that the problem is amplified by top management team (TMT) homogeneity (Rost and Osterloh, 2010). In keeping with the findings of neuroscience (see Chapter 3), it seems that behavioural research points to the need for greater diversity of knowledge, experience and gender at the top of organizations as a means of combatting the hubris hazard.

ENTREPRENEURSHIP

Entrepreneurs take significant risks in the pursuit of business success. To do so they need to be confident, ambitious and optimistic in deciding to embark on a new venture. A high level of confidence has many advantages, for example it can be beneficial in persuading others to be enthusiastic about joining in a business venturing project, and it can inspire, motivate and assure employees (Busenitz and Barney, 1997). However, the uncertainties faced, the risks involved and the gains to be made also involve a delicate balance between confidence and over-confidence, ambition and over-ambition, and optimism and over-optimism (Haynes et al., 2015). Crossing the line into excess can ultimately bring about the demise of a promising business venture (Busenitz and Barney, 1997; Kramer, 2003).

If proof were needed of the precariousness and perilousness of business venturing, it is salutary to reflect on the failure rates amongst business start-ups. In the UK, it is estimated that more than half of new businesses fail to survive for longer than five years, and the picture is similar in the USA[11] (Figure 5.3). Even in spite of these high failure rates entrepreneurs are boldly optimistic. In a classic study from 1988 of 3000 entrepreneurs who were asked to rate their chances of success, 81 per cent saw their odds of success as 7 out of 10 or better, and a third, extraordinarily, saw their odds of success as 10 out of 10 (Cooper et al., 1988). Needless to say, the consequences of careless over-confidence can be financially catastrophic for individual entrepreneurs and investors, and in the bigger picture entrepreneurial hubris inflates venture failure rates and consumes resources (Townsend et al., 2010). However, as we shall see, hubristic incompetence borne of over-confidence may also have a bright side.

Building on earlier work in strategic management, researchers developed a 'Hubris Theory of Entrepreneurship' to show how over-confident entrepreneurs are more likely to initiate business ventures but also how such ventures are more likely to fail (Hayward et al., 2006). This research helps explain why entrepreneurs start their ventures in the first place when the objective chances of success are on the face of it discouraging. The answer – echoing the basic tenets of Roll's Hubris Hypothesis – seems to be that *they* think *they* know best, and some of them, the successful and luckier ones, plainly do.

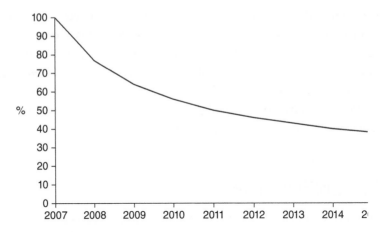

Figure 5.3 New business survival rates in the USA

Source: US Bureau of Labor Statistics at www.bls.gov/bdm/entrepreneurship/entrepreneurship.htm. Reproduced by permission of US Bureau of Labor Statistics

Over-confident entrepreneurs not only ignore base rates but also choose to overlook the failure rate of competitors who have sought to exploit similar opportunities in the past, and under-estimate the strength of the competition (Hayward et al., 2006). They do so in the firm belief that with their abilities and talents – helped along perhaps by a 'lucky hunch' – they will be the ones to overcome the odds (Shane and Venkataraman, 2000: 220). The hazard faced by hubristic entrepreneurs is compounded by the fact that, counter-intuitively, people tend to under-estimate the difficulty of solving the more complex and dynamic problems which typify the business venturing environment (Hayward et al., 2006). Business venturers are at risk from a number of entrepreneurial hubris hazards, as identified by Hayward et al. (2010) (Table 5.6).

Table 5.6 Hubris hazards for entrepreneurs (Hayward et al., 2010)

Under-estimating challenges of complexity and dynamism	Hubristic business founders are likely to be most over-confident in environments with high levels of dynamism and complexity, and likely to be least over-confident when their tasks are neither complex nor dynamic
Privileging abstract business planning over the nuts and bolts of getting things done	Elaborate, high-level business plans are likely to render business founders more optimistic and confident about their ability to meet targets at the expense of completing business-critical tasks
Assuming what worked in the past will work in new venture	As new ventures become more dissimilar to prior ones, hubristic business founders risk exaggerating the extent to which the judgement and skills that they used before will work on new projects

Under-estimating resource requirements	Hubristic business founders are likely to start their ventures with smaller resource endowments and this increases the likelihood that their ventures will fail
Over-committing resources	Hubristic business founders are likely to commit greater resources to a new business opportunity and this increases the likelihood that their ventures will fail

In looking more closely into entrepreneurial hubris, researchers have drawn a distinction between entrepreneurs' expectations of their ability (a belief in their ability to perform certain actions) and their expectations of outcomes (a belief that actions will lead them to success) (Bandura, 1986; Townsend et al., 2010). Inflated expectations of outcome success can seduce individuals who may be both ill-prepared and ill-suited to the task at hand into starting new business ventures and failing subsequently. In addition to outcome expectations, entrepreneurs' ability expectations also play an important role in business venturing (Townsend et al., 2010). As well as over-estimating their chances of success, budding entrepreneurs tend to under-estimate the resource requirements of setting up a business and do not plan for foreseeable problems, thereby further amplifying the chances of failure (Wasserman, 2012).

Research into business start-ups in the USA suggested that entrepreneurs' beliefs in their abilities (ability expectations) was a stronger driver of entrepreneurial behaviour than their beliefs about the outcome (outcome expectations) (Townsend et al., 2010). In other words, it seems that they trust their abilities first and assume that successful outcomes will follow. In business start-ups, entrepreneurs' confidence in their ability appears to be the stronger driving force; if this is so then it may also be the greater danger. Perhaps hubristic entrepreneurs who challenge the odds know logically the chances of success (the likely outcomes) but have such faith in themselves (their perception of their abilities) that they choose to proceed and persist. The threat of hubris in small firms is amplified when business founders who overrate their abilities, are unjustifiably optimistic and run their firms more or less single-handedly, are not subject to the constraints of a board that can temper over-confidence by saying 'no' to reckless decisions (Wasserman, 2012).

LEARNING AND THE LESSONS OF OVER-CONFIDENCE

Failure is a fact of life in the entrepreneurial environment, however there may be a silver lining to the cloud of business venturing failure. The broader and longer-term effects of entrepreneurial failures are not entirely negative on two related counts: the view (1) that society needs over-confident, resilient risk takers; and (2) that there are lessons to be learned from failure in entrepreneurship as well as in all other walks of life.

Over-confidence may be a vital ingredient in taking business into unknown and risky territories where there will inevitably be, because of the nature of the terrain, causalities along the way. And, although hubris may be a factor that contributes to venture failure, the longer-term and broader systemic effects of high levels of confidence, ambition and optimism may be positive. Failure might help to build emotional, cognitive, social and financial resilience which better equips some individuals to rise again from the ashes to build a new or different venture.

Resilience is a second-order and longer-term benefit which overcomes the first-order and immediate costs associated with hubristic over-confidence and the failure of individual ventures (Hayward et al., 2006, 2010). Survivors of hubristic failure may go on to set up new businesses, achieve technology breakthroughs, develop new drugs, and so forth, which they may not have done had they not nosedived at some point along the way. Anecdotal support for the benefits of failure – encapsulated in Nietzsche's aphorism 'that which does not kill us, makes us stronger'[12] – is to be found in the well-known example of Thomas Edison (David, 1992; Hargadon and Douglas, 2001; Hayward et al., 2010). Edison is reputed to have completed more than 10,000 experiments, many of them failures, before he obtained any positive results in developing the first incandescent light bulb. Edison's faith in his ability to achieve success was undiminished, and over the longer term the benefits of his optimism, confidence and ambition overwhelmed the costs of failure along the way (Hayward et al., 2010) (Table 5.7). Tales of well-known business resilience and bounce-back can be sources of inspiration for budding entrepreneurs, but given that such accounts are of exceptional outliers they may fuel an overly rosy optimism on the part of less well-gifted individuals (see Wasserman, 2012).

Table 5.7   Legendary entrepreneurial bounce-backs

Arianna Huffington	Rejected by 36 different book publishers before finally getting her second book accepted for publication. *Huffington Post* was founded in 2005 and panned by critics, largely for poor quality and limited potential. By 2011, the Huffington Post was receiving over a billion page views a year, and was purchased by AOL for $315 million
Steve Jobs	Got ousted from his own company by John Sculley. Bought Pixar with the intention of developing it into a computer hardware company; it ended up evolving into an award-winning and profitable animation studio. Sold it to Disney for $7.4 billion. NeXT computers failed. Returned to Apple with resounding success. Now one of the world's biggest businesses
James Dyson	Made over 5000 failed prototypes before finding the right design for the bagless vacuum cleaner. Dyson had to rely on his partner's income to stay afloat after his invention failed to gain traction in the British marketplace. Took it to Japan, where it was a success. Royalties helped fund a research facility and factory in England; unique bagless vacuum cleaners eventually gained worldwide success

Source: Inc magazine at www.inc.com/sujan-patel/5-failed-entrepreneurs-who-made-a-big-comeback.html (Accessed 9 March 2018)

The consequences of hubristic over-confidence, over-ambition and over-optimism are not unreservedly negative because they may, in the longer term, yield positive effects, especially in the turbulent venturing environments that entrepreneurs operate in and where recovery plans are in place (Hayward et al., 2006; Wasserman, 2012). For hubristic entrepreneurs driven on by confidence, ambition and optimism, failure can be not only a sobering experience but also, for those who are able and willing to make sense of it, a valuable teacher (Ucbasaran et al., 2013). However, a downside is that hubrists may not be inclined to the critical self-examination, self-regulation and reflexivity that learning from mistakes requires; they may impel themselves on a trajectory which reduces their chances of success and ultimately leads to unintended and unexpected failure (Hmieleski and Baron, 2008). This problem can be hampered by the fact that whilst business failures undoubtedly present opportunities to learn, failure is also a context which generates negative emotions and social costs which can inhibit our learning from mistakes (Shepherd, 2004; Ucbasaran et al., 2013).

Whilst a failed business venture is damaging for the individual concerned, the longer-term and system-wide effects of hubristic failures may not be unequivocally bad. For example, failure borne out of over-confidence can have potential benefits both for the individual and the system. Over-confidence can enhance entrepreneurs' self-efficacy by 'enabling them to feel good' about business venturing and achievement (Hayward et al., 2006: 170). It can also give them the 'wherewithal to move into risky territory' (Vecchio, 2003: 314). In this way, the ebullience, exuberance and energy of hubrism could actually be adaptive, albeit risky, in enabling entrepreneurs to deal with the high information-processing burdens in volatile and uncertain environments, in coping with the resultant stress and anxiety, and in promoting decisiveness (Hmieleski and Baron, 2008).

Entrepreneurial leaders must take considerable risks to be successful, and enthusiasm and confidence may also help founders to attract greater resources to the benefit of stakeholders and the wider society (Haynes et al., 2015; Hayward et al., 2006). The popular business press is replete with examples of confident, ambitious and optimistic leaders who have the courage and conviction to act on novel, risky projects that more risk-averse individuals might avoid, whereas timid, indecisive and defensive individuals will resist opportunity and therefore be unlikely to make the big breakthroughs that drive whole industries forward (Hayward et al., 2006). For example, when he was a teenager Michael Dell's grandiose aspiration was that he 'wanted to compete with IBM' (Hayward et al., 2006: 170). Dell learned from costly mistakes which made him less susceptible to hubris (Hayward, 2007). Dell also combined his ambition and resistance to hubris with a curiosity that has inspired him to continually seek out new ideas, keep pace with change and stay ahead of competitors.[13]

Conclusion

It is ironic that hubristically driven failure in entrepreneurship and business management more generally may be useful in that it can convey information about what might or might not work to other executives or business venturers who are then at liberty to either ignore the relevant information or resourcefully exploit it to their own advantage (Hayward et al., 2006). And, given that unrealistic optimism and the illusion of control are pervasive if people are ignorant of, or oblivious to, the chances of bad things happening, they may fail to take sensible steps to avoid negative outcomes (Langer, 1975; McKenna, 1993; Thaler and Sunstein, 2008; Weinstein, 1980; Weinstein and Klein, 1996). Consequently, if entrepreneurs or executives are running excess risks because of being overly optimistic or overly confident in their ability to control events, they are likely to benefit from board-level or policy-level interventions which re-calibrate their ambitions and expectations and push them in the right direction (Thaler and Sunstein, 2008). Executive toe-holders, advisors and vigilant, strong and independent boards, which are themselves actively monitored, are the linchpin in combatting the excesses of CEO hubris (Hambrick and Jackson, 2000; Heracleous and Luh Luh, 2002; Minichilli et al., 2007; Ranft and O'Neill, 2001).

Further Reading

Nixon, M. (2016). *Pariahs: Hubris, reputation and organizational crises*. Faringdon: Libri.
Sadler-Smith, E. (2016). Hubris in business and management research: A 30-year review of studies. In P. Garrard and G. Robinson (eds) *The intoxication of power: Interdisciplinary insights*. Basingstoke: Palgrave, pp. 39–74.

NOTES

1. http://blogs.lse.ac.uk/behaviouralscience/2016/05/24/what-is-behavioural-science-at-the-lse (Accessed 16 October 2017).
2. www.behaviouralinsights.co.uk (Accessed 16 October 2017).
3. For a discussion of the 'nudge' concept, see Thaler and Sunstein (2008).
4. www.theguardian.com/public-leaders-network/2015/jul/23/rise-nudge-unit-politicians-human-behaviour (Accessed 16 October 2017).
5. www.nobelprize.org/nobel_prizes/economic-sciences/laureates/2017/thaler-facts.html (Accessed 22 October 2017).
6. www.national-lottery.co.uk/games/lotto/game-procedures (Accessed 2 November 2017).
7. Google Scholar citation metrics, 16 October 2017.

8. 'Whereas overconfidence relates to an overestimation of one's certainty regarding current "facts" (i.e. information), the illusion of control refers to an overestimation of one's skills and consequently his or her ability to cope with and predict future events' (Simon et al., 2000: 118).

9. https://chiefexecutive.net/years-ceo-year-henry-scheins-stanley-bergman (Accessed 17 October 2017).

10. www.cbc.ca/radio/tapestry/pride-and-compassion-1.3815584/donald-trump-a-case-study-for-hubristic-pride-1.3815587 (Accessed 14 March 2018).

11. www.telegraph.co.uk/finance/businessclub/11174584/Half-of-UK-start-ups-fail-within-five-years.html (Accessed 21 October 2017). https://www.bls.gov/bdm/entrepreneurship/entrepreneurship.htm (Accessed 21 October 2017).

12. www.psychologytoday.com/blog/insight-therapy/201008/what-doesnt-kill-you-makes-you-weaker (Accessed 22 October 2017).

13. https://hbr.org/2015/09/why-curious-people-are-destined-for-the-c-suite (Accessed 15 February 2018).

6

AN ORGANIZATIONAL APPROACH

WISE WARNING

Μηδὲν ἄγαν ('Nothing to excess') (Aphorism inscribed at Delphi, 440 BC)

Introduction

A temptation in studying the rise and fall of high-profile hubrists is to attribute the destructive outcomes of their leadership largely to their personal hubristic incompetence. But to do so risks overlooking the significance of the organizational and wider context in which hubristic leadership is situated. There are a number of important factors in the wider organizational system that need to be acknowledged and accommodated in the analysis of hubristic leadership; these include the organization's goals, its culture, the people, its technologies, the processes through which it seeks to achieve its purpose, and the wider organizational context within which leadership is located.

SOCIOTECHNICAL SYSTEMS

A system-wide analytical approach which holistically embraces the interrelatedness of people, technology, goals, structure, processes and context is 'sociotechnical systems theory' (STS).[1] At the core of sociotechnical theory is the idea that the performance of any organizational system can only be understood if the social and technical aspects are treated as interdependent parts of a complex whole (Cherns, 1987; Eason, 1982; Leavitt,

1965; Mumford, 2006) (Figure 6.1). The interactions between social and technical factors create conditions for intended or unintended outcomes, and successful or unsuccessful organizational performance.

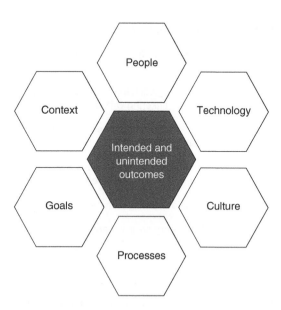

Figure 6.1.   The sub-systems of a sociotechnical approach to hubris

Source: https://business.leeds.ac.uk/research-and-innovation/research-centres/stc/socio-technical-systems-theory [Accessed 21 July 2018]

Understanding and improving performance involves both the social and the technical in a world where outcomes can be the intended consequences of linear cause-and-effect relationships or they can be the unintended consequences of non-linear, complex relationships. The sociotechnical approach – in acknowledging the interrelatedness and complexity of real-world problems – has provided a large body of actionable knowledge in areas such as employee involvement, work design, risk analysis, behaviour change, performance and productivity, and so on. Moreover, its generality and flexibility give it the capacity to be adapted to almost any organizational situation, and it is open to development (Appelbaum, 1997; Hackman and Oldham, 1980).

So far, this book has focused largely on individual leaders and psychological processes and behaviours, however hubristic leadership can also be – and invariably is – the product of interactions between psychological, social and technological factors. The complex interdependencies that exist between organizational sub-systems (people, technology, culture, goals, processes and context) can create the conditions in which actors fail to manage risks and consequences by over-estimating what can go right, under-estimating what can go wrong and being impervious to criticism and learning (Table 6.1).

Table 6.1   Organizational sub-systems and their relevance to hubris

Organizational sub-system	Relevance to hubris
People	Hubristic leaders; intoxication with power; susceptibility of followers
Technology	Technological hubris; over-confidence in ability of technology to deliver; 'tinkering with nature'; ethics/bioethics
Goals	Over-confidence and ambition; prior successes in achieving goals; expectations
Culture	Corporate hubris; organizational narcissism; organizational culture; tone from the top
Processes	Decision making; communication; team processes
Context	Regulatory environment; governance; markets

The interactions between human behaviour and complex organizational, institutional and technical infrastructures – its complex sociotechnical systems – can give rise to collective over-confidence, over-ambition and a contempt for and complacency towards risk. In a sociotechnical view, the interactions between social *and* technological sub-systems in an organization, rather than the social *or* technological systems in isolation, create the conditions for an organizational hubris to emerge. This may lead to unintended negative consequences, and is more than a simple 'technological hubris' instantiated in a belief in the omnipotence of technology (Burns and Machado, 2009: 25).

HUBRIS: AN AVOIDABLE ACCIDENT WAITING TO HAPPEN?

When hubristic leadership is conceptualized in destructive terms, it is concerned typically with harmful outcomes; likewise, 'accidents' typically involve harmful, and usually unanticipated, outcomes. The Yale sociologist Charles Perrow in his seminal book *Normal Accidents: Living with High-Risk Technologies* (1984), inspired by the Three Mile Island nuclear incident in 1979 (a cooling malfunction caused part of a reactor core to melt), argued that technical systems that are complex and tightly coupled and where there is catastrophic potential (as was the case on Three Mile Island), are susceptible to 'normal accidents' (i.e. accidents that are unavoidable and cannot be designed around). In most organized systems, especially complex sociotechnical ones, sub-systems are so tightly intertwined that if something goes seriously wrong in one of them, the whole system becomes susceptible to unintended negative consequences (Roberts and Bea, 2001).

Perrow's focus was on 'risky enterprises' with 'catastrophic potential' such as chemical plants, aircraft and air traffic control systems, ships, dams, nuclear weapons, space missions, genetic engineering, as well as nuclear power, all of which have the potential to cause significant loss of life. Related to Perrow's 'normal accidents theory' (NAT) is high reliability organizations (HRO) theory. Both NAT and HRO focus on the relationships between technical, organizational and social aspects of a system as a whole, and the consequences of their intertwinings for system failure (Leveson et al., 2009; Roberts and Bea, 2001). HRO principles, as used in air travel for example, offer a potential response to obviating the potentially destructive outcomes associated with hubristic leadership (see Chapter 9). As far as Perrow's specifications of complexity, tight coupling and catastrophic outcomes leading to normal (unavoidable) accidents are concerned, hubris is an interesting case in point. It raises questions around the type of coupling (loose or tight) that existed in complex systems where hubris has been implicated in destructive outcomes, and whether such outcomes were avoidable or unavoidable.

This chapter will use a sociotechnical framework to explore two examples of high-risk technologies (mathematical finance at Long Term Capital Management; and offshore exploration and production involved in the Deepwater Horizon/British Petroleum Gulf of Mexico oil spill), and in both cases destructive, unintended consequences have been explained in terms of 'organizational hubris' (Lowenstein, 2000; Owen, 2011b; Stein, 2003).

DEEPWATER HORIZON/BRITISH PETROLEUM GULF OF MEXICO OIL SPILL

On 20 April 2010, Transocean Ltd's oil-drilling rig Deepwater Horizon (licensed to BP) operating in 5000 feet of water in the Macondo prospect 42 miles southeast of Venice, Louisiana in the Gulf of Mexico, exploded and sank: 11 workers were killed in the accident and 17 others seriously injured. Following the collapse and sinking of the rig, hydrostatic control of the well failed and emergency functions failed to seal the well head; as a result, oil and gas escaped at an estimated rate of up to 70,000 barrels (2.94 million gallons) per day until 3 June when the broken riser pipe was removed and a collection system was installed. Even then it continued to spew oil and gas into the waters of the Gulf until a capping stack was installed on 12 July 2010.

Almost 5 million barrels of oil escaped over a period of four months and washed ashore on beaches and marshlands from Texas to Florida. It wreaked havoc on the marine and coastal ecosystems of the Gulf, and caused extensive damage to the fishing industry along the Gulf Coast.[2] The BP Gulf of Mexico oil spill was the second largest in the history of oil exploration and production (the largest was in the Persian Gulf War in 1991). In January 2018, the total cost to BP of the Deepwater Horizon oil spill after raising estimates for outstanding claims (amounting to over 400,000 cases) was uplifted to £43.7 billion ($65 billion).[3]

The accident investigation revealed that serious process safety system failures contributed to the disaster, including ineffective cement failing to create a seal, major valve failure, the leak not being detected soon enough, and there being no gas alarm on the rig (*New Scientist*, 8 September 2010). Various parties were implicated: the exploration and production company (BP), the rig leasing company (Transocean) and an oil services company (Haliburton). BP's own official technical report into the accident identified at least five key issues relating to the condition of the safety-critical blowout preventer (BOP) system prior to the accident including problems with maintenance, leaks, testing, system modifications and diagnostic practices. In the words of BP's chief executive at the time, Tony Hayward, 'It is evident that a series of complex events, rather than a single failure led to the tragedy', the implication being that there were lessons from the catastrophe for all three main parties rather than it being an indictment of BP's own practices (Elkind et al., 2011). Many have argued, however, that the prime responsibility was BP's, and that a large part of the problem was an organizational hubris that emerged under Hayward's predecessor (Owen, 2011b).

The Deepwater Horizon oil spill was a human tragedy above all else: as noted, 11 workers lost their lives; it was an environmental calamity because of the immediate ecosystem damage that ensued (the longer-term effects on different species have been variable),[4] and it was an economic disaster because of the damage to fisheries and related industries and because of the cost of the clean-up. Moreover, the reputational, as well as financial, damage to BP has been immense.

In spite of the emphasis on technical issues in the various reports, the Deepwater Horizon incident and BP's organizational culture were, in the view of some experts, inseparable. In the 1980s, BP was seen as a bureaucratic organization delivering a profit-per-employee that was half that of Exxon, and in the eyes of some industry insiders it was steady and reliable but slightly 'dull' (Crooks, 2010; Elkind et al., 2011); and to some company insiders it was 'dirty, old-fashioned and short on ethics or environmental principles' (Browne, 2010: 81). The critical cultural change came with the appointment of the charismatic John (now Lord) Browne as CEO in 1995 (and who served until 2007). Browne instigated significant organizational change with a focus on growth, bottom-line results, cost reduction, the introduction of tough productivity and profit targets for senior managers, and the delegation of safety to local levels. In parallel with these organizational changes, BP under John Browne became much more ambitious technologically. It pursued large-scale projects that pushed drilling technology to its limits and exploited more and more technically difficult reserves (Crooks, 2010). Moreover, its technological exuberance was exercised in a benign US business context of political stability and low taxes, an oil-friendly stance in the Bush administration and, later, politicking with the Obama administration, which meant that restrictions on drilling operations in the Gulf were gradually relaxed (Crooks, 2010; Elkind et al., 2011).

The organizational and technical changes under the new leadership were a major cultural shift and they delivered short-term shareholder value. In his autobiography *Beyond Business: An Inspirational Memoir from a Visionary Leader* (2010: v), John Browne claimed: 'I transformed a company, challenged a sector and prompted business and political leaders to change', and the book's marketing material declared a story of engineering feats 'which in many ways rival those of going to the moon'.[5] Under Browne, BP doubled its revenues, became the largest producer in the USA and was more profitable than its great rival, Shell (Elkind et al., 2011). BP became 'swashbuckling', entrepreneurial and creative, and its geo-engineering deep-drilling aspirations pushed technological boundaries to extremes (Crooks, 2010; Ladd, 2012). Praise was lavished on Browne who attainted celebrity CEO status: he was Britain's 'most admired CEO', branded 'The Sun King' by the *Financial Times*, was knighted by Her Majesty the Queen, and was the UK's most highly paid chief executive in 2004.

The turning point came around 2005, two years before Browne's departure as CEO: BP began to experience a string of safety-related issues that culminated in the Deepwater Horizon blowout. A series of infringements and accidents in the USA contributed to the company having one of the worst safety records in the industry, including two serious pre-Deepwater incidents (Elkind et al., 2010). The 2005 refinery explosion in the declining 71-year-old Texas City installation BP inherited from Amoco (at which fires and leaks were routine) killed 15 workers and injured almost 200. Corrosion, as a result of a failure to properly test and clean ageing pipes in BP's Prudhoe Bay, resulted in a spill of more than a quarter of a million gallons on Alaska's North Slope (Elkind et al., 2011) (Figure 6.2).

BP's 'aggressive new policies to slash costs, quadruple the company's assets, fire safety engineers, and pursue high-risk, high-reward projects' in the Browne years have been cited as a major contributory factor (Ladd, 2012: 107). The cultural change and technical exuberances were also ensconced in a wider organizational, political and regulatory context that was propitious for organizational hubris to emerge. As noted above, the Bush administration was oil-friendly, Vice President Cheney was keen to meet the demands of the oil industry by expediting offshore drilling, and the atmosphere was one of 'lax regulatory inspection, compliance and corporate hubris', and this was amplified during the Obama administration (2012: 108).

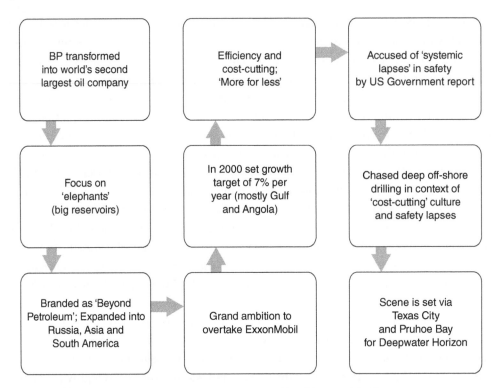

Figure 6.2   BP's trajectory towards Deepwater under (Bower, 2010)

The investigation by Elkind et al. (2011), which included in-depth interviews with Browne's successor Tony Hayward, identified significant cultural failings. Some BP directors themselves were of the view that Browne was overly ambitious in cutting costs too quickly and too savagely, and in its ascendency under Browne, BP 'flew too close to the sun' and never looked down or back; instead, every next initiative had to be bigger than the last, and imagination and boldness were rewarded (Elkind et al., 2011). Meanwhile, the emphasis on improving safety tended to emphasize individual worker occupational safety, reducing 'slips, trips and falls' and neglect process-related safety matters (Elkind et al., 2011). For example, the US Chemical Safety Board commented on the lack of operating discipline, and the toleration of serious deviations from safe operating practices in BP. The lack of attention to and awareness of safety issues meant that signals that preceded incidents, and might have prevented them from happening, were sometimes missed (Elkind et al., 2011).

The Deepwater Horizon oil spill represented a high-risk engineering venture executed in what has been described as a 'poor safety culture' where key decision makers were 'over-confident in a blowout preventer [BOP] used at extreme depths and under unanticipated conditions' (Sylves and Comfort, 2012: 88). As BP's third major safety incident in the USA, Deepwater Horizon has been judged not to be the product of a rogue blow-out caused by a local lapse in judgement; rather, its root causes have been attributed to systemic safety and cultural issues (Crooks, 2010; Elkind et al., 2011; Ladd, 2012; Sylves and Comfort, 2012). Although BPs own report admitted 'oversight mistakes', it also blamed Transocean and Haliburton. That said, most independent assessments place the prime responsibility on BP itself (Elkind et al., 2011). According to Professor Robert Bea of the University of California at Berkeley's Marine Technology Centre for Risk Mitigation, the natural hazards of this environment combined with human malfunctions such as 'hubris, arrogance, greed, ignorance, [and] indolence' formed the perfect storm for a disaster (Bea, 2011:6).[6]

The Deepwater Horizon case demonstrates the interaction between lapses in human judgement (as a result of over-confidence) and the highly damaging consequences that can result from the catastrophic breakdown of large-scale sociotechnical systems (Sylves and Comfort, 2012). As a result of the Deepwater Horizon oil spill, a number of measures have been proposed which could help mitigate the hazards of organizational hubris in similar contexts, including better regulation and testing of safety process technology, more stringent regulation of exploration and production operations in deep waters, improved corporate safety culture, and information sharing amongst oil and gas companies in deep-water drilling technologies. However, focusing solely on technical issues is less likely to militate effectively against organizational hubris of the type that was witnessed at BP. Organizational hubris emerges out of the interactions between organizational sub-systems and these are typically the most complex and difficult problems to solve. The opportunities for organizational hubris to materialize in the future are exacerbated given that dependence on large-scale, increasingly complex sociotechnical systems is expanding rapidly. Adding artificial intelligence and robotics to the mix only amplifies the risks and potential for significant negative unintended consequences to materialize sooner or later.

LONG TERM CAPITAL MANAGEMENT

Long Term Capital Management (LTCM) was a multi-billion-dollar private investment (hedge fund) management firm. It had 16 partners (including two Nobel Prize Laureates, a former Vice Chairman of the Federal Reserve Bank, and a cadre of elite Wall Street traders) and employed around 200 staff headquartered in Greenwich, Connecticut, about 40 miles from Wall Street. LTCM managed investments for a relatively small number of extremely wealthy clients.

LTCM was founded in 1994 by John Meriwether, a 'congenial' and 'cautious' former Salomon Brothers trader. LTCM had on its staff some of the finest and best-earning mathematical finance brains, many of whom joined the company from Salomon with

Meriwether, including the two most 'celebrated' traders Victor Haghani and Lawrence Hilibrand (Lowenstein, 2000). LTCM was given scientific cachet by the inclusion on its board of two 'young professor' Nobel laureates, Robert C. Merton and Myron S. Scholes (who won the Nobel Prize in economics in 1997 for 'a new method to determine the value of derivatives' – the Black–Scholes formula).[7] At its peak in the mid-1990s, LTCM notched up trading profits that were the envy of Wall Street (its average annualized return in its first three years of trading was 35 per cent) (Figure 6.3). However, by 1998 LTCM had got into $4.6 billion of debt and had to be bailed out by a consortium of 13 other banks, which took over its portfolio at the behest of the Federal Reserve Bank, lest contagion spread to the rest of the financial and wider economic system. But why did this happen?

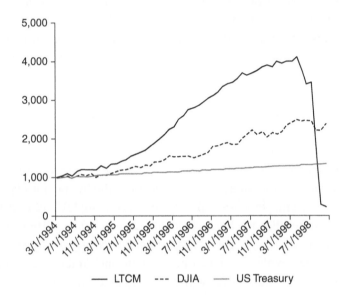

Figure 6.3   Value of $1000 invested in LTCM compared to Dow Jones Industrial Average (DJIA) and US Treasury Bonds (US Treasury)

Source: Wikimedia Commons/JayHenry

LTCM traded widely in government bonds and derivatives. The core technology of LTCM's success was in the so-called Black–Scholes formula (an options pricing model) and the associated VaR (Value at Risk) calculations. The combination of human brain and computational power gave LTCM's young male traders – some referred to them as 'eggheads' – supreme confidence in their predictions (Lowenstein, 2000: 12) (Table 6.2). However, in the view of the eminent economist Meghnad Desai, LTCM was so heavily leveraged that it courted disaster, operating as it did on high ratios of debt to equity (the 'leverage' or 'gearing') estimated to be between 50:1 and 250:1 compared to 2:1 in other hedge funds (Desai, 2015; Stein, 2003). The models were based on rational actor assumptions which gave them a cold, calculating predictability that a market of 'hot emotional' human beings did not have, and therein lay the Achilles heel of LTCM's alchemy (Lowenstein, 2000).

Table 6.2   Organizational narcissism at LTCM (Stein, 2003)

Pride	Encouraged by adulation, became persuaded that there were no limits to LTCM's power and knowledge
	Uniquely special, nigh-on perfect organization; LTCM as the 'Rolls Royce' of hedge funds
	In a unique and invulnerable market niche; only they had worked out how to operate in it risk-free
Contempt	Perception on Wall Street of being haughty; reputation for treating other firms and traders with disdain
	Arrogance to the point of thinking they were dealing with 'idiots' they could pick off routinely
	Disrespect for other highly reputable firms (e.g. Goldman Sachs, Chase Manhattan, etc.)

Source: Stein (2003)

By 1998 Wall Street had caught up and rivals were operating with similar models. One consequence of this was that trades were operating on smaller and smaller margins; as a result, LTCM had to borrow money to do more of them and it branched out from bonds into equities (Lowenstein, 2000). On the back of the 1997 Asian currency and 1998 Russian debt crises – both highly unpredictable high impact events – the markets stopped behaving in the way the mathematical models had predicted; LTCM went into freefall. 'Black Swan' (high impact, low probability) events such as currency and debt problems in Asia and Russia were outside the scope of the models. Investors watched the value of their assets plunge and panicked. Between August and September 1998, the value of a dollar invested in LTCM in March 1994 fell from £3.50 to 25 cents. The driving force behind LTCM's terminal blunder was one of organizational hubris, and the principal culprits in the affair were CEO John Meriwether and his young and brilliant but arrogant and over-confident trading team (Lowenstein, 2000). They placed supreme self-assurance and optimism in their mathematical and computational skills; Wall Street was also culpable by duping itself into believing the technology and the traders to be infallible. Everyone involved, by assuming that there was little or no risk, courted calamity.

LTCM's technological assumption, that the market was inherently rational and that investors were cold, calculating machines, was hubristically over-confident, not to say misguided and arrogant (Stein, 2003).[8] The reality was that volatility and unpredictably turned the market hot and emotional, fear spread and investors moved into the much less risky bond market. By summer 1998 LTCM was losing $100 million a day; the business model and its rational assumptions were exposed as a hubristic house of cards. The disaster LTCM had been flirting with ensued so quickly as to take most people by surprise. Its imminent collapse exposed the major US banks to massive potential losses (including Bear Stearns, Chase Manhattan, Goldman Sachs, JP Morgan, Merrill Lynch, Morgan Stanley and, ironically, Lehman Brothers). The situation was desperate, and required intervention and bailout from the US Federal Reserve. LTCM was primed to expose America's largest banks to $1 trillion in default risks. In the view of some finance experts, had the worst happened it could have taken the entire financial system with it.

LTCM's 'riches to rags' debacle – at the hands of what they themselves referred to as its 'extreme event' – has been described as a 'tragedy for its partners' (Lowenstein, 2000: 219). Hilibrand, who was the most over-confident and 'cock-sure' of the traders and had been worth close to half a billion dollars, was broke; he had to plead with his bank to spare him the ignominy of personal bankruptcy, and other partners lost most than 90 per cent of their wealth (Lowenstein, 2000: 219). The press had a field-day of schadenfreude, dubbing them as pampered rich kids, and *Time* labelled them 'The Brightest and the Brokest'. Portentously, Alan Greenspan admitted that by orchestrating a Fed-led bailout he may have encouraged future risk taking and increased the odds of a financial disaster happening again (Lowenstein, 2000: 229–30), which of course it did with further ruinous consequences a decade later.

LTCM fell prey to what the *Financial Times* referred to as the 'hubris trade' that defines every cycle: 'what worked before suddenly doesn't'.[9] In this case, organizational hubris was rooted in LTCM's over-bearing self-assurance. There could be no doubt about LTCM's collective brain power, but the culture of the organization brazenly exaggerated and extravagantly over-evaluated its powers of prediction (Stein, 2003). Everybody was 'enamoured with their intellect', some likened it to 'Kennedy's inner circle – Camelot! They had the brightest and the best'; when one of the principal partners, Myron Scholes (he of the 1997 Nobel Prize in Economic Sciences), was asked at a golf weekend whether he had more money or more brains Scholes replied 'Brains, but it's getting close!' (Lowenstein, 2000: 84).

LTCM's hubris enticed them to take extreme risks in what turned out to be highly volatile financial markets populated by investors who were ultimately human beings, not machines, and as such were prone to nervousness, anxiety and irrationality. In trying to make sense of what went wrong, researchers have suggested that one reason was that LTCM fell prey to an 'organizational narcissism': an exaggerated pride and inflated evaluations of the power of their mathematical technology and licence to take extreme risks. Not only that, they showed scorn, low regard and callous contempt for other firms (Lowenstein, 2000; Stein, 2003) (see Table 6.3). Although many of the outward manifestations of organizational narcissism became apparent as events progressed, hubris was there from the inception, a lurking presence below the surface. Unlike BP in which organizational hubris was an emergent property of its sociotechnical system, at LTCM organizational hubris was endemic and built into the fabric and functioning of its socio-technical system (Stein, 2003).

Table 6.3   Intellectual and technological resources at LTCM

Top-notch resumés from Ivy League universities, Wall Street firms and US government
Merton and Scholes Nobel Prize in Economic Sciences (Black–Scholes theorem)
Lavish praise: 'one of the most elegant and precise models any of us have ever seen' (from a Chicago School economist)
Claims that Merton and Scholes are 'on a par' with Pascal and Gauss in understanding risk
One Partner (David W. Mullins, ex-MIT, Harvard and Fed) claimed to be world authority on financial collapses
Used most sophisticated, powerful and up-to-date computer hardware and software

Stein's (2003) analysis of LTCM's organizational narcissism from a Freudian psychoanalyt-ical perspective reveals parallels with narcissistic personality disorder: (1) the organization is felt by its members to be very special and to embody unique qualities; (2) members experience an inauthentic, exaggerated hubristic pride in their achievements; (3) the organization is in a 'delusional realm' (p. 529) in which it is, in its own estimation, flaw-less; (4) there is an unconscious imperialism whereby anything of value outside of it is hard to tolerate; and (5) delusions are ascribed to authorize arrogance, contempt and the dishonouring of others (cf. hybris; see Chapter 2). The organizational narcissism identi-fied by Stein (2003) predisposed LTCM to hubris.

Organizational hubris was an intrinsic feature of LTCM's people, culture, technol-ogy, processes, goals and context; it was an inherent property of a sociotechnical design pervaded by hubris (Stein, 2003). The core feature of the technological sub-system was, as noted above, the Value at Risk (VaR) programmes underpinned by the Nobel Prize-winning Black–Scholes method. The hubrism in the maths was that it adorned events that were inherently uncertain with a certitude, for example that the Asian currency and Russian debt crises were highly improbable but high-impact events (Lowenstein, 2000). In its organizational hubris, LTCM's sociotechnical system failed to accommodate the possibility of highly improbable events occurring in the wider context and impacting the whole system. The technology, in which the traders had unwavering confidence, predicted what one would lose on a normal day, but failed to make bets for when a Black Swan appeared.

The author of *The Black Swan: The Impact of the Highly Improbable* (2007), Nassim Nicholas Taleb, describes the LTCM architects of the technology, Scholes and Merton, as suffering from 'Black Swan blindness'. His argument illustrates a fundamental point about organizational hubris both at LTCM and more generally: LTCM defended Black Swan risk taking simply because it could not see the extreme event coming, however as Taleb points out we have to make the conceptual leap and arrive at the insight that precisely because 'we do not see these events coming, we need to be robust to them' (p. 341). Mathematically perfect reasoning is less important in sociotechnical systems than reasoning based on real-world ecological assumptions which accommodate people, technology, culture, context, procedures and metrics. If unintended consequences are to be guarded against, then complexity and chance must be acknowledged.

PLANNING FOR EXTREME EVENTS

Managers in high-risk environments make well-intended efforts to guard against highly improbable events. Nonetheless, they are at the mercy of the unintended negative consequences as a result of interactions between interconnected organizational sub-systems. Planning for extreme events involves large-scale system-level responses that can provide critical functions. For example, planning for the unlikely but catastrophic event of an earthquake in a major city that lies on a fault zone entails the provision of robust transportation, telecommunications, water, power, gas and sewerage systems (Sylves and Comfort, 2012).

These are not 'preventative medicines', since controlling earthquakes is intractable and will happen sooner or later; instead, they are measures that are put in place to counter the effects if and when the extreme event happens. However, in planning for the extreme event of 'nemesis-as-an-outcome-of-hubris' in business management, it is possible to rely on prevention since, unlike earthquakes, hubristic leadership is a process in which stakeholders have some agency and its negative consequences do not have to happen. The extreme events that helped to bring down LTCM were not a one-off. History repeated itself in the 2007/08 financial crisis and its aftermath. For example, in the post-mortem into the failure of one of the largest UK banks, Halifax Bank of Scotland (HBOS), an official Bank of England report (2015) highlighted the role that interconnectedness in the system played in creating vulnerabilities to Black Swan events, but in spite of the lessons of LTCM the warning signs were ignored or overlooked (see Table 6.4).

Planning for extreme events with what Taleb refers to as an 'an open mind' goes some way to minimizing their potential negative consequences. Moreover, it is possible to increase the likelihood of bad outcomes from extreme events if actors convince themselves hubristically that highly improbable, as opposed to impossible, events cannot happen (Taleb, 2007). In the case of mitigating the effects of an earthquake, for example, the vulnerability of citizens would be intensified by failures to first acknowledge

Table 6.4   The role of the external environment in the failure of HBOS and other UK banks in 2007/2008

The Failure of HBOS: External economic environment
'Halifax and Bank of Scotland merged during a period of heightened corporate activity, in the middle of an economic cycle that had begun in the early 1990s. UK domestic economic growth had been relatively steady since the recession of the early 1990s, resulting in an extraordinarily long period (around 60 quarters) of continuous expansion. The growth in the financial services sector was more than twice as fast as the economy as a whole, averaging 6% per annum in the decade preceding the crisis, and increasing its share of nominal gross domestic product (GDP) to around 10%. Confidence in the future prospects of the economy was reflected in both bank and non-bank equity prices, which rose steadily from the start of 2003 until 2007.' (Paragraph 10)
'As the benign conditions persisted for longer and longer, many perceived that a new paradigm of economic stability had been established. Commentators under-estimated the risks that were building up in advanced economies as low interest rates and cheap – often cross-border – funding flattered banks' performance, and complex innovation increased the interconnectedness of financial firms.' (Paragraph 11)
'The financial and economic trends in the run up to the crisis were unsustainable. Some of the incipient risks were identified and highlighted by central banks, regulators and other analysts but many of the trends had been evident for many years, in some cases decades, without risks crystallising in developed economies. Few predicted the severity and longevity of the crisis that was to occur.' (Paragraph 12)

Source: Bank of England PRA and FCA (2015, Paragraphs 10–12, p. 17)

the possibility of such an event occurring and, second, compounded by failing to foresee and anticipate the consequences of managing a major city without roads, power, telecommunications, water, power and sewerage. As well as requiring the management of relevant technical factors, the management of risk in such situations also requires the management of human factors such as complacency that are likely to hinder effective preparations for or responses to extreme events.

Protection from such effects is a sociotechnical issue and as such is also an organizational culture issue. Further evidence for how an organizational culture can allow collective hubris to flourish is to be found in the example of NASA at the time of the Space Shuttle Columbia disaster in February 2003. Columbia was returning from its 28th mission when, with 16 minutes to touchdown, it broke up over Texas. All seven crew members perished. The cause of the accident was a piece of foam that broke off during launch, damaging the leading edge of the left wing which caused it to incinerate on re-entering the Earth's atmosphere. This was the second shuttle disaster: the Space Shuttle Challenger failed catastrophically in 1986 following a controversial decision to launch in extremely cold temperatures. An accident investigation board determined that NASA's culture was partly to blame because it stifled dissenting views (Mason, 2004). The parallels with the cultural problems at Deepwater Horizon are palpable. Table 6.5 summarizes the Columbia case.

Table 6.5 Cultural markers of organizational hubris at NASA (Space Shuttle *Columbia* disaster) (Mason, 2004)

Success built on culture of technical excellence and risk awareness

NASA early culture shaped by German rocket pioneer Werner von Braun

Original technical culture characterized by discipline, technical excellence, 'hands-on' strategy, awareness of risk and failure, and open communication

Transition to different culture

Dedication to flawless performance replaced in early 1970s under Nixon administration when embarked on re-useable spacecraft programme with emphasis on efficiency and reproducibility at expense of safety and technical excellence

Managerialism ('faster, better, cheaper' mantra from the top of organization)

Hierarchical managerialism; stronger demarcation of decision-making power according to levels

Substantial decision-making power accorded to senior managers

Fundamental norms of questioning, enquiry and originality replaced by norms of silence, self-protection and standardization

Early warning signs of hubris in Challenger disaster

'Culture of production': engineers had to prove that a major calamity would very likely occur to convince senior managers that it was necessary to take preventative action

Sense of invincibility as a result of previous successes under technical culture as justification for increased risk

---

The unintended negative consequences of hubris in the organizational system can only be understood and mitigated if both the social and the technical aspects are treated as interdependent parts of a complex whole. This entails the recognizing and understanding of interactions between technology, people, culture, goals and process sub-systems (Table 6.6).

Table 6.6 Sociotechnical systems analysis of LTCM and Deepwater Horizon BP Oil Spill in the Gulf

Sub-system	Deepwater Horizon oil spill (2010)	Collapse of LTCM (1998)
Destructive outcome	11 deaths; 2nd biggest oil spill; marine and coastal ecosystem damage; fishery damage and disruption; $65 bn cost to BP; long-term reputational harm	$1 tn dollar exposure; risk to entire financial system; bailout by banks overseen by Fed; bankruptcy of LTCM; short-term reputational harm to finance industry
Technology	Deep-water drilling rig; well components; blowout prevention (BOP) stack and control systems; encourages risk taking	Mathematical finance; Black–Scholes formula; Value at Risk (VaR); computer algorithms; rational actor assumptions

Sub-system	Deepwater Horizon oil spill (2010)	Collapse of LTCM (1998)
People	Hubristic CEO (Browne); operator (BP); platform leasing company (Transocean); contractors (Haliburton)	Partners; traders; high-wealth clients; Nobel Prize-winning economists
Culture	Risk seeking; variable safety record in Gulf and related operations in USA; pushing boundaries; ignoring 'heavy' warnings (Texas City, Prudhoe Bay)	Organizational narcissism; omnipotence; omniscience; over-confidence; arrogance; hubristic pride; contempt; arrogance; invulnerability; 'primitive grandiosity'; stellar intellectual reputation; high self-regard; acquisitiveness; elitism
Goals	High-risk, high-reward projects; cost reduction; increase in assets; chasing and overtaking rivals	Low risk trading; wealth maximization; pre-eminence in markets; beating the opposition
Processes	Deep water oil and gas exploration and production; process safety	Absolute return trading strategies; high financial leverage; arbitrage; hedge fund trading
Context	Oil-friendly administration; lax federal oversight; depleting oil reserves; more extreme environments; fragmentation of responsibility; Minerals Management Service (Dept of Interior) exemptions from impact assessments*	Intense competition; cost and overhead reduction; weak financial regulation; instability in Asian and Russian (default on local currency bonds) markets and financial systems; wider banking system; Fed safety net
Organizational hubris	Emergent out of the Deepwater Horizon sociotechnical system	Innate to LTCM sociotechnical system

Note: *http://e360.yale.edu/features/the_gulf_of_mexico_oil_spill_an_accident_waiting_to_happen (Accessed 27 February 2018)

LTCM's processes, like BP's operations in the Gulf of Mexico, were embedded in a highly complex sociotechnical system where knock-on effects can happen very quickly and uncontrollably, where processes are driven by complex, sometimes 'opaque', modern technologies, and where events can take on a life of their own. If organizational hubris was prevalent at BP it bears the hallmarks of an emergent phenomenon; organizational hubris at LTCM, on the other hand, bears the hallmarks of innateness. Both, in their different ways, were 'accidents waiting to happen' where destructive outcomes accrued as a result of actors' hubristic over-confidence in their own abilities and their technological prowess.

LTCM and BP laboured under some illusion of control; organizations, like people, prefer to be able to exercise control over events and their environments, and being unable to do so is a source of insecurity and pessimism, whereas being in control can be a source of safety and optimism (Highhouse, 2001). Organizational hubris appears to entail a rejection of the idea of uncontrollable risk; instead, in a hubristic culture all risky situations are viewed as a challenge to be overcome. In hubristic organizations, actors collectively assume they are 'the special ones' with the power to prevail over contexts, contingencies and chance. Paradoxically, the perceived accuracy of prediction is a source of danger and risk because it leads actors to be over-confident in their ability to predict and control events beyond the parameters of the domain and to pay insufficient attention to deviations from the model as a result of the effect of high-impact, highly improbable events (Burns and Machado, 2009).

The study of complex adaptive systems that are non-linear and dynamic suggests that larger-scale patterns with new properties can emerge from interactions between sub-systems at the local level (Lansing, 2003). The actions that actors take in one sub-system introduce unpredictability and flux across the whole, and actors who hubristically assume they can over-control the organization may end up bringing about destructive outcomes; from this viewpoint, organizational hubris can be thought of as an emergent property of a complex adaptive system (Snowden and Boone, 2007). As technology advances rapidly, new hazards emerge. Research into the role of artificial intelligence and machine learning in financial markets by the Financial Stability Board has identified the possibilities for increased risk from the use of highly complex and opaque systems by multiple actors distributed across potentially volatile global business and trading environments[10] (Table 6.7).

Table 6.7   Risks from unintended consequences of AI and machine learning in financial services

Artificial intelligence and machine learning in financial services: Unintended consequences and 'nasty surprises'
'Artificial intelligence (AI) and machine learning are being adopted rapidly for a range of applications in the financial services industry including assessing credit quality, price and market insurance contracts and automating client interaction. Also hedge funds, broker-dealers and other firms are using AI and machine learning to find signals for higher uncorrelated returns and to optimize trade execution.
A major risk comes from the widespread use of "opaque models" which could result in unintended consequences. If multiple firms develop trading strategies using AI and machine learning models but do not understand the models because of their complexity, it would be very difficult for both firms and supervisors to predict how actions directed by models will affect markets.

Artificial intelligence and machine learning in financial services: Unintended consequences and 'nasty surprises'

When the models' actions interact in the marketplace, it is quite possible that unintended, and possibly negative, consequences could result for financial markets. The hazards emanate from:

- New and unexpected forms of interconnectedness between financial markets and institutions
- Emergence of new systemically important players who fall outside the regulatory perimeter
- Lack of interpretability or auditability of AI and machine learning methods

The widespread use of opaque models may result in unintended consequences and the introduction of AI and machine learning requires adequate testing and 'training' of tools to ensure applications do what they are intended to do

---

Source: Extract from FSB (2017: 34)

Adding artificial intelligence and machine learning to the sociotechnical mix creates a new hazard, especially if computers and robots turn out to be as prone to hubris as human beings are. AI and machine learning could amplify the risk of 'nasty surprises' emerging from complexity.[11]

SOCIOTECHNICAL HUBRIS

In the Daedalus–Icarus myth, Icarus' hubris was a product both of the social (he and his father were frustrated in their desire to leave Crete, contained against their will by the powerful King Minos and the technological (wax and feathers). Icarus's hubristic delusion of control was a *sociotechnical hubris* borne of the ambition to escape and over-confidence in his father's high-risk technology (wax and feathers); his contempt in the end was not for the gods but for nature and its laws.

Sociotechnical hubris can be framed as a moral question. The philosopher Mary Midgley discussed this issue in relation to animal rights and recklessness in food production technology. In the UK in the early 1990s, the so-called 'mad cow disease' (bovine spongiform encephalopathy, BSE) epidemic reached its peak, affecting 180,000 cattle with almost 1000 new cases being reported each week. It led to the mass slaughter of cattle and led to 178 human cases of 'variant Creutzfeld-Jakob Disease' (vCJD). Both BSE and vCJD are fatal. BSE is passed between cows through the practice of re-cycling bovine carcasses for meat and meal protein which is fed back to other cattle. Contamination occurs in humans through ingesting affected meat. Meat producers engaged wantonly in such practices in order to provide cheap meat to the highly competitive UK grocery retailing sector.

Midgley sees this in terms of a 'getting what you asked for' argument, but this does not mean that there is a simple linear cause-and-effect relationship at work or that 'wickedness always gets its just desserts'. However, the issue of mad cow disease does have both a causal and a moral aspect in that: (1) society ought not to be exploiting living creatures in this way in the first place; (2) it is a gross technological insult to nature; and (3) it should come as no surprise, therefore, that there are unintended negative consequences because they flow directly from the 'moral obtuseness that goes with greed' (Midgley, 2004: 149). A similar moral obtuseness can be found in the excesses of hubristic leadership and organizational hubris.

The sociotechnical hubris at LTCM and BP invited unintended negative consequences that emanated from complex interactions between people, technology, goals, culture, processes and context. More broadly, interactions between people and technology on a global scale are having deleterious effects on the Earth's climate systems. Perhaps in our collective sociotechnical hubris we are showing arrogance towards and contempt for nature and its laws. The eminent ecologists Paul Ehrlich and Anne Ehrlich in their book *One with Nineveh: Power, Politics and Human Consumption* (2009) framed this as a hubris that 'induces people to believe that the environment can somehow be put on hold and repaired later if society deems it necessary and throws enough money and new technology at it' (p. 9).

Conclusion

The cutting-edge technologies that were used at LTCM and in Deepwater Horizon had the potential to deliver both highly positive and negative outcomes, and each did both in their different ways and at different times. A danger exists when the complexity and novelty of innovations exceed the capacity of actors to understand them fully and anticipate their potential impacts. Burns and Machado (2010: 97) likened this to a so-called 'Frankenstein effect' whereby societies are confronted by complex sociotechnical systems that generate emergent processes which are not fully knowable or controllable in advance, and are imbued with the capacity to 'generate negative, unintended consequences'. Mary Shelley's novel *Frankenstein* cautioned against the hubris that turned a medical doctor into a mad scientist (Hård and Jamison, 2013) and highly rational actors acting in concert are capable of extraordinary feats of exaggerated self-confidence, self-deception, blindness and commitment to illusions of control. Organizational hubris is an avoidable accident waiting to happen.

Further Reading

Perman, R. (2013). *Hubris: How HBOS wrecked the best bank in Britain*. Edinburgh: Birlinn.
Tourish, D. (2018). Dysfunctional leadership in corporations. In P. Garrard (ed.) *The leadership hubris epidemic: Biological roots and strategies for prevention*. Basingstoke: Palgrave Macmillan, pp. 137–62.

NOTES

1. For a definition of STS, see https://business.leeds.ac.uk/research-and-innovation/research-centres/stc (Accessed 28 February 2018).
2. www.epa.gov/enforcement/deepwater-horizon-bp-gulf-mexico-oil-spill; https://archive.epa.gov/aed/aed_archive_03/web/html/bpspill.html (Accessed 27 February 2018).
3. www.reuters.com/article/us-bp-deepwaterhorizon/bp-deepwater-horizon-costs-balloon-to-65-billion-idUSKBN1F50NL (Accessed 27 February 2018).
4. www.nature.com/scitable/blog/eyes-on-environment/the_road_to_recovery_a (Accessed 3 March 2018).
5. www.ft.com/content/50a1508e-175f-11df-87f6-00144feab49a (Accessed 1 March 2018).
6. https://phys.org/news/2010-07-technology-disasters-trail-hubris.html (Accessed 3 March 2018).
7. Fischer Black died in 1995 at the age of 57, hence he did not receive the Nobel Prize because it is not awarded posthumously, although in awarding the prize the Royal Swedish Academy gave prominence to Black's contribution in their citation (www.nobelprize.org/nobel_prizes/economic-sciences/laureates/1997/press.html, Accessed 3 March 2018).
8. www.nytimes.com/books/00/09/24/reviews/000924.24norrist.html (Accessed 27 November 2017).
9. www.ft.com/content/5858e968-ed00-11e5-888e-2eadd5fbc4a4 (Accessed 27 November 2017).
10. The Financial Stability Board (FSB) is established to coordinate at the international level the work of national financial authorities and international standard-setting bodies, in order to develop and promote the implementation of effective regulatory, supervisory and other financial sector policies: see www.fsb.org.
11. www.telegraph.co.uk/business/2017/11/01/artificial-intelligence-could-bring-nasty-surprises-warns-financial (Accessed 13 March 2018).

7
A RELATIONAL APPROACH

WISE WARNING

'Those friends thou hast, and their adoption tried, grapple them to thy soul with hoops of steel. Give every man thy ear, but few thy voice; Take each man's censure, but reserve thy judgment.' (Spoken by Polonius, *Hamlet*, Act I, Scene III)

Introduction

In leadership, relational processes are the things that leaders and followers bring to their interpersonal exchanges (Uhl-Bien, 2006: 656). In the relational approach, leadership is viewed as a dynamic two-way influence exchange between a leader and follower aimed at achieving mutual goals, and in this respect it is concerned with processes between persons as much as with persons themselves (Uhl-Bien, 2006). Leadership exchanges can be between bosses and subordinates or peer-to-peer (Schaubroeck and Lam, 2002). In terms of its epistemology, the relational leadership research has adopted both positivist/entity-based and social constructionist perspectives (Epitropaki et al., 2018). A relational-type approach sheds light on two aspects of hubristic leadership: (1) how two-way interpersonal exchanges between a leader and a follower can provide a check and balance on leaders' hubris ('toe-holding') and correspondingly what can happen if these constraints are removed; and (2) how three-way interactions between a leader, a group of followers and the context in which their relationships are situated, can bring about destructive outcomes emanating from a process of hubristic leadership. In studying these two-way and three-way relationships, the chapter will explore how a toe-holding relationship can constrain hubris and how a toxic triangular relationship can enable it.

TOE-HOLDING DYADIC RELATIONSHIPS

Many leadership theories emphasize the leader (as in trait-based approaches) or followers and context (as in situational leadership theory). Both assume that followers are a largely homogeneous group in terms of their one-to-one relationships with the leader. But this assumption is an over-simplification and is not especially helpful in understanding hubristic leadership. An alternative is to focus on the unique relationships that leaders have with specific followers. 'Leader–member exchange' (often shortened to 'LMX') theory does not treat followers as an 'average' group, but instead it puts the unique interactions between a leader and a follower (i.e. member) centre-stage (Henderson et al., 2009).

Leader–member exchange theory was first proposed in the 1970s (Dansereau et al., 1975). Its foundations are in social exchange theory (SET), one of the most influential paradigms for understanding workplace behaviour (Emerson, 1976). From the perspective of social exchange theory, relationships between a leader and a follower can evolve over time into trusting, loyal and mutual commitments. These exchanges are governed by 'exchange rules' and expectations of reciprocity (Cropanzano and Mitchell, 2005; Dulebohn et al., 2012; Emerson, 1976). The origins of social exchange theory can be traced back to the 1920s and the works of the anthropologist Bronisław Malinowski, and the foundational contributions to the field include Thibaut and Kelley's *The Social Psychology of Groups* (1959), Homans' *Social Behaviour* (1961) and Blau's *Exchange and Power in Social Life* (1964).

One reason why a social exchange perspective, and the leader–member exchange theory in particular, is potentially insightful for understanding hubristic leadership is because it focuses on the micro-features not of the leader's personality in isolation (as the behavioural and Hubris Syndrome approaches tend to do), but rather of the relationship between a leader and a follower. In so doing, it does not assume leaders treat all followers the same (for example, they may be more trusting of some and more suspicious of others) and opens the way for the analysis of particular types of relationship that leaders have with followers (for example, the special relationship that a senior leader may have with a trusted peer or deputy such as a chairman, deputy prime minister or vice president, or secretary of state). An assumption of the relational approach is that hubristic leadership is embedded in the social relations between a leader and their follower(s).

As one of the dominant approaches to relational leadership, leader–member exchange theory focuses on: (1) leader characteristics, for example personality traits, charisma, expectations of followers, and contingent reward behaviour, and in the case of hubris leaders' over-confidence, over-ambition and recklessness; (2) follower characteristics, for example competence, personality traits, positive and negative affect and locus of control, and in hubristic leadership followers' collusion or compliance; and (3) quality of leader–member relationships, for example perceived similarity, liking, assertiveness, trust, reciprocity, and in the case of hubristic leadership a follower praising the leader and the leader legitimizing the follower (Dulebohn et al., 2012; Epitropaki et al., 2018; Graen and Uhl-Bien, 1995; Martin et al., 2016). In leader–member exchange theory's original formulation, the link between a leader and a follower is referred to as a 'dyadic linkage' and is typically a 'vertical dyadic linkage' between a boss and a subordinate.

In this approach, qualitative differences in leader–member exchange relationships are recognized, for example a 'low leader–member exchange' is characterized by formal, contractual-type exchanges, whereas 'a high leader–member exchange' is characterized by mutual respect, affect, support, loyalty and felt obligation (Martin et al., 2016). Trust is central to a high-quality leader–member exchange, and in essence leader–member exchange can be thought of as a trust-building process (Bauer and Green, 1996; Liden et al., 1993; Scandura and Pellegrini, 2008). Leaders and members (followers) develop trust through social exchanges, with the expectation that positive exchanges will continue (Figure 7.1).

Owen describes a toe-holder as a 'trusted advisor' who is not dependent on the leader, who can hold up a 'metaphorical' mirror to the leader, and who can encourage and enable the leader to critically and objectively reflect on their dispositions and behaviours (2016: 23) – see Figure 7.1. The term was first applied to Louis Howe, Franklin D. Roosevelt's ('FDR') trusted advisor, to whom FDR gave 'licence to dissent' (Owen, 2018: 167) and for whom Howe 'provide[d] the toe-weights' (Rowley, 2011: 64). See Table 7.2 later in the chapter for an outline of the FDR/Louis Howe exchange which is archetypal of the toe-holder relationship.

Figure 7.1 Toe-holder dyad

The cornerstone of high-quality leader–follower exchange is the development of mutual trust through repeated and close interpersonal experiences, common values, beliefs, goals and attitudes and, in politics, shared ideologies. In highly developed, high-quality leader–member relationships, followers are trusted by the leader and there are reciprocal exchanges and reciprocal interdependencies. Both parties bring something of value to the relationship, the parties interact and the history of their interchanges builds the relationship to a point of equilibrium or balance (Brower et al., 2000). In the case of hubristic leadership, for example, the point of equilibrium could be an optimal level of restraint on a leader's exuberance. The existence or emergence of dissimilarities and differences between leaders and followers (for example, as a result of a leader's 'intoxication with power') may create detachment and distance, and the diminution of trust, respect and obligation may lead to a breakdown of the leader–follower relationship (Newcombe and Ashkanasy, 2002).

Leader–member exchange researchers also make a distinction between in-groups and out-groups. In early formulations of leader–member exchange theory, followers become members of an 'in-group' or an 'out-group' based on how well they work with the leader. Relationships between the leader and members of the in-group are characterized by a high degree of mutual trust, respect, obligation and reciprocal influence ('higher quality'), whilst relationships between the leader and individual members of the out-group are more formalized and characterized by lower trust, respect, obligation and reciprocal influence ('lower quality') (Graen and Uhl-Bien, 1995). Relational leadership researchers have also focused on differential relationships between individual leaders and members of the work group (so-called 'leader–member exchange differentiation') (Henderson et al., 2009). Another development is the idea of 'leader–member triads' (Offstein et al., 2006). In a hubristic leadership process, differential triadic relationships within a group can result in the creation and marginalization of an out-group who do not share the leader's aspirations and ambitions, and the privileging of an in-group whose views align with those of the leader and lead to tensions between the in-group and the out-group (see 'toxic triangle' below).

As well as explaining the marginalization of individuals and out-groups, the centrality of reciprocity and trust in a relational-type approach is a useful idea in helping to understand how political leaders and CEOs develop special peer-to-peer relationships. In government settings, a relational-type approach can help to explain how presidents and prime ministers develop special, high-quality relationships with trusted deputies or senior ministers (as in Margaret Thatcher's close professional relationship with her deputy from 1983 to 1988, William Whitelaw) or non-elected advisers (as in Tony Blair's close professional relationship with his press secretary Alastair Campbell). It can help to explain how highly effective business leaders develop mutually beneficial relationships with special 'counsellors', as in Michael Dell's relationship with Mort Topfer marked by 'constant communication' which multiplied their 'individual capacities for success' (Dell and Fredman, 1999: 114).

The role of such individuals is important in understanding how negative outcomes associated with a hubristic leadership process come about. In the case of hubristic leadership, the toe-holding (in the sense of holding back and restraining) exchange is a special type of relationship between a hubristic leader and a particularly trusted follower. The waning of the toe-holding relationship may create the conditions for a hubristically inclined leader's hubris to emerge fully-fledged, as was the case in the relationship (a toe-holding dyad) between British First World War Prime Minister David Lloyd George and his restraining Chancellor of the Exchequer, Andrew Bonar Law. (Figure 7.2)

David Lloyd George, Liberal, Prime Minister, 1916 to 1922

One of the 20th century's most famous radicals. First and only Welshman to hold office of prime minister. Remembered as man of great energy and unconventional outlook in character and politics. Acclaimed as 'man who had won the war'. His 1918 Liberal–Conservative coalition won huge majority. Lloyd George remained a controversial figure; his own party could not decide whether to support or abandon him. Largely disregarded problems facing the Liberal party, preferring to work for himself.

Andrew Bonar Law, Conservative, 1922 to 1923 (Lloyd George's Chancellor)

Won Conservative party leadership in 1911 as compromise candidate. At outbreak of war, offered government support of Conservatives in coalition. Worked closely with Liberals. Admired Lloyd George, declined the premiership in favour of Lloyd George. Given senior position in Lloyd George's war cabinet. Great mutual trust between both leaders. Well-coordinated political partnership. Lost his two eldest sons in war. Health deteriorated. Became prime minister himself briefly from 1922 to 1923.

Figure 7.2   Leader (Lloyd George) and follower (Bonar Law)

Source: www.gov.uk/government/history/past-prime-ministers/david-lloyd-george; www.gov.uk/government/history/past-prime-ministers/andrew-bonar-law (Accessed 10 March 2018)

David Lloyd George/Andrew Bonar Law Toe-holding Dyad

David Lloyd George (1863–1945) was prime minister in the UK's Liberal–Conservative coalition government from 1916 to 1922. He is perhaps best remembered and widely credited as 'the man who won the war'. In the words of a former UK Labour Prime Minister James Callaghan:

Throughout his career, Lloyd George was buoyant, dynamic and brimming with the self-confidence that every prime minister must have. Lloyd George knew the war must be won and he knew he was the man to do it. His drive, his lack of convention, his persuasiveness, carried people with him to believe in victory. Even his foremost opponents conceded: 'He is the only man who can win the war.' Lloyd George was one of the two outstanding war-time prime ministers of the 20th century. Whether he or Churchill should wear the palm is a close-run thing, but both of them outstrip the rest of us.[1]

Two factors contributed to Lloyd George's success during the war years (Owen, 2011a). First was the collaborative and conciliatory way in which he ran the War Cabinet. Second was the constraints placed on his hubristic tendencies by Andrew Bonar Law (1858–1923). As well as being the leader of the Conservative Party, Bonar Law was also appointed by Lloyd George as his Chancellor of the Exchequer in the war-time coalition.

There was a high level of mutual trust between the prime minister and his chancellor. Lloyd George described it as the 'most perfect partnership in political history' (*War Memoirs*: 421). For Lloyd George, 'it was essential to secure' Bonar Law's 'good will and approval' (*War Memoirs*: 370) and, in spite of their political differences (a Liberal prime minister and a Conservative chancellor), Lloyd George was never 'remotely conscious' of Bonar Law's party political association (*War Memoirs*: 191) (Figure 7.3).

Figure 7.3 Lloyd George–Bonar Law toe-holder dyad

Whilst Lloyd George was by nature an optimist, Bonar Law was a pessimist 'who anticipated trouble everywhere and every time, and mostly exaggerated it' (*War Memoirs*: 426). If Lloyd George over-estimated what could go right, this was balanced by Bonar Law who over-estimated what could go wrong. According to Lloyd George, Bonar Law's favourite phrase was 'There is lots of trouble ahead!' (*War Memoirs*: 427). They developed a routine where every morning after breakfast Lloyd George submitted his imaginative ideas to the scrutiny of Law whose critical and practical mind constrained Lloyd George's exuberance and creativity. Their relationship is analysed in terms of actors, processes and relationships in Table 7.1.

Table 7.1   Actors, processes and relationship in the Lloyd George–Bonar Law toe-holder dyad

Actors	'There never were two men who constituted such a complete contrast in temperamental and mental equipment' (*War Memoirs*: 423). Bonar Law lacked confidence (he had declined being prime minister before Lloyd George took office). He said of himself 'If I am a great man, then a good many great men of history are frauds.' Judged by Lloyd George to be 'meekly ambitious' with an 'inherent diffidence which caused him to distrust his own judgement' coupled with 'conscientiousness and caution' (*War Memoirs*: 427). Lloyd George was by nature an optimist, whilst Bonar Law was a pessimist 'who anticipated trouble everywhere and every time, and mostly exaggerated it' (*War Memoirs*: 426); his favourite phrase was 'There is lots of trouble ahead!' (*War Memoirs*: 427).
Processes	'Bonar's first impulse, when a project or prospect was placed before him, was to dwell on its difficulties and dangers. I found that idiosyncrasy useful and even exhilarating ... He had an incomparable gift of practical criticism ... Sometimes I felt the force of his criticism was so great as to be insuperable, and I abandoned the project altogether; at other times I felt it necessary to alter or modify the idea in order to meet some obstacle I had not foreseen but which he had pointed out ... I never failed to listen to his views and give full weight to them' (*War Memoirs*: 425–6).
Relationships	For Lloyd George, Bonar Law's 'good will and approval it was essential to secure' (*War Memoirs*: 370). Lloyd George was never 'remotely conscious' of Bonar Law's opposing political party association (*War Memoirs*: 191). Described by Lloyd George as the 'most perfect partnership in political history' (*War Memoirs*: 421), '[events] brought Mr. Bonar Law and myself into a close partnership, and laid the foundations of a mutual understanding and real friendship which is one of the happiest of my political memories' (*War Memoirs*: 403).

However, after the 1918 general election, in which the coalition won a landslide, Bonar Law's influence on the prime minister began to wane. It was at this time that Lloyd George 'began to develop hubris syndrome' (Owen and Davidson, 2009: 6). In Owen's estimation, Lloyd George went on to become 'potentially [the] most hubristic Prime Minister of the last century' (2011a: 14). Lloyd George's demise was attributed by Lord Beaverbrook to his hubris:

> The Greeks told us of a man in high position, self-confident, so successful as to be overpowering all others. Then his virtues turn into failings. He committed the crime of arrogance. His structure of self-confidence and success came tumbling down. He struggled against fate but he was doomed. (Beaverbrook, 1963, cited in Owen, 2011a: 15)

In tracing Lloyd George's fall from grace, a critical event – some might argue the tipping point – in his decline was when his toe-holding relationship with Bonar Law waned. Bonar Law had recently lost his two sons in the war and 'ill health drove him from companionship and collaboration'; the separation was felt by Lloyd George 'more deeply than any I have endured during my political life' (*War Memoirs*: 422). Without Bonar Law's restraining force, Lloyd George's leadership style and diplomacy became intuitive, erratic, confused and ill prepared (Owen and Davidson, 2009). In his rise, Lloyd George 'contained himself' by means of his exchanges with the prudent and reliable Bonar Law; in his decline and the absence of Law's counsel, his respect for Cabinet diminished accordingly and his demise occurred because he allowed the hubristic temperament which surfaced after his wartime successes to run unconstrained (Owen and Davidson, 2009).

Restraining Relationships in Toe-holding Dyads

The value of a relational-type approach in understanding hubristic leadership is that it can shed light on how the potential for intoxication of power and prior success can be moderated by a toe-holding dyadic relationship. Lloyd George and Bonar Law developed a high-quality peer-to-peer exchange based on respect, loyalty, commitment, support, obligation and trust. They came from different political parties but had compatible goals at a time of great national crisis (the First World War). High levels of mutual respect and mutual affection motivated and enabled the follower to restrain the leader and the leader to heed the intelligent restrainer. In their exchanges, Bonar Law was the 'no-man' that Lloyd George needed rather than the 'yes-man' he needed least, and it was this which helped to keep the leader grounded. Lloyd George was charismatic, whereas Bonar Law was not and they differed in many other respects. Rather than their dyadic relationship being based on perceived similarity, it was based on perceived complementarity and was a highly effective exchange in keeping the hubristic impulses of the leader in check. By way of further illustration, the toe-holder dyad relationship between President Franklin D. Roosevelt (1882–1945) and his Secretary Louis McHenry Howe (1871–1936) is shown in Table 7.2.

The idea of the toe-holding dyad is as relevant to understanding and constraining hubristic leadership in business management as it is in politics. Volvo's Pehr Gyllenhammar was a visionary CEO who tried to push through radical change, but his over-estimation of his own abilities, his over-confidence in his personal vision and a deafness to the naysayers contributed to his downfall (Maccoby, 2000). Gyllenhammar was most effective at Volvo when he had an obsessive toe-holder in the form of Chief Operating Officer Håkan Frisinger to act as a check on his exuberance and keep the business focused on quality and cost (Maccoby, 2000). On the other hand, Michael Dell described his highly productive relationship with his special 'counsellor' Mort Topfer as one in which 'We've come to know that two heads are better than one. Mort and I have complementary strengths so we each focus on areas where we can contribute the most value' (Dell and Fredman, 1999: 114).

High-quality social exchanges between a leader and a toe-holder hold hubrists in check. But toe-holding a hubrist is a challenge, not least because senior leaders, by definition, occupy the upper echelons of politics and business, where not only is it difficult to curb their power and influence, it is also hard for those without vested interests to get close enough to them to identify warning signs.

Table 7.2   Franklin D. Roosevelt–Louis Howe toe-holder dyad

Franklin D. Roosevelt was the 32nd President of the United States from 1932 to 1945. His record of impressive achievements was tarnished by his failed attempt at packing the Supreme Court with liberal-leaning Democrat justices who would support him in order to pass his New Deal in 1937. His court-packing plan ran into stiff opposition and severe difficulties and eventually foundered. It was perhaps the biggest failure and embarrassment of his presidency, and has prompted scholars of Roosevelt's life and achievement to ponder: 'The mystery remains of why such a talented leader so mishandled such an important issue' (Black, 2003: 419). One possible answer is that, although he does not appear to have succumbed to Hubris Syndrome, he did show clear signs of hubris and the potential for the syndrome (Owen and Davidson, 2009). His hubris was held in check by his toe-holder, Secretary to the President, Louis Howe. Howe was Roosevelt's 'streetwise sidekick' who could speak frankly and on first-name terms to him and check his hubris (Hoogenboezem, 2007: 145). One of the reasons Roosevelt chose Howe to be close to him was precisely because he would argue with him. Roosevelt encouraged and expected dissent from Howe, and he got it with exchanges such as 'You damned fool' or 'Goddammit Franklin, you can't do that', and 'That is the stupidest idea I've ever heard of' (Owen, 2018: 167). Howe described himself as the president's 'no man'. Howe was aware of the importance of their relationship and remarked shortly before his untimely death in 1936 that 'Franklin is on his own now'. The court debacle packing was just a year later. Unlike Lloyd George, Roosevelt appears to have recognized how Louis Howe compensated for shortcomings in his presidential style and after Howe's death brought other toe-holders into his immediate orbit, including his wife, his Secretary of Commerce Harry Hopkins and Personal Secretary to the President, Marguerite 'Missy' Le Hand, to keep him in check.

TOXIC TRIANGLE RELATIONAL APPROACH

The 'toxic triangle' is a model of destructive leadership (Chapter 1). It is based on the assumptions that leadership of any type emanates from leaders' motivation and ability to lead, followers' desire for direction and authority, and the circumstances in which leadership is enacted (Padilla et al., 2007) (Table 7.3). The toxic triangle model adds a situational dimension to the individual and the relational aspects and provides an integrative framework for understanding how the phenomenon and process of hubristic leadership becomes associated with unintended negative consequences.

Table 7.3   The three domains of the toxic triangle (Padilla et al., 2007)

Domain	Description
Destructive leaders	Attributes such as charisma, narcissism, personalized use of power, hubris, etc.
Susceptible followers	Conformers (e.g. individuals with unmet basic needs, negative self-evaluations); ambitious and selfish colluders who share leader's world views
Conducive environments	Instability, perceived threat, particular cultural values, absence of checks and balances, institutionalization, etc.

The toxic triangle model has been used to explore the destructive outcomes associated with various types of destructive leadership, including Fidel Castro's leadership of Cuba (Padilla et al., 2007), the Penn State scandal (Thoroughgood and Padilla, 2013) and the controversy at Bristol Royal Infirmary in the UK (Fraher, 2016). Given that hubristic leadership is a type of destructive leadership, the toxic triangle model is a useful framework to explore how the exchanges in relationships and interactions between a hubristic leader, susceptible followers and conducive context lead to destructive outcomes (Figure 7.4).

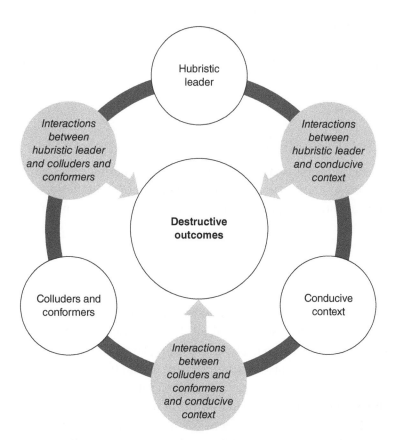

Figure 7.4   Interactions between domains in a generic toxic triangle of hubristic leadership (Adapted from Padilla et al., 2007)

There are few who doubt that the decision to invade Iraq in 2003 led to destructive outcomes. For example, Nobel economics laureate Joseph Stiglitz (2008) referred to it as the '$3 trillion war', and eminent political scientists consider it to be America's worst foreign policy decision (Smith, 2016). A study published under the auspices of the Costs of War Project by the Watson Institute for International Studies at Brown

University in 2013 estimated that the cost of the Iraq war could grow to more than $6 trillion over the next four decades (counting benefits to veterans and interest charges) and that it has led to the death of at least 134,000 Iraqi civilians, and over 4000 US military personnel. The deepening of Shiite–Sunni divisions and the insurrection by ISIS fundamentalists have been attributed to the conditions that the invasion and subsequent events created and amplified in Iraq and the wider region (Chomsky and Barsamian, 2017). In what follows, the destructive leadership process which led to the 2003 invasion of Iraq is treated at some length and will be analysed in terms of: (1) Bush as a hubristic leader (with an over-reliance on instinct and intuition; low openness to experience and low integrative complexity; appeals to high moral authority); (2) susceptible followers (active colluders; cautious restrainer; anticipatory complier); and (3) the conducive context (pre-9/11 and 9/11 and beyond).

Bush as a Hubristic Leader

Three systematic and habitual aspects of Bush's decision-making style contributed to his hubrism: (1) his over-reliance on his instinct and intuition; (2) his low openness to experience and low cognitive complexity; and (3) his appeals to a higher moral authority (i.e. God).

Over-reliance on instinct and intuition

Intuitions are affectively charged judgements that arise quickly and involuntarily (Dane and Pratt, 2007). Bush self-defined his decision style in these terms: 'I think it's just instinctive. I'm not a textbook player. I'm a gut player' (Woodward, 2002: 137). His approach was to choose a course of action intuitively, and because 'I'm the commander [...] I don't need to explain' (Woodward, 2002). Bush valued this approach in himself and in others: 'People have either got good instincts or they don't ... They trust you or they don't' (Smith, 2016: 73–5). Some have described his decision-making style pejoratively as 'macho Texan cowboy' (Dunn, 2003: 279). More sympathetically, a White House veteran staff member described Bush as 'a top down, no-nonsense, decisive macho leader who set his eye on the far horizon and doesn't go wobbly in getting there ... To lead, in his book, is to decide' (Smith, 2016: 151).

Intuition can have advantages in uncertain and dynamic conditions when it is based on extensive experience and domain-relevant expertise (Kahneman and Klein, 2009; Sadler-Smith and Shefy, 2004). On the other hand, in its naïve form intuition exposes decision makers to well-documented errors and biases (see Gilovich et al., 2002). For example, previous research has described a process whereby unbridled intuition crowded-out rationality in Bush's decision making in an area, foreign policy, where he had little prior experience or relevant expertise (Claxton et al., 2015). Given that intuitions are prior analyses (i.e. experiences) frozen into habit and the capacity for rapid response through recognition (Simon, 1987: 63), to rely on intuition with a weak experience base is a potential source of error and bias (Kahneman and Klein, 2009).

Low openness to experience and low integrative complexity

Additional personality-related and cognitive factors contributing to Bush's hubris were his low openness to experience and low integrative complexity (Simonton, 2006). Individuals low on openness to experience show little proclivity for or receptivity to matters such as aesthetics (e.g. an appreciation of art or music), ideas (e.g. intellectual curiosity) and novel actions (e.g. trying out new activities and visiting novel places). Individuals who are low on integrative complexity tend to see things from a single perspective – their own. Additionally, since they do not take alternative points of view into consideration, the integration of new or incongruous information becomes unnecessary and redundant (Simonton, 2006). Low levels of integrative complexity have been found in groups such as hardline communists in the Soviet leadership and extreme Islamic fundamentalists in al Qaeda and the Taliban (Suedfeld and Leighton, 2002; Tetlock and Boettger, 1989). Low openness to experience is associated with a greater reliance on heuristics (McElroy and Dowd, 2007); low-integrative-complexity individuals tend to rely on tried-and-tested mental short cuts, and to gather and interpret information according to familiar patterns ingrained in mental models and stereotypes (Wong et al., 2011).

Appeals to higher moral authority

A further aspect of Hubris Syndrome identified by Owen and Davidson (2009) is the appeal to a higher moral authority and being accountable, ultimately, to a higher court such as 'history or God' (p. 1398). Former UK Prime Minister Tony Blair used this in support of his decision to invade Iraq (Owen, 2011a). In this regard, a transformative event in Bush's life may have been his encounter with evangelical Christianity in 1985 via the preacher Billy Graham. His faith appears to have been central to his transformed persona. In the events leading up to the Iraq invasion and beyond, Bush relied on his faith to claim direction and purpose and to assert a moral high ground. More mundanely, he relied on his faith daily by beginning every cabinet meeting with a prayer for divine guidance (Smith, 2016: 169), and also credits his faith with helping him to 'quit drinking' in the 1980s (Bush, 2010: 34).

Summary

Bush, by his own admission (2010: 1), has a 'habitual personality'; his decision style melded instinct and intuition with low openness to experience and low integrative complexity allied to a strong religious faith. Pulitzer-prize-winning journalist Ron Suskind captured the 'Bush style' succinctly in a *New York Times* article shortly after the Iraq invasion: 'He truly believes he's on a mission from God. Absolute faith like that overwhelms a need for analysis. The whole thing about faith is to believe things for which there is no empirical evidence.' *Washington Post* journalist Bob Woodward remarked similarly in summing up an interview in which Bush referred to intuition and instinct no less than a dozen times: 'his instincts are almost his second religion' (2002: 342). Bush's style resonated with a simple and emotionally charged 'good-versus-evil' binary discourse; it was popular and best exemplified in his State of the Union address on 29 January 2002: 'States like [Iran, Iraq and North Korea], and their terrorist allies, constitute an *axis of evil*, arming to threaten the peace of the world.' The unforeseen events of 9/11 were focal in imbuing Bush's presidency with meaning; he became accountable to history (Owen, 2011a) and his mission was part of God's plan: 'Our responsibility to history is already clear: To answer these attacks and rid the world of evil' (Woodward, 2004: 67).

Susceptible Followers

Pivotal status is accorded to followers in destructive leadership theory and previous research has identified two types of follower: 'conformers' and 'colluders'. In their dyadic exchanges, each participates actively in the leader's agenda and both are driven by self-interest, but their motivations and their exchanges with the leader are quite different (Padilla et al., 2007). In the case of the Iraq invasion, active collusion emanated from a shared world view and mutual ideology, attempts were made at cautious restraint (toe-holding) and conformance emerged from group processes – for example, intragroup conflict, groupthink and political out-manoeuvrings.

Researchers have also identified an 'anticipatory complier' follower type (Mitchell and Massoud, 2009). Based on a reformulation of Janis's (1982) seminal 'groupthink' concept, Mitchell and Massoud (2009) argued that in a group that is dominated by a strong leader 'anticipatory compliance' is engaged in by individuals who have a loyalty towards the leader, know the mind of the leader, are motivated to support her or him, and make it their business to go along with whatever the leader proposes without being explicitly told to do so.

Based on the above formulation, three follower types characterized by different types of dyadic exchanges can be identified in the Bush administration in the lead-up to the decision to invade Iraq in 2003: (1) 'active colluders'; (2) a 'cautious restrainer'; and (3) an 'anticipatory complier'.

Active colluders

Bush prided himself on being 'The Decider', as someone with a flair for instinctive responses (Smith, 2016). However, the reality seems to be that many of the important decisions were driven by a shared ideology with and advocacy of a tight-knit, core group of advisors consisting of Vice President (2001–09) Dick Cheney, Secretary of Defence (2001–06) Donald Rumsfeld, and Deputy Secretary of Defence (2001–05) Paul Wolfowitz. Together, they embodied an ideologically driven 'collective hubris' that was a significant factor in the administration's decision-making processes (Owen, 2011b: 146).

Dick Cheney (Vice President): as an experienced and conservative hardliner, Cheney was the most formidable presence in the West Wing of the White House. *Washington Post* veteran Bob Woodward described him as a 'steamrollering force' (2004: 4). As vice president, Cheney did not present a threat to Bush since he had no presidential ambitions of his own (Smith, 2016: 156–8). Bush gave Cheney responsibility for intelligence, and unlike most previous holders of the office, he had unprecedented involvement and influence. For example, Cheney participated in the National Security Commission (NSC) meetings, was party to the president's morning CIA briefings and headed up the selection process for a team which helped to simultaneously shape and constrain the options presented for Bush's consideration (Beinart, 2010; Mitchell and Massoud, 2009; Smith, 2016). Cheney's chief of staff was I. Lewis 'Scooter' Libby, a protégé of the neoconservative hawk Paul Wolfowitz (see below), who by virtue of his position was a 'power center unto himself, [and] a force multiplier for Cheney's agenda' (Woodward, 2004: 48). In the build-up to the invasion, Cheney's intense focus on Saddam Hussein and Iraq regime change was seen by some colleagues as a disquieting obsession bordering on a 'fever' (Woodward, 2004: 4).

Donald Rumsfeld (Secretary of Defense): Rumsfeld was a renowned, politically dexterous Washington administrator and bureaucrat. He had been Cheney's mentor, and was described by Henry Kissinger, no less, as the most ruthless government official he had ever met (Beinart, 2010; Smith, 2016). Rumsfeld's reputation was as a 'haughty, self-styled transformer' who was convinced that he knew better than the generals about what needed to be done and how to do it (Isikoff and Korn, 2006: 16). During the process leading up to the invasion and afterwards, Rumsfeld is said to have worked hard to marginalize Colin Powell (see below); he is also reputed to have had little time for Condoleezza Rice's office of the National Security Adviser (Gellman, 2008; Mitchell and Massoud, 2009). Eventually, in the critical opinion of his biographer, 'hubris and miscalculation' brought down an administrator considered widely to be amongst 'the best and brightest of his generation' (Graham, 2009: 12).

Paul Wolfowitz (Deputy Secretary of Defense): Wolfowitz completed the triumvirate of active colluders. He was driven by a deeply entrenched neoconservative political and philosophical ideology. He believed in moral absolutes and held a strong antipathy towards the Iraq regime dating back to the 1980s. He was the 'intellectual godfather' (Woodward, 2004: 21) in shaping the administration's aggressive and forceful Middle East policy (Smith, 2016: 181). Wolfowitz ascribed to the 'Rumsfeldain logic' of absence of evidence (e.g. of weapons of mass destruction) not being taken as evidence of absence (Woodward, 200: 290), and he and others (including Rumsfeld) made no secret of a fierce advocacy for toppling Saddam Hussein in their open letter to President Clinton on 26 January 1998:

> The only acceptable strategy is one that eliminates the possibility that Iraq will be able to use or threaten to use weapons of mass destruction. In the near term, this means a willingness to undertake military action as diplomacy is clearly failing. In the long term, it means removing Saddam Hussein and his regime from power. That now needs to become the aim of American foreign policy.

The coalition of active colluders drove a foreign policy agenda that was unremittingly aggressive towards Saddam Hussein and his regime pre-9/11. Its vision was to change the post-Cold War balance of power of the region by removing Saddam Hussein and replacing him with a regime aligned with the USA so as to further American interests in and dominance of the Middle East (Smith, 2016).

Cautious restrainer

Political leaders' hubris can be held in check by the intelligent and cautious restraint of a trusted confidante (toe-holder) who is prepared to speak truth to power (Owen, 2016). A potential toe-holder for Bush's hubris was Secretary of State Powell. However, the dynamics of the leader–follower exchanges in the administration meant that Powell's restraining role had a limited effect.

General Colin Powell was a veteran of the Vietnam, Panama and first Gulf War. He had been National Security Adviser under Reagan (1987–89) and Chairman of the Joint Chiefs of Staff under G. H. W. Bush (1989–93). On becoming president, George W. Bush appointed Powell, with little hesitation or consultation, to the position of Secretary of State. In contrast to the president's style, Powell's predisposition was towards intelligent restraint emanating from the considered judgement, informed by extensive experience, that foreign policy was not about wholesale regime change but more to do with 'holding things together, keeping all hell from breaking loose, [and] incremental change', even if it meant sticking with a distasteful regime that one knew, rather than deposing and replacing it with a potentially volatile unknown (Beinart, 2010: 322). As the 'reluctant warrior' (Woodward, 2004: 78), Powell's intelligent restraint did not always align well with the president's 'go-with-your-gut' attitude, nor did it fit with the long-held ambitions of the active colluders regarding Iraq.

Moreover, Powell and Bush failed to develop the kind of personal chemistry that the president thrived on and trusted implicitly (Woodward, 2004).

Unlike active colluders such as Wolfowitz, who thought that getting rid of Saddam Hussein was not only necessary but 'would be relatively easy' (Woodward, 2004: 21), Powell was concerned with the aftermath of any invasion. He knew, as an accomplished military strategist, that the Iraqi army was no match for the US armed forces but he was concerned about the unpredictable and unintended consequences of a war which would be 'unforeseen, dangerous and hard to control' (Powell, 2012: 209). Powell never bought into the idea that Iraq would transform, within 90 days of Baghdad being successfully occupied, into a stable democracy, and he was very doubtful even that Saddam's elimination 'would be worth a war' (Powell, 2012: 211).

Powell saw his remit as advising and warning Bush as to the challenges and dangers of war in Iraq, but he did not see it as being his responsibility to tell Bush what to do. As far as Powell was concerned, it was the president as wartime commander-in-chief who decided ultimately (De Young, 2007; Mitchell and Massoud, 2009). As someone who, in Cheney's words, 'had major reservations about what we were trying to do' (Woodward, 2004: 411), Powell was outside of the active colluder in-group, and although, according to Wolfowitz, he gave their project 'credibility' (Woodward, 2004: 411), Powell also represented a challenge to its interests and purposes. Powell ended up marginalized such that his cautious restrainer role became transformed into that of reluctant conformer (Beinart, 2010; Isikoff and Korn, 2006; Smith, 2016; Woodward, 2004).

Anticipatory complier

Leaders, such as Bush, whose predisposition is towards instinct, intuition, simplicity and the 'big picture' in preference to restraint, intellect, complexity and detail need 'devil's advocates', 'toe-holders', 'naysayers', 'critical friends' and 'no men/women' to contain their impulses and curb their hubris (Kets de Vries, 1990; Miller and Ireland, 2005; Owen and Davidson, 2009; Sadler-Smith and Shefy, 2004; Shimizu and Hitt, 2004). Therefore, what Bush needed least was congenial flatterers who would do his bidding without question, inhibit deliberation and work unremittingly to achieve his goals and those of his in-group of closest advisors (Mitchell and Massoud, 2009; Smith, 2016).

Bush appointed Condoleeza Rice, who had been his chief foreign policy aid during the campaign, to the post of National Security Adviser. The person in this role would be expected to be an 'honest broker' who maintained a flow of accurate, relevant and up-to-date information to the president for his scrutiny. However, in Smith's (2016) critical assessment, the team around Bush 'failed utterly when it came to presenting him with the full range of policy alternatives' and it was Rice who appeared to take it on herself to paper over divisions, reduce complexity and 'provide Bush with what made him most comfortable' (Smith, 2016: 154–5).

Social intuition is a form of social cognition whereby one individual accurately 'reads' another's motivations and intentions (Lieberman et al., 2004). Rice was finely attuned in meetings to others' (especially Bush's) aims and purposes; she could read 'twitches', and, if confrontation threatened, could 'intuit where it [the meeting] was headed and shape it' to suit the president's wishes (De Young, 2007: 334). In so doing, Rice in effect secured advantage for the dominant coalition of active colluders against any effective opposition from other individuals or sub-groups within the administration, or from government agencies.

Rice was skilled in accommodating the president's gut instincts without being explicitly told to do so (McLellan, 2008). She saw herself as his 'enabler' and 'enforcer' who could translate his intuitions into policy, but also 'reinforced his wrong impulses' and nurtured his hubris when she should have been slowing him down, holding his toe and encouraging him to think through the complications and consequences of critical issues (Smith, 2106: 186). Her skills in anticipatory compliance made her an important instrument in and advocate for the decision to invade (Mitchell and Massoud, 2009). And, as an anticipatory complier, Rice was in effect an 'echo chamber' for Bush's intuitions, and by extension for the aims of the active colluders (Figure 7.5).

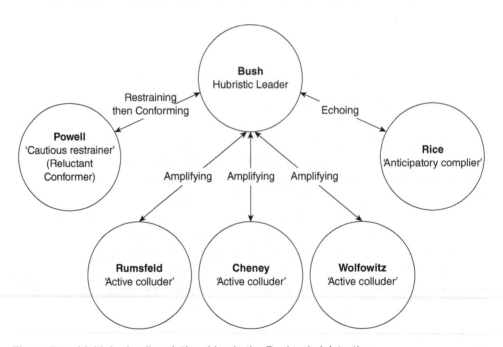

Figure 7.5   Multiple dyadic relationships in the Bush administration

Summary

Bush was by nature an impulsive and intuitive leader; as a result, he did not question the assumptions and beliefs that were the basis of the strong ideological stance he shared with his closest associates – the exchanges created an in-group which fostered group-think. Whilst intuition is an undoubted leadership strength, it also presents shortcomings which need to be countered by checks and balances. The anticipatory complier in the administration (Rice) did not provide such a balance; instead, she appears to have pro-vided an 'echo chamber' for Bush's instincts which probably helped push the centre of gravity towards the neoconservatives. Likewise, the cautious restrainer (Powell) could not, in the end, offer an effective check against the president's determination to go to war, even though he himself appears to have been sceptical as to the practicalities and purpose of an invasion. Dynamics and manoeuvrings in the exchanges within the senior team eventually reduced Powell's role from cautious restrainer to that of reluctant conformer. The active colluders, on the other hand (Cheney, Rumsfeld and Wolfowitz), were moti-vated by a strong neoconservative ideology in which America was seen to have the right to take unilateral action to advance its interests in geopolitically important arenas post-Cold War, and served as amplifiers for Bush's intuitions in their exchanges with him.

Conducive Context

Bush and his administration were embedded in a pre-9/11 geopolitical context, and the decision to invade Iraq and oust Saddam Hussein's regime, which had been long sought after by active colluders, appears to have been catalyzed by the events of 9/11 itself.

The pre-9/11 context

The pre-9/11 context had three significant elements: the Gulf War (1990–91); the post-Cold War neoconservative intellectual climate; and terror attacks on US personnel and facilities.

Gulf War: George H. W. Bush (George W.'s father) led America in the Gulf War against Iraq (1990–91) in response to Saddam Hussein's invasion of Kuwait. Military action was endorsed by the United Nations Security Council Resolution 678 and implemented by a coalition of forces from 35 nations. Bush Senior was criticized by some for not press-ing the successful campaign on to a full-scale advance on Baghdad and the removal of Saddam Hussein from power. However, he was reluctant to do so because it would have entailed occupation and significant human and political costs. Bush Senior's intelligent restraint was seen by some as a failure of leadership and by others as a missed opportunity, especially those in the White House and Pentagon, such as Wolfowitz, with long-held ambitions to 'remake' the Middle East. According to Woodward (2004), Rumsfeld thought Bush senior was 'weak, [and] lacking in substance' (2004: 17). Iraq, for the colluders, was unfinished business.

Post-Cold War neoconservative intellectual climate: neoconservatism rose to prominence in the USA in the 1970s and offered a blend of liberal democracy, idealism and hawkish foreign policy which rejected modern liberalism. It is associated with the works of various political scientists (e.g. Fukuyama, 1992) and conservative intellectuals (e.g. Irving Kristol who received the Medal of Freedom from Bush in 2002). Two of the most prominent and influential neoconservatives under Reagan and George W. Bush were Richard Perle (Chairman of Bush's Defense Policy Board Advisory Committee, 2001–03) and Paul Wolfowitz (see above). The controversial Defense Planning Guidance Report ('Defense Strategy for the 1990s') proclaimed explicitly America's status as the post-Cold War global superpower and charted a path for unilateral action to protect and extend America's interests in the Middle East and beyond. Some have criticized it as a 'hammer looking for nails' policy (Beinart, 2010). The thinking behind it informed the military stance of the so-called 'Bush Doctrine' and was a significant element in the leadership's hubristic posture towards regime change in Iraq.

Terror attacks on the USA at home and abroad: the conducive context of the Bush administration's hubristic leadership process was compounded by the fact that the USA had already been subjected to various fatal terrorist attacks both on home (1993 World Trade Center truck bombing) and foreign soil (attacks on the US embassies in Kenya and Somalia in 1998). According to Woodward (2004), in the lead up to 9/11 the then CIA Director George Tenet had 'explicitly warned [Bush] about the seriousness and immediacy of the bin Laden threat' (p. 24). Against this background, it was the 'hawkish' Wolfowitz (Woodward, 2004: 21) who led the anti-Iraq intellectual and ideological charge within the administration, driven by the conviction that Saddam was the mastermind behind much of the world's terrorism pre-9/11 (Isikoff and Korn, 2006; Smith, 2016: 175).

The 9/11 context and beyond

Several interrelated contextual factors contributed to the likelihood of invasion: 9/11 itself, the Afghanistan campaign, the diminished role of the United Nations and the role of the media.

9/11: what happened on 11 September 2001 was one of those shocking and surprising calamities that change the course of history and after which the world suddenly became significantly more irrational and unpredictable (Owen, 2011a). Post 9/11 the question in the Bush administration was not 'if' and 'why' the USA would go to war with Iraq, but 'how' and 'when' (Beinart, 2010; Isikoff and Korn, 2006; Smith, 2016). For example, on the day of the attack, Woodward (2004) reports that in a note Rumsfeld had mused about whether to 'hit S.H. @ same time – not only UBL' (p. 25). The speech Bush gave on the day of the attacks, in which he enunciated what became known as the 'Bush Doctrine', encapsulated the president's mindset: (1) the attacks on New York and Washington were an unequivocal act of war; (2) the USA was now engaged in a 'war against terror'; (3) as a result, an entirely new set of rules come into play; and (4) the USA would make no distinction between terrorists and those nations who harbour or support them and would attack them unilaterally as well if necessary. Pre-emption was axiomatic on the basis that 'you cannot defend against terrorism', and in the wake of 9/11 it was felt that the most serious threat the USA faced was an attack using a nuclear weapon or chemical agent inside the country's borders (Woodward, 2004: 34). In the unfolding circumstances, Bush and his team were unlikely to listen to advice about what it should not do, and this served to intensify the hubristic leadership process.

Afghanistan campaign: prior successes fuel hubris (see Chapter 5). The first significant response to 9/11 was military action to attack al Qaeda and the Taliban in Afghanistan. Operation 'Enduring Freedom' was designed to prevent the Taliban from providing a haven to al Qaeda by using Afghanistan as a base of operations for terrorist activities. The Afghanistan operation served two purposes: it was a focal response to bin Laden, but it also provided a 'noise level' under which forces could be moved into the region in readiness for the Iraq invasion as the 'groundwork for war' (Woodward, 2004: 61–2). US support for the Northern Alliance against the Taliban and al Qaeda proved to be highly successful (Fairweather, 2014). The Taliban capital Kandahar fell on 7 December 2001 and Bush's popularity rating rode on the crest of the wave of victory (Eichenberg et al., 2006). Military success in Afghanistan emboldened Bush's hubrism and amplified his confidence in an Iraq invasion (Smith, 2016; Woodward, 2004).

Diminishing role of the United Nations (UN): the machinations of this hubristic leadership process were intertwined with a diminished UN role. The UN did not pass any resolution in support of the invasion, however it did provide the most high-profile platform for a justification for the invasion and unilateral action if necessary, with or without international approval. The cautious restrainer-cum-reluctant conformer Secretary of State Powell was centre-stage. In the febrile post-9/11 atmosphere, Powell struggled against impossible odds to concoct a diplomatic solution that would be acceptable to Bush and the active colluders. He wanted to intensify Hans Blix's inspections process by increasing their intrusiveness whilst continuing with a military build-up alongside working hard for UN approval for military action if Saddam's regime did not conform (Isikoff and Korn, 2006: 176).

Powell's combination of intelligent restraint and tactful juggling did not sit well with the president's de-cluttered mind. Issues came to a head in Powell's 5 February 2003 speech to the United Nations in the weeks leading up to the invasion in which he presented evidence claiming that Saddam Hussein was actively seeking a nuclear weapons' capability. With hindsight, Powell's reluctant conformance seems to have been against his nature and better judgement (De Young, 2007; Powell, 2012). Powell made what turned out to be a series of inaccurate allegations based on dubious evidence which subsequently unravelled and damaged his reputation and legacy.

In the absence of United Nations' approval and in spite of exhortations not to proceed from various world leaders, the USA and the UK (under the leadership of Prime Minister Tony Blair) sought and received approval from the US Congress (297 to 133, House of Representatives; 77 to 23, Senate) and the UK Houses of Parliament (412 to 149) respectively, which authorized military action against Iraq. The decision to invade received support and approval from across the political spectrum both in the USA (29 out of 50 Democratic senators voted in favour) and the UK (254 Labour members voted in favour).

Role of the media: previous research has found that media praise and 'celebrity status' fuel hubris (Hayward, 2007; Hayward and Hambrick, 1997; Li and Tang, 2010). Pre-9/11 Bush was not noted particularly for his eloquence or charisma (Bligh and Kohles, 2009), however post-9/11 his rhetoric, under the guidance of West Wing speechwriter Michael Gerson (responsible for the 'axis of evil' address), became infused with a rhetorical and charismatic tone (Bligh et al., 2004; Davis and Gardner, 2012; Smith, 2016). Bush was transformed in the eyes of the press and public from a president mocked regularly for his linguistic shortcomings to someone who exuded 'steel and eloquence'. Moreover, the administration's binary discourse reflected an 'either/or' construction of reality, and as such was suited ideally to a political culture dominated by mass media. TV channels provided the president with a platform for his hubris. His approval rating shortly after the commencement of the war surged by 15 percentage points (Eichenberg et al., 2006) (Table 7.4).

Table 7.4 Conducive context for decision to invade Iraq (Padilla et al., 2007)

Context	Description
Pre 9/11	Gulf War (1990–91): unfinished business for active colluders
	Post-Cold War neoconservative intellectual climate: political scientists (Fukuyama) and conservative intellectuals (Kristol)
	Terror attacks on US at home and abroad: World Trade Center, Kenya and Somalia
Post 9/11	9/11: 'Bush Doctrine' and 'war against terror'
	Afghanistan campaign: Operation 'Enduring Freedom'
	Diminished role of United Nations: Powell's speech, approval in US Congress and UK Parliament
	Role of the media: re-presentation of Bush ('steel and eloquence')

Summary

Previous research shows that hubris is more likely to emerge in environments that are complex, uncertain and dynamic because these conditions create opportunities for enhanced leader discretion, untrammelled improvisation and executive over-reach (Li and Tang, 2011; Tang et al., 2015). The environment post-9/11 was highly volatile and favoured a chain of command decision-making process headed up by a president who saw himself as an assertive 'wartime' commander-in-chief without any need to manage the risks by explaining his decisions to anyone or listening to advice about what should not be done (Woodward, 2004). Propelled forward as he was by over-confidence, moral rectitude and religious certitude, the president seemed to have been oblivious to alternatives and insensible to the potential consequences of his actions (Smith, 2016).

Dubious links between terrorism and Saddam Hussein gave impetus to an imperative for invasion and regime change in Iraq that was propelled forward relentlessly once a hubristic leadership process had taken hold. The active colluders within the administration were complicit in bringing about the longer-term destructive outcomes associated with the invasion by appealing to an over-simplified interpretation of the geopolitical context (Beinart, 2010; Isikoff and Korn, 2006; Smith, 2016). Powell was the only member of the senior team who had combat experience but his informed and cautious approach was at odds with the zeal of the active colluders (Woodward, 2004). In the role of 'moderate negotiator' versus Rumsfeld the 'hard-line activist' (Woodward, 2004: 23), Powell became increasingly sidelined as events moved forward swiftly. Post-9/11 the exchanges within Bush's senior team were such that beneath the surface it became fractured and bifurcated (Smith, 2016; Woodward, 2004).

The 9/11 context presented a set of propitious circumstances for a hubristic leadership process to emerge. Throughout this, Bush consistently displayed many of the hallmarks of hubris (Claxton et al., 2015), foremost amongst which was an 'unwavering personal certainty about his decisions' (Anderson, 2011: 233). Powell's efforts at reining in presidential hubrism ended up being to no avail (Woodward, 2004). The president and the active colluders, enabled by anticipatory compliance and impervious to cautious restraint, 'had already made this decision for military action. The dice had been tossed. That's what we were going to do'.[2] The invasion of Iraq on 20 March 2003 was the outcome of a process of hubristic leadership, and its unintended negative consequences have turned out, in the view of many expert commentators, to be long-term destructive and destabilizing, both regionally and globally.

Amplifying Hubris in a Toxic Triangle Relationship

The exchanges between the domains of hubristic leader, colluding, conforming and complying followers and a propitious context in a toxic triangle of hubristic leadership, increase the chances of destructive outcomes. These outcomes are emergent joint accomplishments because of multiple agents (leaders, colluders, conformers, compliers, protagonists, restrainers, etc.) interacting in open-ended ways to produce unforeseen outcomes.

The toxic triangle of hubristic leadership resonates not only with a relational-type approach, it also echoes some of the principles of systems thinking in that rather than seeking to isolate and split domains, it seeks to weave them together, embrace complex relations and acknowledge connectivity, recursiveness and emergence (Tsoukas and Dooley, 2011; Weick and Roberts, 1993). Recursion is an important phenomenon in these

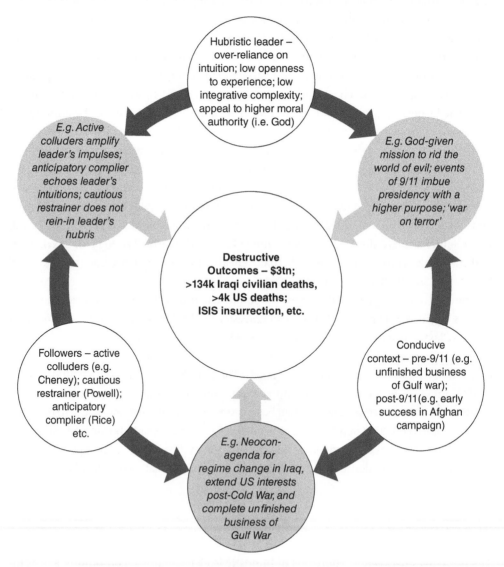

Figure 7.6   Toxic triangle of hubristic leadership in the decision to invade Iraq in 2003

interactions (see Feldman and Pentland, 2003; Giddens, 1984). The three domains of hubristic leadership are recursively linked in the literal sense of 'running back' (*recurrere*) from context to leader (for example, the events of 9/11 prompted a habitual instinctive response from Bush), from leader to context (for example, the invasion deepened sectarian Shiite/Sunni divisions in Iraq), and likewise from leader to followers and back, and from followers to context and back. Mapping the relationships between domains offers deeper insights than does simply considering each domain in isolation (Figure 7.6).

Seen in this way, hubristic leadership as a collective, collusive and contextual phenomenon and process is not reducible to a consideration of the three domains in isolation. The complexity whereby each domain has enabling/constraining and producing/reproducing effects on the others needs to be acknowledged in any analysis of the process of hubristic leadership by focusing on domains and their interactions over time (see Chapter 8). The toxic triangle of hubristic leadership attempts to articulate an approach which is sensitive to structure, agency, process, context and time (Giddens, 1984; Toulmin, 1990). In the relational view, hubristic leadership emanates from the three-way interactions between leader, followers and context, whereby relationality, situatedness and temporality create the conditions for the emergence of destructive outcomes.

In a process of hubristic leadership, as opposed to purely destructive types of leadership such as bullying or tyranny in which there is intent to harm, there is usually no explicit or deliberate intention on the part of the leader to bring about destructive outcomes. The attributes of and the interactions between the three domains of hubristic leader, colluding, conforming or complying followers and a conducive context are such that there is an increased likelihood of destructive consequences ensuing. Bush and his active colluders' high-risk behaviour was intentional and volitional; they over-estimated what could go right and under-estimated what could go wrong. They could have chosen goals and actions from amongst other, ultimately less destructive alternatives and could have managed the risks more effectively, but they chose not to do so.

Hubrists ally over-confidence with displays of contempt and arrogance; consequently, one of the ways in which hubristic decision makers fail to manage risks appropriately is by not listening to advice from toe-holders, cautious and intelligent restrainers or 'wise warners' about what they should not do. In the case of the Iraq invasion, vulnerabilities to the potentially destructive consequences were not managed appropriately and advice (for example, from the French president, the German chancellor, Vladimir Putin, Kofi Annan and the personal envoy of Pope John Paul II) fell on deaf ears. The destructive consequences of these decisions were not accidental, not because there is a provable causal link between hubristic leadership and subsequent destructive outcomes, but because emergent effects and unintended negative consequences materialized that were invited by and more likely to occur because of complex, unpredictable and dynamical interactions between leader, followers and context over time.

Potential early warning signs of hubristic leader behaviours based on the Iraq case include: (1) excessive confidence in one's judgement and ability to 'get things done' through impulse and instinct; (2) scorning accountability for one's actions in the unshakeable belief that their decisions and the actions which emanate from them will be vindicated in the long run by history or a higher authority; (3) seeing things from a single perspective – one's own and that of active colluders; (4) imperviousness to or being shielded from information that conflicts with one's instincts and beliefs, rendering the integration of countervailing information inconvenient and unnecessary; and (5) irrational exuberance combined with rigid ideology.

Conclusion

Viewed from a relational perspective, hubristic leadership, and its outcomes, is not located in or is the product of a hubristic leader acting in isolation from followers and contexts. Hubristic leadership is the product of interactions between an assemblage of interconnected domains; it emerges holistically out of the open-ended exchanges between leader, followers and context which are recursively intertwined and unfold over time to produce patterns of events that generate both intended and unintended consequences. The possibilities that hubristic leadership create for unintended negative consequences are significant and cannot and should not be ignored by organizational actors. The hazard that hubristic leadership poses is amplified in times of volatility, uncertainty, complexity and ambiguity, and is compounded when leadership is enacted through exchanges between leaders and followers who are oblivious or indifferent to the longer-term and systematic effects of their immediate actions.

Further Reading

Owen, L. D. (2018). Heads of government, 'toe-holders' and time limits. In P. Garrard (ed.) *The leadership hubris epidemic: Biological roots and strategies for prevention*. Basingstoke: Palgrave Macmillan, pp. 165–78.
Smith, J.E. (2016). *Bush*. New York: Simon and Schuster.

NOTES

1. www.theguardian.com/books/2002/oct/19/highereducation.biography (Accessed 30 September 2017).
2. Comment made by Powell in an interview in 2016: www.pbs.org/wgbh/frontline/article/colin-powell-u-n-speech-was-a-great-intelligence-failure (Accessed 14 March 2018).

8
PARADOX AND PROCESSUAL APPROACHES

WISE WARNING

'I am wiser than this man; it is likely that neither of us knows anything worthwhile, but he thinks he knows something when he does not, whereas when I do not know, neither do I think I know; so I am likely to be wiser than he to this small extent that I do not think I know what I do not know.' (Plato, *Apology of Socrates*, 21d–e)

Introduction

This chapter explores hubristic leadership from two related viewpoints – paradox theory and a process perspective. These two perspectives can help us to understand: the relationships between leaders' strengths and weaknesses, and excesses and deficiencies of leader capabilities; how hubristic leadership can impel organizations towards unintended negative consequences. It concludes with a practical question which sets the scene for the final chapter: if hubristic leadership can impel a leader or an organization on a trajectory towards a precipitous fall, how can leaders know if and when they are treading the fine line that divides success from failure and how might they avoid crossing it?

HUBRISTIC LEADERSHIP: A PARADOX PERSPECTIVE

Hubristic leadership manifests paradoxically when the leadership strengths that are instrumental in building success can seduce some leaders into using them to excess, and thereby unintentionally create the conditions for negative outcomes. And, as we have seen, in over-reaching themselves, hubristic leaders precipitate not only their own decline and demise, they can also damage others and risk bringing about far-reaching destructive outcomes. Hubristic organizations follow a similar pattern of behaviour. Examples of business failures show repeatedly that the factors that drive success, when taken to dangerous extremes because of hubristic over-confidence, over-ambition, arrogance, contempt and pride, can cause the demise of once respected and successful leaders and the decline of once-outstanding companies. Looking at hubristic leadership from the perspectives of paradox theory and process philosophy can help us to better understand how hubris can sometimes impel highly successful leaders and businesses on a trajectory towards self-initiated destruction.

Paradox

A paradox is a persistent contradiction between two mutually interdependent elements, such as 'profit and purpose', 'stability and change', 'self-focus and other-focus' (Lewis, 2000; Schad et al., 2016). A paradox is constructed in management when oppositional tendencies, for example 'collaboration and control' or 'exploration and exploitation', are brought into proximity to each other in ways that engender anomalies, contradictions, incongruities and tensions (Ford and Backoff, 1988: 89). Tensions are an underlying source of paradox and may be good or bad, and as such paradoxes are a 'double-edged sword' (Lewis, 2000: 763). On the positive side, tensions can fuel virtuous cycles that unleash creativity and exceptional performance; negative-side tensions, on the other hand, can spur vicious downward spirals (Miron-Spektor et al., 2017). For example, a collaboration–control tension in corporate governance could generate negative outcomes because by being overly collaborative, boards can foster groupthink, whilst over-control by a CEO could foster mistrust between board members (Sundaramurthy and Lewis, 2003). The mismanagement of the tensions in the 'focal paradox', in this case control–collaboration, can result in actors becoming trapped in a vicious downward spiral which can lead to destructive outcomes (Lewis and Smith, 2014).

Viewed constructively, the acceptance and resolution of tensions within an organizational paradox is a mechanism whereby actors can work with a 'both/and' mindset and thereby thrive on tensions (Lewis and Smith, 2014: 129). Paradox researchers often adopt an optimistic orientation in sympathy with a positive organizational scholarship ethos (Cameron and Dutton, 2003). In so doing, their concern is with managing paradox to go beyond vicious spirals by embracing 'both x and y' rather than 'either x or y'. However, given that the aim here is to understand the relationship between hubristic leadership and destructive outcomes, the focus is, inevitably, on the downsides and also how they might be avoided.

By failing to manage the tension within a focal paradox, actors tend to behave defensively (e.g. blaming others, as in the case of BP in attributing responsibility to Transocean and Haliburton at Deepwater Horizon), and even though this can maintain order and reduce anxiety in the short term, it can ultimately have the effect of fostering opposite, unintended negative consequences (Lewis, 2000: 763). One such example of the negative dynamics of organizing paradoxes in collaboration–control is when senior managers call for middle-manager involvement but impose strict limits on middle-manager discretion, thereby splitting the paradox between middle managers' contribution and senior managers' control (O'Connor, 1995). A further hazardous aspect of organizational paradox is that it tends to be associated with surprises or unintended consequences, the outcomes of which can be positive or negative (Davis et al., 1997; Sitkin and Beis, 1993, cited in Lewis, 2000). In the case of hubristic leadership – framed as a type of destructive leadership – the dynamics of the paradox are not constructive and the outcome is typically a negative unintended consequence that comes about as a 'nasty surprise'.

Tensions in paradoxes arise from relationships between opposing elements, such as 'old-versus-new ways of doing things' (referred to as a 'learning paradox'), 'control-versus-flexibility' (an 'organizing paradox') and 'other-versus-self' (a 'belonging paradox') (Lewis, 2000). Hubristic leaders, in being overly confident and overly dismissive of the counter-vailing opinions of others, end up positioning themselves at the 'self' and 'control' extremes of these polarities. Moreover, hubristic leaders are often resistant to learning or listening to contrary opinion; instead, they adhere to the conviction that they – rather than, for example, naysayers, devil's advocates or the market – know best. In so doing, they gravitate away from the more constructive pole of the paradox towards the more unconstructive end.

The negative consequences that arise from such polarisings are ubiquitous and persistent forces that challenge long-term success and can ultimately lead to destructive outcomes (Lewis and Smith, 2014). The situation can be compounded when leaders, rather than staying with a tension and the uncertainties it engenders long enough to make sense of and learn from it, commit two further errors by: (1) gravitating towards those factors most under their control and those things within their understanding which worked well in the past; and (2) choosing to work most closely with colleagues with a similar mindset who are much more likely to confirm rather than contest the leader's views (Vince and Broussine, 1996). For example, in the Space Shuttle *Columbia* disaster, tensions were intensified rather than tempered when engineers who were opposed to the launch were told in no uncertain terms to 'take off their engineering hat and put on their management hat' (Mason, 2004). This amplifies rather than ameliorates polarisations, and gives rise to short-sightedness, narrow-mindedness and groupthink which further accentuate negative-side tensions (Lewis, 2000). This tension is consistent with the observation that hubrists tend to look for excuses and scapegoats, and seek to pin the blame on others (Collins, 2009; Petit and Bollaert, 2012).

Polarising against others and away from learning can result, ultimately, in leader derailment (Hogan et al., 2010).

Paradox of Hubristic Leadership

Leadership strengths such as direction, communication, flexibility, commitment and openness are typically thought of as good things.[1] They are akin to leadership virtues, and are normally associated unquestioningly with success. Other examples are shown in Table 8.1. The incongruity at the heart of the paradox of hubristic leadership is that strength can be associated with failure, but how can strengths produce failures?

Table 8.1 Leadership strengths and their corresponding weaknesses

Strength	Hubristic weakness (based on Hubris Syndrome)
Benign influence	Becomes a narcissistic propensity to see world as arena for exercising power/seeking glory ('It's all about me')
Positive alignment	Becomes over-identification with the organization ('I am this organization')
Healthy energy	Becomes messianic manner and tendency to exaltation (speaking in the 'royal we' or third person)
Sound judgement	Becomes excessive confidence ('just trust me, I know')
Proper ambition	Becomes exaggerated self-belief, bordering on omnipotence ('we can do anything')

Hubristic leadership is a paradox of 'strengths-into-weaknesses'. One of the problems of how strengths are framed typically in management and leadership discourse is that they are taken indisputably as open-ended and positive. Abundance is construed as unconditionally good, and in such a milieu it is not possible to have 'too much of a good thing', and any notions of excess are papered over (Halse et al., 2007). In this regard, hubris is a form of deviance which brings about excesses that operate in several ways: (1) it is excess of confidence or ambition and a corresponding deficit of the virtue of humility, and is associated with contempt and arrogance and the disrespecting and dishonouring of the 'other' (cf. hybris, Chapter 2); (2) it is an excess (as a result of over-confidence and over-ambition) of leader behaviours (such as decisiveness or boldness) or organizational capabilities (such as innovation and flexibility); and (3) over-confidence and over-ambition act on such strengths to turn them into weaknesses (Figure 8.1). The strengths-into-weakness paradox can be analysed at the organizational (macro) level and the individual leader (micro) level.

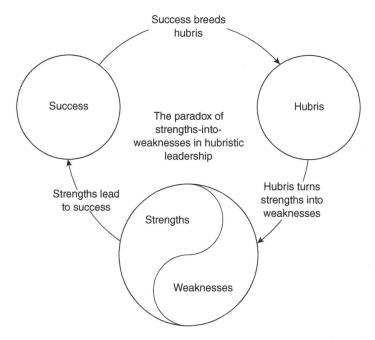

Figure 8.1   The paradox of strengths-into-weaknesses in the hubristic leadership process

Paradox of Hubristic Leadership at the Organizational (Macro) Level

Miller, in his book of the same name, termed the strengths-into-weakness paradox *The Icarus Paradox* (1990). He named it so because the power of Dædalus son's wings was his greatest asset, but his over-confidence in the power of flight that his wings gave him led to a reckless abandon. He flew too close to the sun, and his power literally melted away and his demise followed. The same paradox applies to hubristic leaders: 'their victories and their strengths often seduce them into the excesses that cause their downfall' (Miller, 1990: 3). The principle of Miller's paradox is that the causes of success (i.e. a boss's or business's strengths) when over-extended – because of hubristic over-confidence, recklessness and contempt – become the cause of failure. Three important points follow: (1) leaders have free will, therefore they are volitionally over-confident, reckless or contemptuous; (2) in over-extending their strengths, they are not engaging in deliberately destructive behaviours; (3) nevertheless, they are complicit, albeit unintentionally, and must take their share of the responsibility for any damaging outcomes which ensue.

Miller attributes the process of decline to four, what he terms, 'time-bomb' trajectories (i.e. 'focusing', 'venturing', 'inventing' and 'de-coupling') identified from his detailed studies of corporate decline in once-successful US corporations. In Miller's Icarus Paradox, a business's core strengths, categorized in terms of its strategies, goals, structure and culture, are practised to such an excess that they bring about decline. In the focusing trajectory, quality-driven craftsmen-type organizations become rigidly controlled, detail-obsessed tinkerers, and strengths such as quality leadership morph into the weakness of technical tinkering. In the venturing trajectory, growth-driven, entrepreneurial builders become impulsive, greedy imperialists expanding their businesses helter-skelter into areas they know little about, and strengths such as building morph into the weakness of gratuitous over-expansion. In the inventing trajectory, pioneers with unrivalled R&D capabilities and state-of-the-art operations become utopian escapists run by scientists and technologists who squander resources on grandiose technical schemes, and strengths such as innovation morph into the weakness of high-tech escapism. In the decoupling trajectory, salesperson-type organizations with unparalleled branding and marketing become aimless bureaucratic drifters obsessed by a sales fetishism, and strengths such as brilliant marketing morph into the weakness of bland proliferation (Table 8.2).

Table 8.2   The four trajectories and respective strengths and weaknesses in Miller's 'Icarus paradox' (Miller, 1992)

Trajectory		Configuration	Strategy	Goals	Culture	Structure
Focusing	From	'Craftsman'	Quality leadership	Quality	Engineering	Orderly
	To	'Tinkerer'	Technical tinkering	Perfection	Technocracy	Rigidity
Venturing	From	'Builder'	Building	Growth	Entrepreneurial	Divisionalized
	To	'Imperialist'	Overexpansion	Grandeur	Gamesman	Fractured
Inventing	From	'Pioneer'	Innovation	Science-for-society	R&D	Organic
	To	'Escapist'	Hi-tech escapism	Technical utopia	Think tank	Chaotic
Decoupling	From	'Salesperson'	Brilliant marketing	Market share	'Organizational man'	Modestly decentralized
	To	'Drifter'	Bland proliferation	Quarterly numbers	Insipid and political	Oppressively bureaucratic

In terms of the Icarus metaphor, Miller likened strengths in the areas of strategy, goals, culture and structure to the feathers and wax which makeup the business's wings and enable it to soar (its 'configuration'). However, when businesses use these wings and the power it gives them to fly too close to the sun, the wax holding the feathers together begins to melt – the configuration breaks down, strengths become weaknesses and the business 'crashes and burns'.

Miller illustrates his model with the case of ITT where, under the leadership of president and CEO Harold S. Geneen, its great successes in diversification and seemingly controlled decentralization eventually became a fanatical and all-consuming, end-in-itself way of life of obsessive expanding, diversifying, merging and acquiring rather than a well thought-through business strategy. Geneen's hubris led the company into ever-more ambitious, grandiose and sometimes hostile acquisitions that were further and further removed from the business's telecoms and technological core operations. The acquisitions of businesses as diverse as Sheraton Hotels, Avis Car Rental and Continental Baking were just three out of a hundred Geneen acquisitions which eventually made ITT by 1977, with 375,000 employees across 80 countries, the largest conglomerate on Earth.

Miller cites this as an example of the venturing trajectory gone badly wrong under Geneen's hubristic leadership. It led ITT to amplify a sensible, measured expansion strategy that had paid off handsomely into a senseless drive for diversification at all costs. ITT failed to coordinate and control the diversity it had created and 'balance the bulk'. As a result, product lines became neglected and outmoded, different business units experienced major operating problems and returns fell sharply. Geneen's successor was forced to sell off business units in a desperate attempt to revive a 'flabby agglomeration' (Miller, 1990: 7). ITT's very success paved the way into dangerous excesses and the eventual decline of a once outstanding company. A highly successful builder morphed into a grossly gratuitous imperialist. Perhaps the most telling insight is that none of this was intended (no leader, no matter how hubristic, would set out to wreck a business) but that the forward momentum at ITT was unstoppable (the process took on a life of its own); as a result, nemesis became inevitable.

One of the principal sources of momentum that impelled businesses on these various downward spirals from strength to weakness and success to failure is what Miller refers to as a 'leadership trap' whereby success has several important and negative side-effects on leaders themselves: (1) it reinforces leaders' preconceptions and tethers them to tried-and-tested approaches (consistent with the negative pole of the learning paradox above); (2) it makes leaders over-confident and prone to excess and complacency; and (3) leaders end up taking too much pride in and credit for prior successes and taking too seriously the praise of acolytes and admirers in business, in media and in wider society (consistent with the 'self' pole of the belonging paradox above). Ultimately, such individuals become arrogant, conceited and obstinate, resenting and ignoring contrary voices; they end up 'isolating themselves from reality' (Miller, 1992: 30) and in so doing they become 'resolutely blind' to the possible negative consequences of their hubris (Kets de Vries, 1993: 94).

Paradox of Hubristic Leadership at the Leader (Micro) Level

One of the biggest dangers for leaders who become detached from reality is derailment. Consistent with the strengths–into–weaknesses paradox, the personality psychologists Joyce and Robert Hogan and colleagues have identified how leaders can become detached and derailed as a result of over-using their strengths. The Hogan Development Survey (Hogan, 2009) measures 11 potentially derailing characteristics which are categorized into three major styles of conflict: (1) 'trying to succeed by intimidation and avoidance of others'; (2) 'trying to succeed by charm and manipulation'; and (3) 'trying to succeed by ingratiating and building alliances' (Hogan and Hogan, 2001). In trying to succeed by intimidation and avoidance of others, positive characteristics such as cautiousness (which Hogan associates with conscientiousness) and scepticism (associated with an ability to navigate organizational politics) morph into paralysis through fear and cynicism. The two Hogan conflict styles that are most relevant to hubristic leadership are trying to succeed by charm and manipulation and trying to succeed by ingratiating and building alliances (Morgan, 2017; see Table 8.3). In trying to succeed by charm and manipulation, hubristic leaders become, for example, self-absorbed, unwilling to admit to making mistakes and inclined towards taking ill-advised risks. In trying to succeed by ingratiating and building alliances, leaders become perfectionistic micromanagers whilst followers become eager to please and reliant on the leader for guidance (see Kaiser et al., 2008).

Table 8.3 The transformation of leader strengths into derailers through 'moving against' and 'moving towards' others (Hogan, 2009; Hogan and Hogan, 2001)

Dimension	HDS* scale	Strength	Derailer
Succeeding by charm and manipulation	Bold	Ambitious and self-confident	Self-absorbed; unwilling to admit mistakes
	Mischievous	Charming and friendly	Manipulative; prone to impulsiveness and overly risky decisions
	Colourful	Expressive, lively and fun	Prone to dramatics and attention-seeking behaviours; disorganized and distracted
	Imaginative	Creative, outside-the-box thinkers	Prone to impractical, idiosyncratic and even eccentric behaviours
Succeeding by charm and manipulation	Diligent	Careful and meticulous	Perfectionism; micro-managing and hyper-critical
	Dutiful	Eager to please	Overly reliant on others for guidance; reactive; reluctant to take independent actions

Note: *HDS = Hogan Development Survey

One of the biggest challenges that senior leaders face, once they acknowledge that they may be at risk of hubris, is determining where to draw the line between what constitutes an excess or a deficiency of their own strengths and/or the business's capabilities. In this sense, good leadership judgement is akin to 'practical wisdom'; in Aristotelian terms, this is 'prudence', or *phronēsis*, which entails being 'able to deliberate rightly about [judge] what is good and advantageous' (*Nicomachean Ethics*, Book VI, Chapter V). Since hubris is often concerned with executive over-reach, the crucial judgement that a leader must be able to make is what level of a strength constitutes an excess rather than a deficiency. Under particular conditions for particular leaders, the point of excess that marks the margin of effective leadership becomes obscured. This is the potentially fatal tipping point at which the executive themselves and the organization they lead is exposed to the risk of crossing the Rubicon between the right amount of a strength and too much of it. It is not possible, unfortunately, to make generalized claims about what 'too much of a good thing' looks like, but self-awareness is a starting point. Leadership is situational, and what constitutes a perilous excess of a given strength in one context may not necessarily be self-defeating in another. Walking the hubris tightrope of excess versus deficiency is a significant leadership challenge. Whilst it is easy to fall off the leadership tightrope, staying on it can be one of a leader's biggest challenges, especially in turbulent business environments.

Conceptualizing hubristic leadership as a paradox of 'strengths-into-weaknesses' unravels some taken-for-granted assumptions about the idea of abundance in leadership and management discourses, and offers an alternative way of thinking about hubris. The paradox of hubristic leadership is a hazard to particular actors in particular circumstances at particular times, and to ameliorate the risk it is crucial that actors' responses take account of their context by mindfully perceiving the particulars of the situation (Yan, 2009). The paradox of hubristic leadership invites a process of rising and falling, precipitated by a failure on the part of leaders to navigate effectively the tensions in, and walk the tightrope between, an excess and a right amount of the strengths which contributed to prior successes. Leaders must sometimes incline towards excess (to push the boundaries of possibility), whilst at other times they must veer in the opposite direction (to avoid over-reaching themselves), but the extent to which they should do so is a matter of the finest practical judgement.

HUBRISTIC LEADERSHIP: A PROCESS PERSPECTIVE

If hubris is a pathology of 'epidemic' proportions in leadership (Garrard, 2018), we might glean a better understanding of it from a detailed study of the course of the disease. Moreover, if 'prevention is better than cure', then a challenge for leaders, managers and researchers might be to practise a preventative medicine that identifies the early warning signs of incipient hubris and avoids the condition in the first place or cures it before the disease can fully take hold (Chapter 9 offers some suggestions in this regard). In such a view, time is of the essence. A 'process perspective' offers deep insights into the ebbing and flowing, and unfolding and emerging, of hubristic leadership over time by revealing the granularities in the processes of rising and falling.

Process Philosophy

The idea of 'process philosophy' – in common with several of the ideas discussed in this book – originates with the ancient Greeks. The first process philosopher was Heraclitus (c. 535–475 BC), a pre-Socratic for whom reality 'at bottom [was] not a constellation of *things* at all but one of *processes*' (Rescher, 1996: 9–10, original emphases). It was Heraclitus who remarked famously that you cannot step in the same river twice (i.e. a river is not an object but an ever-changing flow): 'the river where you set your foot just now is gone – those waters giving way to this, now this' (Heraclitus' *Fragments*, 41). The theme of flow, temporality and duration has continued throughout western philosophy in the works of 'processists' such as Leibniz, Hegel and Bergson, and especially in the works of American pragmatist philosophers such as Peirce, James, Dewey and Whitehead (for a historical analysis of key thinkers in process philosophy, see Helin et al., 2014).[2]

In process ontology, and its underlying process metaphysic, the world is viewed as being made up of processes rather than 'things' (as in a 'substance philosophy') (Langley et al., 2013; Rescher, 1996). Process philosophy prioritizes activity over substance, process over product, change over persistence and novelty over continuity (Rescher, 1996). Its fundamental contentions are that: (1) time and change are principal categories of metaphysical understanding; (2) processes are more fundamental than things; (3) substances, persons, nature as a whole and even God are best understood in process terms (Rescher, 1996: 31).

Analytically, the world viewed through the process lens is a transience composed of events and experiences (processes) which can be further decomposed into other, smaller events and experiences (micro-processes) (Langley et al., 2013). All experience is 'owned' (i.e. by an agent), however processes need not necessarily be 'owned' (Rescher, 1996). Transformative processes detached from substantial things are fundamental to process philosophy and these can be classified as 'owned processes' representing the activity of agents (for example, the chirping of birds), or as 'unowned processes' which are 'free floating' in that they do not represent the activities of actual agents (for example, a fluctuating magnetic field) (Rescher, 1996).

Process ontology comes in 'weaker' and 'stronger' forms; the former treats processes as important but reducible to the action of things, whilst the latter deems actions and things to be instantiations of process complexes (Chia and Langley, 2005). Interactions between intentional actions and contextual conditions can result in changes that produce unintended consequences that can be decisive in shaping outcomes positively or negatively; the connections with hubristic leadership and the potential it creates for consequences that are unintendedly destructive are palpable. In the stronger process view, 'unowned processes' instantiated in uncertainty and indeterminacy are a recurrent, nemesis-like shadowy presence (MacKay and Chia, 2013: 211).

In management research, a process has been defined as 'a sequence of individual and collective events, actions and activities unfolding over time in context' (Pettigrew, 1997: 338). Process research aspires to catch 'reality in flight' and is concerned with the phenomenon of transience and questions of how and why things become, emerge, develop, grow, transform and terminate over time (Hernes, 2014; Langley, 1999; Langley et al., 2013; Pettigrew, 1997). Process philosophers claim that their approach has advantages over substance-oriented approaches for the study of 'non-natural persons', such as corporations, because from the processists' perspective such entities can be considered 'process complexes'. In the process view, 'things' are complex bundles of coordinated processes (process complexes) that possess a functional unity that is open-ended and flowing (Rescher, 1996: 112).

Process philosophy is an important but somewhat overlooked perspective for the study of leadership in organizations (Dinh et al., 2014). As far as empirical methods are concerned, process researchers search for patterns in processes which shape trajectories and consequences (Pettigrew, 1997). Langley (1999) identified several different strategies for making sense of organizational processes, including those shown in Table 8.4.

Table 8.4   Research methods for processual analysis (Langley, 1999)

Research strategy	Description
Narrative strategy	Researchers construct a detailed story from the data which has embedded plots and provides themes as a preliminary step in preparing a chronology for subsequent analysis
Alternate template strategy	Researchers propose several plausible but different interpretations of events. For example, Allison (1971), in the study of the Cuban missile crisis, offered three retellings of events in terms of 'rational actor', 'organizational process' and 'political' models, and then selected the most theoretically plausible versions
Visual mapping strategy	Appealing for the analysis of process data because it allows for the movement of events (e.g. key personnel changes, design problems, negotiations) along dimensions (e.g. operations, finance, technology) to be shown simultaneously in the form of a 'process flowchart'
Temporal bracketing	The timescale of the process is decomposed into successive phases which possess, in the researchers' interpretation, internal coherence and continuity and discontinuities at their boundaries

These research strategies should be seen as 'generic approaches' which are neither exhaustive nor mutually exclusive, but each approach is useful in processual analysis because it helps to address and fix attention on anchor points that enable empirical materials to be structured; it also determines which elements are accorded more attention than others (Langley, 1999: 694).

Process of Hubristic Leadership

Based on an analysis of 11 major corporate declines, Collins (2009), in his study of *How the mighty fall*, identified five stages of degeneration which he compared to a staged disease which is harder to detect (the victim may appear to be a picture of health on the outside) but easier to cure in the initial stages. The process can become irreversible once the final stage is locked into. The five stages that Collins identified were 'hubris borne of success', 'undisciplined pursuit of more', 'denial of risk and peril', 'grasping for salvation' and 'capitulation to irrelevance or death'. The details of Collins' research approach is given in his 'fallen company selection criteria' (2009).

Collins presents a stage-based view, however he is not a process researcher and his work on corporate decline is not a processual analysis as such (cf. MacKay and Chia, 2013; Langley, 1999; Langley et al., 2013). Nonetheless, Collins' findings are useful as an illustrative example of the narrative account he gives (using methods analogous to narrative, temporal bracketing and visual mapping; see above) of the rise and fall of major businesses (e.g. Bank of America, Motorola, Rubbermaid) and in which hubristic leadership was implicated prominently. As such, it presents one of the few studies – albeit much higher on practical relevance than on processual rigour – of hubristic leadership in business management viewed through the lens of time. Collins (2009) depicts the falling process in terms of 'key markers' for each of the five stages, as shown in Figure 8.2, but he is keen to point out that not 'every marker means you have the disease' (p. 43).

Stage 1 – Hubris borne of success ('self-aggrandizing'): success is viewed as deserved rather than being hard-earned, fortuitous or even fleeting; leaders believe that success is, and will continue to be, theirs by right. Leaders neglect to reflect on and renew the business's 'primary flywheel' that gave it success in the first place. Leaders fail to ask penetrating and critical questions; as a result, they fail to leverage new insights and there is a corresponding decline in reflexivity and learning (Collins, 2009).

Stage 2 – Undisciplined pursuit of more ('escalating'): leaders embark on an unsustainable quest for growth based on prior success, setting ever higher expectations and putting inordinate and intolerable pressure on people, culture and systems. The organization begins to 'fray at the edges' (Collins, 2009: 63). Leaders push the business in directions that do not fit with the company's core values, or focus on things that it could not be 'the best' at, or which are unlikely to drive the organization forward. In addition, there is

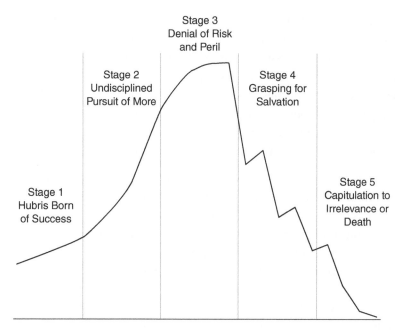

Figure 8.2   Five stages of corporate decline

a declining number of the right sorts of people in the right roles. A culture of discipline and responsibility is replaced by one of bureaucracy and control. The personal interests of those in power are placed above those of the organization. Senior leaders allocate more money, privileges and fame to themselves (Collins, 2009).

Stage 3 – Denial of risk and peril ('denying'): leaders accentuate the positive, wallow in praise and publicity and discount or explain away the negative. Leaders make big bets (for example, on mergers and acquisitions or the overly risky use of technologies) that fly in the face of experience, naysayers, markets and the facts. Over-confidence in their own judgement elevates the risk that they could 'blow a hole below the [ship's] water-line' (Collins, 2009: 81). Hubristic leaders stifle dialogue and debate, they engineer shifts towards consensual groupthink or even a dictatorial interpersonal style, and seek to externalize blame for setbacks and failures. Rather than confronting systemic and structural issues, the business constantly re-organizes and downsizes. Leaders become imperious and detached, and their rhetoric and the symbols of power with which they surround themselves amplify and accentuate detachment from the real world (Collins, 2009).

Stage 4 – Grasping for salvation ('clinging on'): leaders look for silver bullets, for example that game-changing acquisition or innovative technology, so as to catalyse much-needed salvation. Likewise, the board may seek a 'saviour' in a new charismatic and transformational leader. Leaders become hasty, reactive and panicky; small positive signs are hyped up, creating the conditions for a cycle of disappointment. A hyperbole of superficial change predominates rather than intelligently restrained, dispassionate analysis of the systemic and structural issues that could be spelling the business's impending demise. The ability to articulate what the business stands for evaporates; values erode 'to the point of irrelevance' (Collins, 2009: 101); for employees, the business becomes just another place to work and pick up a pay check. Chronic restructurings drain resources, energy, trust and commitment; strategy is dictated by circumstance (Collins, 2009) and forces beyond the leader's control.

Stage 5 – Capitulation to irrelevance or death ('capitualting'): the organization spirals out of control, options narrow and hope fades. At this point, the Rubicon has likely been crossed and 'lock-in' has occurred. Collins (2009) concludes with the frank observation that perhaps not all companies deserve to last, and maybe the world is better off without some of them and it is perhaps better that they perish rather than continuing to inflict their inadequacies on stakeholders, shareholders and wider society (Collins, 2009).

Not all the companies studied by Collins reached Stage 5. One that Collins depicts as going through the entire rise and fall cycle was the 'Zenith Radio Corporation'. It was founded in the 1920s, and during its heyday Zenith was the biggest player in the manufacture of radios, black-and-white TVs and colour TVs in the USA. Today, with the closure of its last US factory in 1998 and Chapter 11 Bankruptcy in 1999, Zenith is a shadow of its former self; the company still exists as a US research and development division of South Korea's LG Electronics. Zenith's rise and fall is described below as Collins (1990) has it, but with the addition of a preliminary 'Stage 0' which describes Zenith's rise to become the pinnacle of radio and TV manufacturing in the USA, and from which went into a decline. To younger audiences, the demise of Zenith is likely to have little resonance, however to an older US generation Zenith was an iconic radio and TV manufacturer (Figure 8.3).

Phase 0 ('Scaling the heights'), 1920s–1950s: the business was founded by radio enthusiasts Karl Hassel and Ralph H. G. Mathews, almost but not quite on a 'kitchen table', as the Chicago Radio Laboratory in 1919. It began life as a small manufacturer of radio equipment and was formally incorporated as the Zenith Radio Corp. in 1923. At this time, the charismatic entrepreneur and adventurer Eugene F. 'The Commander' MacDonald, CEO from 1923 to 1958, and a man who was the 'supremely if not irrationally confident',[3] took the helm. Famous for its highly distinctive 'lightning bolt logo' and marketing strapline 'the quality goes in before the name goes on', Zenith's major innovations included the first portable radio in 1924, first mass-produced radios in 1926, first push-button tuning in 1927 and automobile radios in the 1930s. Further innovations followed with home television sets in 1949 (its TV sales topped $100 million in 1950), TV remote controls in the 1950s, the worldwide standard for FM stereo radio in the 1960s, and so on.

Figure 8.3 Marketing material for the once iconic Zenith Radio Corporation

Source: Reproduced by kind permission of Zenith Electronics LLC

Phase 1 (Hubris born of success), 1950s and 1960s: with more than 15,000 employees in seven Chicago plants and $500 million in sales in 1966, Zenith was the leading manufacturer of black-and-white televisions; its share price generated returns of more than ten times the market. It was sceptical about colour TV – in the words of 'The Commander':

> Someday, the technical and service problems of colour TV will be solved. When that day comes, we will offer you a line of outstanding colour sets. In the meantime, we will not try to make an experimental laboratory of dealers and the public. We will keep colour in our laboratories until it is ready.[4]

More importantly and worryingly for Zenith, foreign competition in consumer electricals began to gain traction but this was arrogantly discounted: 'the Japanese (the *Japanese* for goodness sake, with their cheap products) could not possibly pose a serious threat to the Great American Quality [Zenith] Brand' (Collins, 2009: 108, original emphasis).

Phase 2 (Undisciplined pursuit of more), late 1960s and early 1970s: with a breakthrough in colour TV, an exponential increase in demand and an expansion of manufacturing facilities, Zenith surpassed RCA as the leading manufacturer of colour TV sets. It made a 'big bet' on pay TV but this failed as it was over-ambitious and too far ahead of its time. Zenith developed a reputation as a 'fast follower' of innovative technologies. It increased its manufacturing capacity and moved some plants overseas and automated production (laying off 25 per cent of its US workers). The business doubled its debt-to-equity ratio to 100 per cent and adopted a confrontational approach towards Japanese competition. The business attitude was captured in a speech given by Zenith chairman Joseph S. Wright in 1972 using 'trade war' rhetoric, accusing the Japanese of dumping at less than fair value, and redolent with protectionist and other overtones: 'the only way that the Japanese image can get any lasting polish in this country is by Japan's really dismantling some of the apparatus she has created to take advantage of us in the areas of trade'.

As and aside:

A similar tone was echoed on 2 March 2018 in a tweet by President Trump: 'When a country (USA) is losing many billions of dollars on trade with virtually every country it does business with, trade wars are good, and easy to win. Example, when we are down $100 billion with a certain country and they get cute, don't trade anymore-we win big. It's easy!' An unintended negative consequence of the president's trade war occurred when the iconic American brand Harley Davidson moved some of its production overseas in response to tariffs. The president's actions amounted to 'friendly fire' which harmed the very workers he was seeking to protect.[5]

Phase 3 (Denial of risk and peril), mid 1970s: the business began to suffer from a lack of competitiveness with Japanese imports and a corresponding manufacturing over-capacity. It lowered prices in a battle for market share, took on more debt and its profitability was driven down. Blame was externalized to Japanese trading practices, a struggling US economy, labour unrest, oil shocks, and so on. The unpalatable state of affairs for Zenith bosses was that Japanese, Taiwanese and South Korean manufactures were able to sell electronic consumer goods in the USA at prices significantly below what American companies could afford to offer. Zenith doggedly pursued a protectionist strategy and filed law suits in 1974 against the Japanese charging violation of Antitrust Laws and Anti-Dumping Act of 1914, seeking $900 million in damages.

Phase 4 (Grasping for salvation), late 1970s and 1980s: the business ominously posted its first loss in decades in 1977. In response to challenging times, it jumped at every available opportunity ('if we have any plan at all, it's that we'll take a shot at everything', Zenith senior leader, cited in Collins, 2009: 158), including video cassette recorders, video discs and cable TV decoders. Financial problems were compounded and it increased its debt-to-equity ratio to 140 per cent. In the early 1980s, Zenith abandoned the radio business, but around the same time a potential salvation appeared in the form of its Zenith Data Systems (ZDS) division. The business reflected the change in its re-naming to Zenith Electronics Corporation and became the second biggest manufacturer of IBM-compatible PCs. Between 1980 and 1989, ZDS generated more than half of Zenith's revenues and contributed to its profits.

This was a crucial vectoring point in the Zenith process. In Collins's view, 'under the right leadership and in the right circumstances Zenith "could have become Dell or Compaq"' (Collins, 2009: 110). However, the success of ZDS was never going to be enough to offset the impact of competition in the consumer electronics business to which it was structurally and culturally wedded. In an unfortunate juxtaposition of events, the US courts ruled in favour of Japanese manufacturers (following an appeal process), and millions of dollars in legal costs were incurred by Zenith and other co-plaintiffs. By 1985 computer sales had risen from $249 million in 1984 to $352 million, but this could not offset the haemorrhaging in its consumer electronics business. By the year end, the company was nearly $8 million in the red.

Phase 5 (Capitulation to irrelevance or death), late 1980s and 1990s: Zenith held on to its failing TV business too long and used ZDS to finance research into the bright future of HDTV, technologies that ultimately would yield hundreds of millions of dollars in royalty revenues to Zenith and LG. Zenith's financial position became unsustainable in the 1980s. It had half a billion dollars of debt and shrinking cash reserves (less than 5 per cent of liabilities). Zenith bosses decided to sell its computer business in 1989 to Groupe Bull in the hope this would improve its ability to compete in the ferociously competitive consumer electronics market. They used the $511.4 million received from Bull to pay off short-term debt and some of its long-term obligations. The struggling TV and consumer electronics business dragged Zenith towards its demise with mounting year-on-year losses. Five per cent of the business was sold to Korea's LG in a technology-sharing agreement. In 1995 LG increased its stake to a controlling 55 per cent. Zenith filed for Chapter 11 Bankruptcy in 1999 and LG bought the remaining 45 per cent in exchange for debts. The one viable part of the business left, its set-top box division, was sold to Motorola in 2000.[6]

Phases in the rise and fall of Zenith are depicted in a process flowchart (Table 8.5): 'scaling the heights', *flourishing*; 'hubris borne of success', *self-aggrandizing*; 'undisciplined pursuit of more', *escalating*; 'denial of risk and peril', *denying*; 'grasping for salvation', *clinging on*; and 'capitulation to irrelevance or death', *capitulating*.

Table 8.5 Process flowchart for the rise and fall of Zenith Radio Corporation (based on Collins, 2009)

	Phase 0, 'flourishing' (1920s–1950s)	Phase 1, 'self-aggrandizing' ('50s/'60s)	Phase 2, 'escalating' (late '60s/early '70s)	Phase 3, 'denying' (mid-'70s)	Phase 4, 'clinging on' (late '70s/'80s)	Phase 5, 'capitulating' (late '80s/'90s)
Innovation and Technology	Founded by radio enthusiasts 1919; Zenith Radio Corp in 1923; numerous innovative firsts (portable radio; push-button tuning; car radios; home TV; remote controls; FM stereo radio; home video cassette recorders)	Leading manufacturer of black and white TVs; sceptical about colour TV	Breaks through in colour TV; surpasses RCA as leading colour TV maker; Pay TV fails, too ahead of its time	Develops reputation as 'fast follower'	Jumps at all opportunities; salvation appears as Data Systems Division (DSD) 79; Becomes Zenith Electronics Corporation; 2nd biggest manufacturer of IBM-compatible PCs; leaves radio business in early '80s	Holds on to failing TV business too long in the face of unassailable competition from the Far East in consumer electronics
Operations and Finance	In 1920s was 12th in $400 million industry; survives Great Depression; in 1941 was 2nd in $600 million industry	Shares return more than ten times market; financial peak in 1966 with 15,000 employees in seven Chicago plants; $500 million in sales	Exponential increase in demand, expands manufacturing facilities; Moves plants overseas, automates production (lays off 25% of US workers); doubles its debt-to-equity ratio to 100%	Lack of competitiveness, manufacturing over-capacity; Lowers price in market share battle; Takes on more debt; Profits driven down	Posts first loss in decades 1977; Increases its debt-to-equity ratio to 140%; 1980–89 DSD generates more than 50% of Zenith revenues and virtually all profits	Financial position unsustainable, half a billion dollars of debt, shrinking cash reserves (<5%); Forced to sell DSD 1989 to pay off short-term debt; Mounting year-on-year losses in TV business
Competition and Markets	In late 1930s was exporting to 96 countries	Foreign competition in consumer electricals begins to gain traction; discounts Japan as little threat	Confrontational approach towards Japanese competition; accuses Japan of dumping; adopts protectionist overtones	Externalizes blame (Japan, struggling economy, etc.); Far East gains grip on US markets; files $900m anti-trust law suit against Japanese	Court ruled on appeal in favour of Japanese	Sells 5% of business to LG, technology sharing; 1995 LG increases to 55%; LG buys remaining 45%; viable set-top box division sold off in 2000; Chapter 11 Bankruptcy in 1999

Collins (1990) documents examples of other firms who managed to pull themselves out of a descent into destruction, and went on to regain their stature and be even more successful, such as Boeing, Disney and Hewlett Packard. Decline is not a function of forces out of leaders' control, otherwise this could lead to despair. Collins' (2009) view is that decline is far from inevitable it if is caught in the early stages of the process and reversed by 'sound management practices and rigorous strategic thinking' (p. 117), which can protect against the hazards of hubristic leadership.

SUMMARY

The trajectory of hubristic leadership is a paradoxical and largely self-inflicted process of rise and fall (Collins, 2009; Miller, 1990). The high-performing firms studied by Miller (1990) were impelled on a trajectory towards decline by a strengths-into-weaknesses paradox. For example, Digital Equipment Corporation's deterioration began ironically when it was a manufacturer of the highest quality computers and performing spectacularly. However, in common with other businesses that followed this trajectory, success amplified current strategies to extreme levels in a leadership and culture which aggravated this trajectory (Miller, 1990). By the time it had reached the end of its downward spiral, Digital had become an engineering monoculture that produced high-spec machines that were out of sync with the market and consequently 'bombed' (Miller, 1990: 12). Digital did not set out to produce products that would fail or eventually get taken over in a risky acquisition by Compaq, nevertheless they did. The outcome for Digital was unintended, unanticipated and negative. Likewise, in Collins's study of the five-phase rise and fall of Zenith, the destructive outcome which emanated from the choices that were taken was neither expected nor intended by those involved. The paradox and the process perspectives show how the unintended consequences of hubristic leadership can influence individual and organizational outcomes in unexpected, negative, and sometimes catastrophic, ways.

In process-theoretic terms, human agency is creatively adaptive (MacKay and Chia, 2013). As far as the process of hubristic leadership is concerned, particularly when conceptualized destructively, the deliberate choices made by human agents turn out to be creatively *maladaptive*. Human agents implicated in a hubristic leadership process seek to cope with a chaotic and messy reality, and in so doing make decisions and take actions which contain the seeds of 'latent possibilities and unintended consequences' in a longer-term future that exist only as potentialities at the time such decisions are taken (MacKay and Chia, 2013: 211). Actors are at the mercy of complexity and owned and unowned processes emanating from the interactions of people, markets, technology, macro-economic factors, political events and so forth within a systemic whole (Rescher, 1996). In such a 'complexification' (Rescher, 1996: 54), hubristic agents are at risk of over-estimating the chances of success and under-estimating what might go wrong, thereby sowing the seeds for unintended negative consequences that have the potentiality to bring about their own failure and the demise of their organization. Well-intentioned choices exercised in ITT and Zenith were overtaken by consequences which eventually dragged down both businesses. The same process of rise and fall is witnessed in the other hubristically driven failures such as LTCM (Chapter 6).

CONCLUSION

The end state in both Miller's paradox and Collins's process is the product of a decline in which strengths turn into weaknesses and arrogance, complacency and rigidity borne of success take hold which propel firms on a downward trajectory which for some, but not all, becomes an uncontrollable spiral into demise (Taleb et al., 2009). The consequences of the paradox and process of hubristic leadership are unanticipated, unintended and destructive. In other examples of hubristic failures in areas such as banking (for example, Royal Bank of Scotland), finance (for example, Long Term Capital Management, LTCM) and engineering (for example, BP and Deepwater Horizon), the damaging and destructive outcomes that accrued were not what the leaders of any of these organizations intended (LTCM did not intend its value would plummet overnight), nor were they expected (BP did not expect a blowout at the Deepwater Horizon installation and a bill of $65 billion). However, negative consequences stemmed from leadership behaviours and organizational cultures that became hubristic on the back of success (a rise) and precipitated a downward spiral fuelled by excess and over-reach (a fall) in a weakly constrained environment. If hubristic leadership impels organizations on trajectories which can vector into a precipitous fall, how can leaders know if they are treading the fine line between success and failure and how can they avoid crossing it?

Further Reading

Collins, J. (2009). *How the mighty fall, and why some companies never give in.* London: Random House.

Furnham, A. (2018). Management failure and derailment. In P. Garrard (ed.) *The leadership hubris epidemic: Biological roots and strategies for prevention.* Basingstoke: Palgrave Macmillan, pp. 69–92.

NOTES

1. From a list of the most important leadership strengths compiled by *Harvard Business Review*: https://hbr.org/2016/03/the-most-important-leadership-competencies-according-to-leaders-around-the-world (Accessed 22 January 2018).
2. For example, for Bergson the direction of intuitive knowing of the flow of lived experience is more faithful to reality than is detached intellective thought.
3. www.madeinchicagomuseum.com/single-post/2016/08/09/Zenith-Bakelite-Tube-Radio-S-17366-by-Zenith-Radio-Corp-c-1950s (Accessed 22 January 2018); https://chicagology.com/silentmovies/zenithradio (Accessed 23 January 2018).
4. www.fundinguniverse.com/company-histories/zenith-electronics-corporation-history (Accessed 23 January 2018).
5. www.bloomberg.com/view/articles/2018-06-25/trump-s-trade-war-harley-davidson-s-a-friendly-fire-casualty (Accessed 22 July 2018).
6. https://en.wikipedia.org/wiki/Zenith_Electronics; www.fundinguniverse.com/company-histories/zenith-electronics-corporation-history (Accessed 23 January 2018).

9

AVOIDANCE
APPROACHES

WISE WARNING

'An ounce of prevention is worth a pound of cure.' (Benjamin Franklin, 1736)

Introduction

Unintended negative consequences can arise when leaders have a false idea of their own worth and over-lofty ambitions, when they over-estimate what can go right, under-estimate what can go wrong, and display arrogance and contempt towards the advice and criticism of others. Hubristic leadership is fuelled by prior successes and praise, and it flourishes where followers conform, comply and collude, and where effective restraining forces and preventive structures are lacking.

So far this book has been about understanding the characteristics and causes and the human, economic and social costs of hubristic leadership. This final chapter will be concerned with how to contain its potentially destructive, sometimes catastrophic, consequences through an avoidance approach. This is analogous to the use of preventative medicine and is based on the assumption that early manifesations of a disease are much easier to cure than its later stages. Five different approaches are suggested which are intended to pick up on and check the early onset of hubris in organizations and institutions: (1) identifying linguistic markers; (2) high reliability organizing; (3) better governance and regulation; (4) avoiding a hubristic organizational culture; and (5) constraining executive remuneration (Figure 9.1).

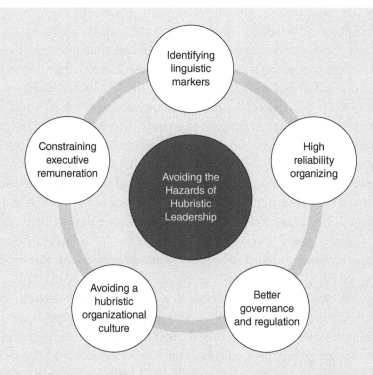

Figure 9.1   Five approaches to avoiding the hazards of hubristic leadership

IDENTIFYING LINGUISTIC MARKERS

One of the challenges that hubris researchers, along with colleagues who research other negatively connoted leadership attributes such as narcissism, face is, not surprisingly, accessing hubrists and narcissists. The problem is doubly magnified when trying to reach hard-to-access groups, for example CEOs or prime ministers, at the top of organizations and institutions. In such situations, researchers and media commentators often have to resort to at-a-distance techniques and measures, for example narcissism researchers have in the past studied CEOs' letters to shareholders and even their signature size (Craig and Amernic, 2011; Ham et al., 2018). For example, Donald Trump's signature is claimed by a member of the British Institute of Graphologists to reflect 'wild ambition, dynamism, bravery and fearlessness' and a 'hunger for power' with a surfeit of 'determination and stubbornness'.[1]

The business arena can be especially challenging because in the upper echelons of organizations much of what is likely to be of interest to hubris researchers goes on behind closed doors. On the other hand, the political arena has the advantage not only that the lives of political leaders tend to be well documented through press, biographical and autobiographical sources, but also that many noteworthy events take place 'live', in the public space. Hubris researchers working in the psychiatry and neuroscience fields have combined theories of natural language use with the techniques of computational linguistics to develop novel techniques for the identification at a distance of early warning signs of Hubris Syndrome in political leaders.

Language in the form of leaders' spoken utterances provides hubris researchers with a 'rich source of biologically eloquent data' for the study of the 'mental and cognitive states of individuals whose written or spoken discourse has been preserved in large quantities' (Garrard et al., 2014: 168). In the case of the UK Houses of Parliament, for example, all debates are recorded permanently and for posterity in the *Hansard* official reports.

Language can serve as a proxy indicator or signal of thoughts, feelings, personality and motivations.[2] Pentland (2010) argued that human beings' surprisingly well-honed ability to read each other is based on thin slices of behaviour which he refers to as 'honest signals'. Honest signals are a reliable communication system which social species are likely to develop to support the coordination of behaviour amongst individuals in a group (Pentland, 2010; Pentland and Heibeck, 2010). Honest signals influence critical social activities such as negotiation, persuasion and decision making, and have been found to be accurate predictors of human behaviour in groups (Ambady, 2010; Ambady and Rosenthal, 1992; Ambady et al., 2006). The signals themselves manifest in a variety of verbal and non-verbal modalities, for example mimicry (Pentland, 2010; Pentland and Heibeck, 2010).

Honest signals manifest through the lexical choices and the linguistic structures used in verbal communication. Language is how people translate their internal thoughts and emotions into a form that others can understand (Tausczik and Pennebaker, 2010). The words people choose to use and the way in which they use them – unconsciously as well as consciously – afford researchers a distinctive and relatively easy-to-access diagnostic and psychological indicator of individuals' mental, social and physical state (Pennebaker et al., 2003). The study of language as an indicator of inner psychological states goes back at least as far as Freud who noted that inadvertent slips of the tongue could apparently reveal a person's hidden intentions via apparent linguistic mistakes – so-called 'Freudian slips' (Tausczik and Pennebaker, 2010). It is perhaps unsurprising that researchers were quick to examine the linguistic patterns in Donald Trump's speeches during the presidential campaign (Table 9.1).

Table 9.1　Linguistic analysis of Donald Trump's campaign speeches for the Republican nomination (October 2015) (Ahmadian et al., 2017)

Explaining Donald Trump via communication style

Psychologists at the University of British Columbia investigated how Donald Trump managed to dominate more experienced competitors in the US presidential election primaries. The researchers analysed 27 speech segments of the top nine Republican candidates (October 2015) using Pennebaker et al.'s (2001) LIWC computerized text analysis software (see below) and supplemented by acoustic analyses of speech recordings, and rated them for grandiosity. Trump scored highest on (1) grandiosity ratings, (2) use of first-person pronouns, (d) greater pitch dynamics, and (e) informal communication (including Twitter usage of all 17 candidates). With 'number of primaries won' as the criterion, the results suggested that Trump benefited from all these aspects of campaign communication style. One of the authors of the study, Delroy L. Paulus of the University of British Columbia, concluded that 'Bottom line is that a politician's vocal style is at least as important as the content of his speeches. In debating with 17 other candidates, [Trump's] political platform differed little from the others. However, his statements were typically more extremely and bombastically worded. The software analyses also singled out a dynamic vocal range, and a strong preference for simple, informal wording.[6]

Numerous studies of unconscious lexical choices reveal clear and consistent differences in language use under various psychological conditions, including positive-versus-negative mood and inferior-versus-superior position in a social hierarchy (Garrard et al., 2014). The signals that natural language use inadvertently gives hearers regarding the speaker's psychological state are referred to as 'linguistic markers' (Pennebaker et al., 2003). The study of linguistic makers has been revolutionized by the advent of high-speed personal computing and advances in statistical techniques. This has enabled linguistic scientists to efficiently analyse enormous volumes of spoken or written utterances which previously they would have had to analyse manually by word counting. For researchers in this area, various tools and techniques are available (see Table 9.2).

Table 9.2　Sample computational techniques for analysing patterns of natural language use

DICTION	DICTION is a computer-aided text analysis program for determining the tone of a verbal message. DICTION searches a passage for five general features ('activity', 'optimism', 'certainty', 'realism' and 'commonality') as well as 35 sub-features. It can process a variety of English-language texts using a 10,000-word corpus and user-created custom dictionaries. DICTION has been used to analyse presidential and campaign speeches, political advertising, public debates and media coverage (www.dictionsoftware.com)
LIWC	Linguistic Inquiry and Word Count (LIWC) uses a word-count strategy based on 2300 words or word stems categorized into 70 hierarchically organized linguistic dimensions in order to access thoughts, feelings, personality and motivations. It uses standard language categories (such as prepositions, pronouns), psychological processes (such as positive and negative emotion), relativity-related words (such as time, motion and space) and content (such as sex, death, home, occupation) (https://liwc.wpengine.com)

Neuroscientists have studied how language use can signal the onset of progressive neurological disease. For example, automated text analysis found striking differences in lexical diversity and lexical characteristics between the texts of the early and late works of the 20th century English novelist Iris Murdoch (Garrard et al., 2004). The changes picked up by the linguistic analysis were associated with and 'almost certainly influenced by' the cognitive decline which characterizes the onset of Alzheimer's disease which Murdoch suffered from (Garrard et al., 2014: 168). Similarly, a study of the parliamentary speeches of UK Prime Minister Harold Wilson (1964–70, 1974–76) suggested that Wilson's later speeches contained pre-symptomatic clues to the Alzheimer's disease that he succumbed to in later years (Garrard, 2009).

Based on the assumption that lexical choices and syntactic structures can be indicative of psychological and cognitive changes, researchers have used linguistic analyses to study the onset and progression of Hubris Syndrome (see Chapter 4). Researchers compared the spoken discourses of two British prime ministers who were identified independently as meeting the criteria for Hubris Syndrome (Margaret Thatcher, 1979–90; and Tony Blair, 1997–2007) with one who did not (John Major, 1990–97) (Garrard et al., 2014). The argument was that clinical features of Hubris Syndrome might be reflected in the language use of 'those suffering from the disorder' (Garrard et al., 2014: 169), as outlined in Table 9.3.

Table 9.3 Features of Hubris Syndrome manifesting in language use (Garrard et al., 2014)

Hubris Syndrome symptom	If present should be associated with	Findings from Garrard et al. (2014)
Symptom 6 ('a tendency to speak in the third person or to use the "royal we"')	Increased usage of 'he/she', 'him/her', 'his/her', 'we/us/our' or the speaker's own name where the first-person pronoun might be expected	'Royal we' became less, rather than more, common in both Thatcher and Blair's discourse. The 'WE-to-I' ratio was higher for hubrists, and peaked coincident with significant successes
Symptom 7 ('excessive confidence in the individual's own judgement and contempt for the advice and criticism of others')	Increased usage of terms such as 'certain', 'sure', 'confident' and 'succeed/success'	Changes in frequencies of words indirectly associated with symptomatic behaviours. Blair was increasingly 'sure', increasingly self-referential in his choice of pronouns ('I' and 'me') and more likely to consider his statements 'important'. Both Thatcher and Blair were decreasingly likely to refer to their 'duties' the longer they stayed in office
Symptom 8 ('exaggerated self-belief, bordering on a sense of omnipotence, in what they personally can achieve')	Increased usage of terms such as 'certain', 'sure', 'confident' and 'succeed/success' (as above)	
Symptom 9 ('a belief that rather than being accountable to the mundane court of colleagues or public opinion, the court to which they answer is history or God')	Increased use of the terms 'history' or 'God'	References to God or 'history' did not emerge as temporal correlates

The researchers found that the first-person pronouns 'I' and 'me' and the word 'sure' showed strong temporal correlations with Blair's time in office (and hence with the progression of Hubris Syndrome). On the other hand, the words 'we shall' and 'duties' both correlated negatively with time in office in the speeches of Thatcher and Blair but not of Major. As well as looking at the absolute frequency of word use, the researchers also looked at the ratio of the first-person plural pronoun ('WE') and first-person singular pronoun ('I'), where higher values indicated greater relative use of 'WE'.

Blair's 'WE-to-I' ratio was significantly higher throughout his term of office than Thatcher's, and Major's was low in comparison to both Blair and Thatcher throughout their time in office. For Blair, the WE-to-I ratio peaked between 1999 and 2001, corresponding to military interventions in Kosovo (1999) and Sierra Leone (2000). At this time, Blair was buoyed up by success and it has been suggested that this coincided with the onset of Hubris Syndrome (Garrard et al., 2014). There was a similar but smaller peak in Thatcher's profile corresponding to her re-election following victory in the Falklands War (1982). Major's WE-to-I ratio was relatively low and flat throughout his time in office. The researchers interpreted these results as providing 'collateral support for the reality' of Hubris Syndrome (2014: 179). It also offers evidence for the proposal that language use may serve as a 'mental blood test' for the syndrome, even though only some, rather than all, of the expected changes in language use were observed (2014: 179; see also Table 9.3).

If Hubris Syndrome is a condition for which aspects of spoken or written speech can be used as a marker of both presence and severity, then this technique could be used as an early warning sign of the onset of hubris in political or business leadership. The comparison of Blair and Thatcher (hubrists) to Major (non-hubrist) suggests that the 'WE-to-I' ratio, the 'sureness', the self-referential tone and according increased 'importance' to one's own utterances, are potential markers for the emergence of hubrism. Linguistic markers present faint (i.e. not easily detectable) but not necessarily weak signals of Hubris Syndrome (a faint, hard-to-detect signal can be a strong indicator that something might be about to go amiss).

The study of business and political leaders' language as a marker of hubris was spotlighted in the 2016 presidential campaign in the USA. Candidate Trump, as he was then, gave a now infamous 45-minute speech announcing his presidential candidacy. In it he used a grand total of 257 self-references (compared to seven mentions of 'America' or 'American'), including: 'I've done an amazing job', 'I beat China all the time – all the time', 'Rebuild the country's infrastructure? Nobody can do that like me', 'I would build a great wall – and nobody builds walls better than me' and 'I will be the greatest jobs president that God ever created, I tell you that!'[3] In his presidency, the hubristic tone from the top was amplified through the medium of Twitter, as in the famous 'stable genius' series of Tweets he made on 6 January 2018:

Now that Russian collusion, after one year of intense study, has proven to be a total hoax on the American public, the Democrats and their lapdogs, the Fake News Mainstream Media, are taking out the old Ronald Reagan playbook and screaming mental stability and intelligence ... Actually, throughout my life, my two greatest assets have been mental stability and being, like, really smart. Crooked Hillary Clinton also played these cards very hard and, as everyone knows, went down in flames. I went from VERY successful businessman, to top TV Star ... to President of the United States (on my first try). I think that would qualify as not smart, but genius ... and a very stable genius at that!

Business researchers have adopted a linguistic approach in the study of CEO speech and hubris, for example Craig and Amernic's (2011) DICTION study of Lord John Browne when he was CEO of BP (Table 9.4). As noted previously, Owen (2011b) has suggested a link between Browne's leadership and organizational changes at BP which may have been implicated in the Deepwater Horizon oil spill (see also Ladd, 2012).

Table 9.4   CEO Language and Hubris (Craig and Amernic, 2011)

Linguistic markers of hubris for Lord John Browne when CEO of BP
Craig and Amernic (2011) used DICTION to explore links between Hubris Syndrome and a CEO's natural language use. Their subject was Lord John Browne of BP who was identified previously as having shown indications of Hubris Syndrome (Owen, 2011a). The researchers offered the following example to illustrate the hubristic tone in Browne's assessment of himself and his moral rectitude (Craig and Amernic, 2011): 'This then is my story ... about the insights I gained as I transformed a company, challenged a sector, and prompted business and political leaders to change. My adventures included going toe-to-toe with tyrants, despots and elected leaders, while bringing them around to my way of thinking' (Browne, 2010: 5). Based on the analysis of Browne's speeches when CEO of BP, researchers identified a 'preliminary diagnostic pattern' for identifying CEO hubristic language: (1) scores above the normal range upper limit for 'tenacity', 'aggression', 'accomplishment' and 'centrality'; (2) scores below the normal range lower limit for 'communication' and 'human interest'.

These techniques are a potentially important diagnostic tool in business and politics because it is impossible, to all intents and purposes, for a hubrist to consciously avoid detection due to the sustained and complex mental effort required to conceal speech patterns (Garrard, 2016). The use of linguistic markers holds considerable promise as a method for the detection of the faint signals (i.e. hard-to-detect but not necessarily weak indicators); moreover, the use of 'big data' and machine learning opens up new opportunities for linguistic analysis (Akstinaite, 2018). Identifying linguistic markers that are warning signs for the emergence of hubristic leadership in both politics and business could help to 'weed out' hubrists before hubristic leadership takes hold (Marquand, 2007; Russell, 2011). Identifying the early signs of hubris in leaders' language makes early invention and cure easier.

HIGH RELIABILITY ORGANIZING

If, as the author of *Normal Accidents* (1984), sociologist Charles Perrow, suggested, complex, interdependent sociotechnical systems are susceptible to catastrophic 'normal accidents', managers can either simply accept that the inevitable is unavoidable and leave it all to the gods, or they can be proactive and take measures to try to prevent such occurrences (see Chapter 6).

The High Reliability Organizing (HRO) model is an approach to managing high-risk operations that seeks to minimize the severity and frequency of disastrous outcomes. The HRO approach was developed by researchers who were interested in understanding how some organizations can operate error-free and avoid catastrophic accidents in high-risk environments for very long periods of time (Roberts, 1990a, 1990b; Roberts and Bea, 2001). In High Reliability Organizations (HROs), 'performance reliability rivals productivity as a dominant goal' (Roberts, 1990a: 102). In placing reliability on an equal footing with performance, HROs: (1) do not try to hide failures but instead use them constructively as windows into the health of the overall system; (2) are able to see how the parts fit together by not focusing on one sub-system at the expense of the whole; (3) expect the unexpected; and (4) empower frontline experts with decision-making powers (Christianson et al., 2011).

HRO researchers have assembled a compelling body of evidence which has shown how seemingly inevitable accidents can be delayed and deferred in many of the high-risk operations that are essential to modern society, including nuclear power, space flight, oil and gas exploration and production, transportation systems, military operations, chemical process plants, and commercial aviation. Proponents of the HRO approach argue that it is possible to 'beat the odds', regardless of the organization's purpose, which means that the HRO approach can be applied to 'soft high-risk' as well as 'hard high-risk' technologies (Roberts and Bea, 2001) for example (1) soft high-risk: the use of 'cutting-edge' mathematical finance technology at LTCM was not risk-free and resulted in negative unintended consequences, and one of the reasons LTCM failed was because it suffered from organizational hubris (Lowenstein, 2000; Stein, 2003); (2) hard high-risk: the Deepwater Horizon incident came about as a result of a blend of hubristic exuberance in chasing ever-greater financial and technical targets, and hubristic leadership and complacency on safety matters (Ladd, 2012; Owen, 2011b).

If the HRO approach could be applied to hubristic organizations as a means of minimizing the risks from the hubris hazard, what HRO-type strategies might be borrowed to prevent destructive outcomes? Research on HROs points to three fundamental principles that such organizations use: (1) HROs aggressively seek to know what they don't know; (2) HROs balance efficiency with reliability; and (3) HROs communicate the 'big picture' to everyone (Roberts and Bea, 2001). By adopting a HRO-type approach, organizations prone to hubris could substantially reduce or eliminate entirely the risk. Table 9.5 shows how the HRO approach could help to reduce risks from the hubris hazard (Sadler-Smith et al., 2019).

Table 9.5   HRO approach and hubris (Roberts and Bea, 2001)

What HROs do	What hubristic organizations do	Using HRO to prevent hubris
HROs aggressively seek to know what they don't know	Hubristic organizations are used to not having problems, delude themselves that they are in total control, think they know best and, as a result, they don't know what they don't know	Train employees to look for anomalies; de-couple sub-systems when problems are discovered and empower employees to act
HROs balance efficiency with reliability	Hubristic organizations aggressively pursue performance at the expense of reliability and risk	Decrease likelihood of destructive outcomes by privileging long-run sustainability, safety and soundness instead of short-run over-exuberance
HROs communicate the 'big picture' to everyone	Senior leaders in hubristic organizations under-communicate and over-control	Employees at all levels are encouraged to communicate openly, especially about situations that seem unusual or problematic and may signal potential problems

Source: Roberts and Bea (2001)

A strong organizational culture is a core characteristic of HROs. Strong HRO cultures rooted in a safety-critical approach encourage team learning, foster interconnections that span silos, reward openness, sharing and problem solving, accord areas of ignorance the same significance as areas of certainty, and allow the authoritative voice of the expert to challenge managerialism (Saunders, 2015). A strong HRO culture could help to immunize organizations against becoming hubristic in the first place.

BETTER GOVERNANCE AND REGULATION

During the financial crisis of 2007/08, three of the largest UK banks had to be bailed out by the taxpayer: HBOS (Halifax Bank of Scotland), Northern Rock and Royal Bank of Scotland (RBS). HBOS was created from the merger of Bank of Scotland (a medium-sized bank specializing in business banking) and the UK's biggest building society, The Halifax, in 2001. The merger offered the opportunity for Halifax to transform itself from a reliance on traditional mortgages and savings into a broad-based commercial corporate bank and to become, in its own estimation, 'a new force in banking' that would challenge the existing 'Big 4' (Barclays, HSBC, Lloyds and RBS). At its peak in 2007, HBOS's market capitalization was £40 billion with a book value of £18 billion. However, only seven years after the merger HBOS shareholders watched in horror as 96 per cent of its peak value vanished almost overnight and what remained was salvageable only by the intervention of the UK taxpayer and its acquisition by Lloyds to the tune of £20.5 billion.

A damning assessment by the Parliamentary Commission on Banking Standards, described the entire HBOS project as being based on a flawed business model where 'perilously high-risk' and 'reckless' lending (Parliamentary Commission on Banking Standards, 2013: 13) and enabled by lax regulation. The report was entitled *'An Accident Waiting to Happen': The Failure of HBOS*. As early as 2004, warning signs of impending disaster began to appear in that 'the Group's growth had outpaced the ability to control risks' (p. 3). According to the report, 'the downfall of HBOS was not the result of cultural contamination by investment banking'; instead, it was a 'traditional bank failure pure and simple. It was a case of a bank pursuing traditional banking activities and pursuing them badly' (p. 44) in an 'inappropriate' culture that was ultimately the responsibility of the CEO, the chairman and the board.

In a follow-up assessment in 2015, the Bank of England Prudential Regulation Authority (PRA) and the Financial Conduct Authority (FCA) concluded that although ultimate responsibility for HBOS's failure lies with its board, the Financial Services Authority (FSA) failed in its regulatory responsibility by failing to 'ensure that adequate resources were devoted to large systematically important firms such as HBOS' and, as a result, the regulators did not step in until it was too late (p. 14). In the final reports, board members were exposed for their hubristic incompetence and weak regulators were exposed for their failure to exercise necessary control. HBOS was an example both of 'how not to run a bank' and 'how not to regulate one'.

How Not to Run a Bank: the PSBC report 'named and shamed' the architects of the organizational hubris that had infected HBOS; their 'self-delusion' was a failure of corporate governance (p. 50) which caused its downfall; and the report recommended that they be barred from undertaking any role in the financial sector: (1) Sir James Crosby (CEO until 2006) was 'architect of the strategy that set the course for disaster' (and who subsequently offered to renounce his knighthood; it was annulled in 2013); (2) Andy Hornby (who took over as the protégé of Crosby in 2006 and prior to which he worked at the grocery retailer Asda) 'proved unable or unwilling to change course'; (3) Lord Stevenson (chairman) presided over the bank's board from its birth to its death and who 'in particular, has shown himself incapable of facing the realities of what placed the bank in jeopardy'.

How Not to Regulate a Bank: the official reports from the PCBS and the Bank of England PRA/FCA (2015) drew attention to the fact that the quality of regulation from the Financial Services Authority was inadequate, for example there was: (1) too much reliance on the use of junior staff without sufficient engagement of senior FSA staff; (2) an inclination towards simplistic 'box-ticking' exercises which detracted from the consideration of more deep-seated strategic and structural issues that could bring the bank down; and (3) a failure on the part of the regulator to follow up on warning signs about the bank's ability to fund itself. During the key phase in which problems were festering at HBOS (2004 to the latter part of 2007), the PCBS report concluded that the FSA regulator 'was not so much the dog that did not bark as a dog barking up the wrong tree' (Paragraphs 16–17, p. 49) (Table 9.6).

Table 9.6   How to create the conditions for organizational hubris to flourish in the banking sector

How Not to Run a Bank

'18. The strategy set by the Board from the creation of the new Group sowed the seeds of its destruction. HBOS set a strategy for aggressive, asset-led growth across divisions over a sustained period. This involved accepting more risk across all divisions of the Group. Although many of the strengths of the two brands within HBOS largely persisted at branch level, the strategy created a new culture in the higher echelons of the bank. This culture was brash, underpinned by a belief that the growing market share was due to a special set of skills which HBOS possessed and which its competitors lacked. The effects of the culture were all the more corrosive when coupled with a lack of corporate self-knowledge at the top of the organization, enabling the bank's leaders to persist in the belief, in some cases to this day, that HBOS was a conservative institution when in fact it was the very opposite. [This report] consider[s] the effects of these cultural weaknesses.'

Source: Parliamentary Commission on Banking Standards (2013, Paragraph 18, pp. 8–9)

How Not to Regulate a Bank

The failings of the Financial Services Authority (FSA) were primarily due to deficiencies in its prevailing approach to the supervision of systemically important firms. The FSA did not see its role as being to criticize a firm's business model. This approach gave rise to a framework with: (1) inadequate resources devoted to the prudential regulation of large systemically important banks; (2) inadequate focus on prudential risk areas of asset quality and liquidity in an apparently benign economic outlook; (3) inadequate consideration of strategic and business model-related risks; (4) risk-assessment practices that were too reactive. Overall, the approach was too trusting of firms' management and insufficiently challenging. The report also noted that the wider political and regulatory environment played a role in that there was a sustained political emphasis on the need for a 'light touch' in its approach and that it was likely that anything more would have been met by complaints of heavy handedness.

Source: Bank of England PRA and FCA (2015, Paragraphs 94–102, pp. 32–3)

If the hubristic demise of the accident waiting to happen that was HBOS offers salutary lessons to politicians, policy makers and executives on how not to run or regulate a bank, what also does it tell us about how to govern and regulate effectively in order to reduce risks and balance reliability with performance? The recommendations for firms (board responsibility, board composition, the relationship with regulators) and regulators (the will to act, the supervision of international groups, conflicts of interest) are summarized in Table 9.7.

Hubristic organizational culture emanating via the 'tone from the top' is not unique to the financial sector. Boards of directors in general are likely to face considerable challenges when presented with proposals by charismatic, powerful, over-confident CEOs

Table 9.7 Recommendations for better governance and regulation in the financial sector (Bank of England PRA and FCA, 2015)

Recommendations for financial firms	Recommendations for financial regulators
Directors must take responsibility as a collective body for not only ensuring that the firm's business model is sustainable but also that the principle of 'safety and soundness' is embedded in organizational culture	Even though it is not a regulator's role to ensure that 'no bank fails', they should, where the risks are high, have the statutory powers to intervene to require a bank to change its business model, even where markets appear benign
Boards of directors should include non-executives with diverse experience from inside and outside the sector, and the board members should have the motivation to explore and challenge key strategies with executives	It is not enough for UK regulators to rely on local regulatory authorities for oversight of consolidated international groups; they should have sufficient understanding of international business to be able to engage effectively with the firm and local regulators
Executives should establish a culture that adheres to the letter and the spirit of regulatory requirements and proactively identify threats to the safety and soundness of the firm and notify regulators when issues seem likely to arise	Financial services regulators should guard against any actual or perceived conflicts of interest arising out of board composition and ensure that the risks associated with including industry practitioners as non-executive directors are managed adequately

whose risk-seeking behaviours are a hazard not only to themselves but also to employees, investors and the industry itself (Haynes et al., 2015; Hayward and Hambrick, 1997). The risks associated with a hubristic tone from the top magnifies and intensifies the imperative for improved board selection and composition processes so that over-confident and irrationally exuberant CEOs are less able to install 'yes men' and 'yes women', and foreground the need for regular and meaningful board evaluations (Conger et al., 1998; Malmendier and Tate, 2005b; Van den Berghe and Levrau, 2004).

In the face of opposition from 'stubborn and arrogant CEOs', firms have a responsibility to organize their governance structures such that the over-confidence of hubristic CEOs can be monitored so that employees, firms and investors are protected from recklessly over-confident decisions (Lorsch, 1995: 111). For example, including outside directors on the board who have the capability and confidence to frustrate a reckless CEO, and splitting the roles of CEO and chair, could also thwart a hubrist's power (Hayward and Hambrick, 1997; Li and Tang, 2010; Van den Berghe and Levrau, 2004). Ambitious and confident CEOs need to be effectively managed by their boards which means honing a delicate and creative tension which both supports and challenges them (Nixon, 2016).

Redressing the gender imbalance at senior levels could also help to offset the potentially destructive effects of testosterone-fuelled hubris by having more female traders, board members and CEOs (Coates and Herbert, 2008; Ghaemi et al., 2016). Boards might also be required to give adequate representation to stakeholder groups (Nixon, 2016).

Table 9.8 summarizes some of the suggestions that practitioners, researchers, policy makers and regulators have offered that could help organizations anticipate and avoid the hubris hazard through improved governance processes.

Table 9.8 Combatting organizational hubris through board composition/structure and board processes/regulation

Board composition and structure	Board processes and regulation
Split roles of CEO and chair; rotate talent through the board	Take collective responsibility for ensuring a sustainable business model
Include non-executives with diverse experience from inside and outside sector and who have capability and confidence to thwart CEO hubris	Embed 'safety and soundness' principle in organizational culture
Ensure risks associated with including industry practitioners as non-executive directors are managed adequately	Hone creative tension within board which supports and challenges the CEO
Guard against any actual or perceived conflicts of interest arising out of board composition	Establish culture that adheres to the letter and spirit of regulatory and safety requirements
Improve board selection and composition processes; avoid recruiting individuals with a predisposition to hubris and narcissism	Proactively identify threats to safety and soundness and notify regulators when issues seem likely to arise
Have adequate representation along important dimensions of diversity; consider stakeholder group representation	Conduct regular and meaningful board evaluations

AVOIDING HUBRISTIC ORGANIZATIONAL CULTURE

At the heart of the HBOS and other failures was an organizational culture that created the conditions for hubris to flourish which then had knock-on effects across the system. The Bank of England (2015) report into HBOS highlighted the aggressive pursuit of growth at the bank which was typical of the sector as a whole. The tone from the top was exemplified by the exuberant rhetoric of senior leaders: 'well ahead of a typically ambitious plan', 'necessity to out-perform expectations', 'we are better than the competition. We can grow faster. We can do this, and this, and this', 'we need sales growth!', and perhaps most tellingly, 'under *no* circumstances can we miss this revised target' (Paragraphs 949–51, p. 219, original emphasis). In HBOS, the tone from the top failed to balance the gung-ho rhetoric with an intelligent restraint that gave due regard to risk and control. This was culturally ingrained both in financial institutions themselves and in wider social norms, and was exacerbated by the light touch of regulators and government.[4]

As a result of the failures of governance and regulation in the financial sector, policy officials and regulators have become alert, though arguably somewhat belatedly, to the dangers of organizational and cultural hubris and its potentially debilitating effects on organizations and the wider industry. Six years after the crash, the then Deputy Governor of the Bank of England (Prudential Regulation), Andrew Bailey, who subsequently became the Chief Executive of the FCA, gave a speech in London in May 2016 cautioning against the culture of hubris which had infected his industry (see Table 9.9).

Table 9.9   Extract of speech by Andrew Bailey (then Deputy Director of the Bank of England) cautioning against a culture of hubris in the finance industry

Andrew Bailey: 'Culture in financial services – a regulator's perspective' (extract)
'Culture has a major influence on the outcomes that matter to us as regulators. My assessment of recent history is that there has not been a case of a major prudential or conduct failing in a firm which did not have among its root causes a failure of culture as manifested in governance, remuneration, risk management or tone from the top. Culture has thus laid the ground for bad outcomes, for instance where management are so convinced of their rightness that they hurtle for the cliff without questioning the direction of travel. We talk often about credit risk, market risk, liquidity risk, conduct risk in its several forms. You can add to that, *hubris risk*, the risk of blinding over-confidence. If I may say so, it is a risk that can be magnified by broader social attitudes. Ten years ago there was considerable reverence towards, and little questioning of, the ability of banks and bankers to make money or of whether boards demonstrated a sufficient diversity of view and outlook to sustain challenge. How things have changed. Healthy scepticism channelled into intelligent and forceful questioning of the self-confident can be a good thing. In turn, culture matters to us as financial regulators because it can, left alone, tend to shape and encourage bad outcomes, but it doesn't have to do that.'

Source: www.bankofengland.co.uk/-/media/boe/files/speech/2016/culture-in-financial-services-a-regulators-perspective.pdf (Accessed 24 February 2018) (emphases added)

The irrational exuberance and over-confidence which typify a hubristic culture can be counterbalanced by assembling top management or venture teams which have a diversity of backgrounds, demographics knowledge, skills and motivations and who are therefore better placed to offer multiple and competing perspectives. Individuals within such teams can act as devil's advocates, prompting re-evaluation of cultural assumptions and biases, and question the acceptance of group decisions, thereby forestalling forceful and overly enthusiastic executives or disrupting compliant and acquiescent groupthink climates (Baron, 2009; Hayward et al., 2006; Janis, 1982; Schweiger et al., 1989; Shimizu and Hitt, 2004). Adding members to senior teams who are more moderate in their optimism, as compared to the leader, could offset hubristic leaders' over-confidence and zeal (Hmieleski and Baron, 2008).

It has been argued by policy makers and regulators that organizational hubris should be added to the list of risks that finance firms face (see Table 9.9) and that steps should be taken not only to single out individual hubrists at senior levels, in order to thwart their recklessness, but also to recognize and correct organizational hubris before it becomes too deeply rooted and its effects corrode the culture of the organization, and the same applies to others sectors and contexts. In the finance industry, the prime responsibility for the organizational hubris which takes hold must rest with the boards of the banks, who have a legal responsibility to the shareholders (Darling, 2012). Boards and senior management teams must take responsibility and ask themselves the question of whether they themselves actually understand the risks to which their organizations may have become exposed. Failure to do so also risks abdicating responsibility to the architects of the high-risk technologies and processes which can be too opaque to be predictable.

Reaching a point at which hubristic leadership is recognized as a 'normal hazard' that can affect senior leaders in business and politics could signal cultural shift; this might then make it more acceptable to put in place institutional constraints that, rather than being seen as threats to the leader, are seen as intelligent safeguards. Hubris may come to be seen as a potential hazard to any occupant of a senior leadership role, analogous to a 'slip, trip and fall hazard' in the workplace. Such an attitudinal and cultural shift might also result in leaders accepting, rather than resisting, organizational, institutional and societal constraining mechanisms on power, such as fixed terms of office, or automatically stepping down or not seeking re-election or re-appointment once the condition has been established (Owen and Davidson, 2009). The eight-year (two four-year terms) constraint on the US presidency and the roles of non-executive directors on company boards are positive examples of such approaches.

Executive education (including executive coaching and mentoring) can effect meaningful cultural change by providing leaders with educational and training experiences which offer objective insights into their knowledge, skills and competencies in relation to those required in senior leadership and business start-up roles, and could: (1) enable leaders themselves to calibrate their actual ability (what they can actually do) versus their ability expectations (what they think they can do); (2) assist them in developing the necessary capabilities in areas where they lack the requisite knowledge and skills. Human resource processes also have a role to play in obviating attempts at accessing the upper echelons of organizations by individuals who lack the fundamental dispositions to succeed, and making entry more difficult for over-optimistic but under-equipped candidates (Townsend et al., 2010).

Training executives and entrepreneurs in effective self-regulation techniques and executive (i.e. meta-cognitive) control strategies could help them to hold their overly confident, ambitious and optimistic tendencies in check (Hmieleski and Baron, 2008). Training in, and the application of, appropriate strategic decision making and long-range planning tools such as scenario planning, mental simulation, counter-factual thinking, 'pre-mortem' and cognitive mapping may help to ground and educate over-confident executives and entrepreneurs as to what they can and cannot accomplish, sensitizing them to and preparing them for what could go wrong (Gaglio, 2004; Huff, 1990; Van der Heijden, 2011).

CONSTRAINING EXECUTIVE REMUNERATION

One of the dimensions of 'The Hubris Factor' identified by strategic management researchers as being associated with negative acquisition outcomes was CEO self-importance measured as CEO relative compensation, i.e. CEO cash compensation divided by the compensation of the second-highest-paid company officer (Hayward and Hambrick, 1997). Relatedly, behavioural finance researchers found that celebrity CEOs (i.e. those who had won CEO of the Year-type awards) tended to extract higher compensation from their business in the form of stock and options (Malmendier and Tate, 2009).

An additional warning sign of a hubris-infected organizational culture might therefore be the emergence of inequalities in CEO remuneration relative to other employees. The authors of a report into CEO remuneration in the USA point to the fact that CEO pay continues to be exorbitantly high and that it has grown far faster in recent decades than typical worker pay (see Table 9.10). The growth of 937 per cent (measured in stock options realized, respectively) from 1978 to 2016 does not reflect correspondingly higher output and the figure is more than 70 per cent faster than the rise in the stock market; and is substantially greater than the 11.2 per cent growth in a typical worker's annual compensation over the same period (Mishel and Schieder, 2017: 2). These inequalities prompt the question of how can individuals who are so highly paid ever fully capture the support of low-paid employees, many of whom may be on zero hours contracts? (Tourish, 2018:141).

Table 9.10   CEO remuneration trends relative to high-wage and typical earners. (Mischel and Schieder, 2017)

Report by Economic Policy Institute (Washington, DC) (2017) looking at trends in CEO compensation*
In 2016 CEOs in America's largest firms made an average of $15.6 million in compensation – 271 times the annual average pay of a typical worker
The 2016 CEO-to-worker compensation ratio of 271-to-1 compares with: (1) a 59-to-1 ratio, in 1989; (2) a 20-to-1 ratio, in 1965
The average CEO in a large firm now earns 5.33 times more than even the earnings of the average very-high-wage earner (i.e. earners in the top 0.1 per cent)
CEO compensation has grown far faster than stock prices (937 per cent, a rise that is more than 70 per cent faster than the rise in the stock market) or corporate profits
11.2 per cent growth in a typical worker's annual compensation over the same period

*Stock options realized in addition to salary, bonuses, restricted stock grants and long-term incentive pay-outs.

Ten years on from the financial crash, 2018 saw a doubling of shareholder rebellions against high executive pay with major companies such as Astrazeneca and Shell experiencing protest notes at AGMs (*Financial Times*, 29 August 2018).

By way of further illustration, in 2016 there was a shareholder rebellion when advertising group WPP set the remuneration package for its founder and Chief Executive Martin Sorrell at £70 million, over 2000 times the average WPP employee. This made him one of the UK's highest paid exectives. In 2018 Sorrell, who was the longest-serving FTSE 100 CEO, resigned ahead of allegations of personal misconduct, which prompted some commentators to remark on how frequently it is with leaders that 'instead of departing gracefully, hubris takes over and they cling on, and on, and then the exit is messy, and in terms of their long, hard-earned reputation, highly destructive.'[5]

In relation to financial acquisitiveness more generally and from the perspective of Aristotelian virtue ethics, the moral philosopher Alasdair MacIntyre, author of the seminal work *After Virtue* (1984), had some harsh words for those he referred to as the 'money men'. MacIntyre frames his critique in terms of the way society has come to see money as a meaningless end in itself (an 'external good') rather than a means to a different and more meaningful end which has an intrinsic worth (an 'internal good'). In MacIntyre's view, traders in financial markets have become dislocated from the uses of money in everyday life, such that money becomes the measure of all things including itself (Cornwell, 2010). MacIntyre goes as far as claiming that the financial sector is, in essence, an environment of 'bad character' because the 'money men', as MacIntyre calls them, in his view transfer as much risk as possible to others, and when there is a crash they fail to take into account the collateral damage to individuals and society emanating from the market crises they played a significant role in precipitating.

The issue of hubristic CEOs paying themselves overly generously (or being enabled to do so by complicit boards or remuneration committees) could be redressed by boards exercising good judgement in limiting exorbitant CEO reward packages, or CEOs themselves mobilizing an internal 'moral compass' to constrain avaricious behaviours and cultivate relevant leader character strengths, such as temperance, accountability, integrity and justice (Crossan et al., 2013a, b; Haynes et al., 2015; Petit and Bollaert, 2012). In avoiding hubris, senior leaders and those who determine their levels of remuneration have to tread a fine line between rewarding performance appropriately and exuberant self-indulgence, and between maximizing sustainable financial returns for the business and the pursuit of profit for the sake of it.

LAST WORDS

Hubristic leadership emanates from leaders' intoxication with power and exaggerated beliefs in their strengths and capabilities. This causes them to over-estimate what can go right and under-estimate what can go wrong. They ignore wise warnings and also overlook the possibility of hard-to-predict, high-impact events. As a consequence, they create conditions which invite unintended negative consequences. Ultimately, hubristic leaders demonstrate a lack of ability to act with practical wisdom (prudence) in the volatile, uncertain, complex and ambiguous situations which typify modern organizational life.

In Aristotle's moral philosophy (The *Nicomachean Ethics*), a prudent person is someone who reasons well and is able to calculate successfully about what is good or bad. A prudent leader is someone who is able to deliberate well about what is good or bad and has the capacity to act with regard to things that are good or bad for themselves and for those whom they lead. Practical wisdom is preserved by the virtue of temperance (*sophrosyne*), and temperance is at the mean between deficiency and excess. Hubristic leaders are intemperate and lose the power to navigate a prudent course between deficiency and excess; they incline towards excess. To avoid such errors, hubristic leaders must notice the excesses which they are liable to commit, and sometimes must drag themselves or be dragged in the contrary direction: 'we shall arrive at the mean by pressing well away from our failing' (*Nicomachean Ethics*, Book II, 1109b). However, in many leadership situations not only is it difficult to find the mid-point between deficiency and excess, in seeking the best course of action leaders sometimes need to incline towards excess at the right time, for the right motive and in the right amount, for example in the pursuit of innovative business ventures.

Given current events in the world's business and political arenas, the subject of hubris could not be more topical or timely, and given its pervasiveness throughout human history it is unlikely disappear from the stage any time soon. The problem of hubristic leadership raises important and thought-provoking questions, problems and challenges that warrant increased attention from politicians, business executives, policy makers, educators, researchers, students, and leaders and managers at all levels in institutions and public and private organizations. Hubris is potent and perilous, and it is only by understanding its characteristics, causes and consequences and containing its hazards that the paradox of hubristic leadership can be resolved and the process of hubristic leadership arrested.

NOTES

1. www.independent.co.uk/news/world/americas/donald-trump-bizarre-signature-us-presi dent-inauguration-graphology-handwriting-a7538536.html (Accessed 22 July 2018).
2. https://liwc.wpengine.com (Accessed 6 March 2018).
3. www.washingtonpost.com/opinions/donald-trumps-festival-of-narcissism/2015/06/16/ fd006c28-1459-11e5-9ddc-e3353542100c_story.html (Accessed 13 April 2016).
4. www.fca.org.uk/news/speeches/culture-financial-institutions-everywhere-nowhere (Accessed 5 March 2018).
5. www.independent.co.uk/news/business/comment/martin-sorrell-scandal-share-price-wpp-allegations-a8400566.html (Accessed 22 July 2018).
6. www.psypost.org/2017/08/psychological-analysis-donald-trumps-speech-patterns-shows-triumphed-gop-rivals-49511 (Accessed 14 March 2018).

REFERENCES

Abed, R. T. (2011). The Hubris Syndrome: Is it necessarily pathological? *The Psychiatrist*, *35*(6), 140–5.

Abramson, N. R. (2007). The leadership archetype: A Jungian analysis of similarities between modern leadership theory and the Abraham myth in the Judaic–Christian tradition. *Journal of Business Ethics*, *72*(2), 115–29.

Ahmadian, S., Azarshahi, S. and Paulhus, D. L. (2017). Explaining Donald Trump via communication style: Grandiosity, informality, and dynamism. *Personality and Individual Differences*, *107*, 49–53.

Akerlof, G. and Shiller, R. (2009). How animal spirits destabilize economies. *McKinsey Quarterly*, *3*, 127–35.

Akstinaite, V. (2018). *Use of Linguistic Markers in the Identification and Analysis of Chief Executives' Hubris*, unpublished PhD Thesis, University of Surrey, 2018.

Al Rahahleh, N. and Wei, P. P. (2012). The performance of frequent acquirers: Evidence from emerging markets. *Global Finance Journal*, *23*(1), 16–33.

Alicke, M. D., Klotz, M. L., Breitenbecher, D. L., Yurak, T. J. and Vredenburg, D. S. (1995). Personal contact, individuation, and the better-than-average effect. *Journal of Personality and Social Psychology*, *68*(5), 804–25.

Ambady, N. (2010). The perils of pondering: Intuition and thin slice judgments. *Psychological Inquiry*, *21*(4), 271–8.

Ambady, N. and Rosenthal, R. (1992). Thin slices of expressive behavior as predictors of interpersonal consequences: A meta-analysis. *Psychological Bulletin*, *111*(2), 256–74.

Ambady, N., Krabbenhoft, M. A. and Hogan, D. (2006). The 30-sec sale: Using thin-slice judgments to evaluate sales effectiveness. *Journal of Consumer Psychology*, *16*(1), 4–13.

Anderson, C., John, O. P. and Keltner, D. (2012). The personal sense of power. *Journal of Personality*, *80*(2), 313–44.

Anderson, T. H. (2011). *Bush's wars*. Oxford: Oxford University Press.

Antoniou, A., Guo, J. and Petmezas, D. (2008). Merger momentum and market valuations: The UK evidence. *Applied Financial Economics*, *18*(17), 1411–23.

Appelbaum, S. H. (1997). Socio-technical systems theory: An intervention strategy for organizational development. *Management Decision*, *35*(6), 452–63.

Armstrong, K. (2005). *A short history of myth*. Edinburgh: Canongate Books.

Ashkanasy, N. M. (2013). Neuroscience and leadership: Take care not to throw the baby out with the bathwater. *Journal of Management Inquiry*, *22*(3), 311–13.

Ashta, A. and Patil, S. (2007). Behavioural finance issues in listing and delisting in the French wine industry: Lessons from the case of Grands Vins Boisset. *Decision, 34*(2), 1–26.

Auvinen, T. P., Lämsä, A. M., Sintonen, T. and Takala, T. (2013). Leadership manipulation and ethics in storytelling. *Journal of Business Ethics, 116*(2), 415–31.

Babiak, P. and Hare, R. D. (2006). *Snakes in suits: When psychopaths go to work.* New York: HarperCollins.

Bandura, A. (1986). *Social foundations of thought and action: A social cognitive theory.* Englewood Cliffs, NJ: Prentice-Hall.

Bank of England Prudential Regulation Authority (PRA) and Financial Conduct Authority (FCA) (2015). *The failure of HBOS plc (HBOS)*, November. Available at: www.bankofeng-land.co.uk/-/media/boe/files/prudential-regulation/publication/hbos-complete-report (Accessed 20 June 2018).

Barber, B. M. and Odean, T. (2001). Boys will be boys: Gender, overconfidence, and common stock investment. *The Quarterly Journal of Economics, 116*(1), 261–92.

Barnard, J. W. (2008). Narcissism, over-optimism, fear, anger, and depression: The interior lives of corporate leaders. *University of Cincinnati Law Review, 77*, 405–30.

Baron, R. A. (2009). Effectual versus predictive logics in entrepreneurial decision making: Differences between experts and novices – Does experience in starting new ventures change the way entrepreneurs think? Perhaps, but for now, 'caution' is essential. *Journal of Business Venturing, 24*(4), 310–15.

Bauer, T. N. and Green, S. G. (1996). Development of leader–member exchange: A longitudinal test. *Academy of Management Journal, 39*(6), 1538–67.

Bea, R. (2011). *Understanding the Macondo Well Failures.* Deepwater Horizon Study Group, Working Paper, January 2011. Berkeley, CA: UC Berkeley.

Beinart, P. (2010). *The Icarus Syndrome: A history of American hubris.* New York: Harper.

Bengtsson, C., Persson, M. and Willenhag, P. (2005). Gender and overconfidence. *Economics Letters, 86*(2), 199–203.

Bennister, M. (2009). Tony Blair as prime minister. In T. Casey (ed.) *The Blair legacy: Politics, policy, governance and foreign affairs.* Basingstoke: Palgrave Macmillan, pp. 165–77.

Berglas, S. (2014). Rooting out hubris, before a fall. *Harvard Business Review*, 14 April. Available at: https://hbr.org/2014/04/rooting-out-hubris-before-a-fall (Accessed 5 March 2018).

Black, C. (2003). *Franklin Delano Roosevelt: Champion of freedom.* New York: Public Affairs.

Blair, T. (2010). *A journey.* London: Arrow.

Blau, P. M. (1964). *Exchange and power in social life.* New York: Wiley.

Bligh, M. C. and Kohles, J. C. (2009). The enduring allure of charisma: How Barack Obama won the historic 2008 presidential election. *The Leadership Quarterly, 20*(3), 483–92.

Bligh, M. C., Kohles, J. C. and Meindl, J. R. (2004). Charisma under crisis: Presidential leadership, rhetoric, and media responses before and after the September 11th terrorist attacks. *The Leadership Quarterly, 15*(2), 211–39.

Bligh, M. C., Kohles, J. C., Pearce, C. L., Justin, J. E. and Stovall, J. F. (2007). When the romance is over: Follower perspectives of aversive leadership. *Applied Psychology, 56*(4), 528–57.

Bodolica, V. and Spraggon, M. (2011). Behavioural governance and self-conscious emotions: Unveiling governance implications of authentic and hubristic pride. *Journal of Business Ethics, 100*(3), 535–50.

Boin, A. and Schulman, P. (2008). Assessing NASA's safety culture: The limits and possibilities of high-reliability theory. *Public Administration Review, 68*(6), 1050–62.

Boje, D. M. (1991). Learning storytelling: Storytelling to learn management skills. *Journal of Management Education, 15*(3), 279–94.

Boje, D. M. (1995). Stories of the storytelling organization: A postmodern analysis of Disney as 'Tamara-Land'. *Academy of Management Journal, 38*(4), 997–1035.

Boje, D. M. (ed.) (2011). *Storytelling and the future of organizations: An antenarrative handbook*. Abingdon: Routledge.

Bollaert, H. and Petit, V. (2010). Beyond the dark side of executive psychology: Current research and new directions. *European Management Journal, 28*(5), 362–76.

Bono, J. E. and Judge, T. A. (2004). Personality and transformational and transactional leadership: A meta-analysis. *Journal of Applied Psychology, 89*(5), 901–10.

Boroughs, M. S. and O'Cleirigh, C. (2015). *Pathoplasticity: The encyclopedia of clinical psychology*. Chichester: John Wiley & Sons.

Bower, T. (2010). The real villain of BP. *The Spectator*, 23 June. www.spectator.co.uk/2010/06/the-real-villain-of-bp (Accessed 14 March 2018).

Boyatzis, R. E. (2014). Possible contributions to leadership and management development from neuroscience. *Academy of Management Learning & Education, 13*(2), 300–3.

Brower, H. H., Schoorman, F. D. and Tan, H. H. (2000). A model of relational leadership: The integration of trust and leader–member exchange. *The Leadership Quarterly, 11*(2), 227–50.

Brown, R. and Sharma, N. (2007). CEO overconfidence, CEO dominance and corporate acquisitions. *Journal of Economics and Business, 59*(5), 358–79.

Brown, A. D., Gabriel, Y. and Gherardi, S. (2009). Storytelling and change: An unfolding story. *Organization, 16*(3), 323–33.

Brown, R. P. and Zeigler-Hill, V. (2004). Narcissism and the non-equivalence of self-esteem measures: A matter of dominance? *Journal of Research in Personality, 38*, 585–92.

Browne, J. (2010). *Beyond business: An inspirational memoir from a visionary leader*. London: Weidenfeld & Nicolson.

Brunell, A. B., Gentry, W. A., Campbell, W. K., Hoffman, B. J., Kuhnert, K. W. and DeMarree, K. G. (2008). Leader emergence: The case of the narcissistic leader. *Personality and Social Psychology Bulletin, 34*, 1–14.

Bryman, A. (1992). *Charisma and leadership in organizations*. London: SAGE.

Burns, T. R. and Machado, N. (2010). Technology, complexity, and risk: Part II – A social systems perspective on the discourses and regulation of the hazards of socio-technical systems. *Sociologia, 62*, 97–131.

Burton, J. and McCabe, E. (2009). *We don't do God: Blair's religious belief and its consequences*. London: Continuum.

Busenitz, L. W. and Barney, J. B. (1997). Differences between entrepreneurs and managers in large organizations: Biases and heuristics in strategic decision-making. *Journal of Business Venturing, 12*(1), 9–30.

Bush, G. W. (2010). *Decision points*. New York: Virgin Books.

Butler, M. J., O'Broin, H. L., Lee, N. and Senior, C. (2016). How organizational cognitive neuroscience can deepen understanding of managerial decision-making: A review of the recent literature and future directions. *International Journal of Management Reviews, 18*(4), 542–59.

Cairns, D. L. (1996). Hybris, dishonour, and thinking big. *The Journal of Hellenic Studies, 116*, 1–32.

Camerer, C. and Lovallo, D. (1999). Overconfidence and excess entry: An experimental approach. *American Economic Review, 89*(1), 306–18.

Cameron, K. and Dutton, J. (eds) (2003). *Positive organizational scholarship: Foundations of a new discipline*. San Francisco: Berrett-Koehler.

Campbell, W. K., Hoffman, B. J., Campbell, S. M. and Marchisio, G. (2011). Narcissism in organizational contexts. *Human Resource Management Review, 21*(4), 268–84.

Campbell, W. K., Goodie, A. S. and Foster, J. D. (2004). Narcissism, confidence, and risk attitude. *Journal of Behavioral Decision Making, 17*(4), 297–311.

Chatterjee, A. and Hambrick, D. C. (2007). It's all about me: Narcissistic chief executive officers and their effects on company strategy and performance. *Administrative Science Quarterly, 52*(3), 351–86.

Chen, S. S. and Wang, Y. (2012). Financial constraints and share repurchases. *Journal of Financial Economics, 105*(2), 311–31.

Cherns, A. B. (1987). Principles of sociotechnical design revisited. *Human Relations, 40*, 153–62.

Chia, R. and Langley, A. (2005). Call for Papers: The First Organization Studies Summer Workshop on Theorizing Process in Organizational Research. 12–13 June, Santorini, Greece.

Chomsky, N. and Barsamian, D. (2017). *Global discontents: Conversations on the rising threats to democracy*. London: Hamish Hamilton.

Christianson, M. K., Sutcliffe, K. M., Miller, M. A. and Iwashyna, T. J. (2011). Becoming a high reliability organization. *Critical Care, 15*(6), 314–18.

Claxton, G., Owen, D. and Sadler-Smith, E. (2015). Hubris in leadership: A peril of unbridled intuition? *Leadership, 11*, 57–78.

Coates, J. (2012). *The hour between dog and wolf: Risk taking, gut feelings and the biology of boom and bust*. London: Fourth Estate.

Coates, J., Gurnell, M. and Sarnyai, Z. (2018). From molecule to market. In P. Garrard (ed.) *The leadership hubris epidemic: Biological roots and strategies for prevention*. Basingstoke: Palgrave Macmillan, pp. 25–56.

Coates, J. M. and Herbert, J. (2008). Endogenous steroids and financial risk taking on a London trading floor. *Proceedings of the National Academy of Sciences, 105*(16), 6167–72.

Coles, A. J. and Coles, A. J. (2009). Fit to decide? *Brain, 132*(5), 1407–20.

Collins, J. (2009). *How the mighty fall, and why some companies never give in*. London: Random House.

Colman, A. (2001). *A dictionary of psychology*. Oxford: Oxford University Press.

Conger, J. A. and Kanungo, R. N. (1987). Toward a behavioral theory of charismatic leadership in organizational settings. *Academy of Management Review, 12*(4), 637–47.

Conger, J. A. and Kanungo, R. N. (1998). *Charismatic leadership in organizations*. London: Sage.

Conger, J. A., Finegold, D. and Lawler, E. E. (1998). Appraising boardroom performance. *Harvard Business Review, 76*, 136–64.

Cornwell, J. (2010). MacIntyre on money. *Prospect Magazine*, 20 October. Available at: www.prospectmagazine.co.uk/magazine/alasdair-macintyre-on-money (Accessed 22 March 2018).

Conger, J. A. (1990). The dark side of leadership. *Organizational Dynamics, 19*(2), 44–55.

Cooper, A. C., Woo, C. A. and Dunkelberg, W. (1988). Entrepreneurs' perceived chances for success. *Journal of Business Venturing, 3*, 97–108.

Costa, P. T. Jr and McCrae, R. (1992). *NEO-PI-R and NEO-FFI professional manual*. Odessa, FL: Psychological Assessment Resources.

Craig, R. and Amernic, J. (2011). Detecting linguistic traces of destructive narcissism at-a-distance in a CEO's letter to shareholders. *Journal of Business Ethics, 101*(4), 563–75.

Craig, S. B. and Kaiser, R. B. (2012). Destructive leadership. In M. G. Rumsey (ed.) *The Oxford handbook of leadership*. Oxford: Oxford University Press, pp. 439–53.

Crooks, E. (2010). BP not prepared for Deepwater spill. *Financial Times*, 3 June. Available at: www.ft.com/content/e1e0e21c-6e53-11df-ab79-00144feabdc0 (Accessed 22 March 2018).

Cropanzano, R. and Becker, W. J. (2013). The promise and peril of organizational neuroscience: Today and tomorrow. *Journal of Management Inquiry, 22*(3), 306–10.

Cropanzano, R. and Mitchell, M. S. (2005). Social exchange theory: An interdisciplinary review. *Journal of Management, 31*(6), 874–900.

Crossan, M., Mazutis, D. and Seijts, G. (2013a). In search of virtue: The role of virtues, values and character strengths in ethical decision making. *Journal of Business Ethics, 113*(4), 567–81.

Crossan, M., Mazutis, D., Seijts, G. and Gandz, J. (2013b). Developing leadership character in business programs. *Academy of Management Learning & Education, 12*(2), 285–305.

Daddow, O. and Schnapper, P. (2013). Liberal intervention in the foreign policy think-ing of Tony Blair and David Cameron. *Cambridge Review of International Affairs, 26*(2), 330–49.

Daly, K. N. and Rengel, M. (2009). *Greek and Roman mythology, A to Z*. New York: Infobase Publishing.

Dane, E. and Pratt, M. G. (2007). Exploring intuition and its role in managerial decision making. *Academy of Management Review, 32*, 33–54.

Dansereau Jr, F., Graen, G. and Haga, W. J. (1975). A vertical dyad linkage approach to leadership within formal organizations: A longitudinal investigation of the role mak-ing process. *Organizational Behavior and Human Performance, 13*(1), 46–78.

Darling, A. (2012). Foreword. In R. Perman (2013). *Hubris: How HBOS wrecked the best bank in Britain*. Edinburgh: Birlinn.

David, P. A. (1992). Heroes, herds and hysteresis in technological history: Thomas Edison and 'The Battle of the Systems' reconsidered. *Industrial and Corporate Change, 1*(1), 129–80.

Davidson, J. R., Connor, K. M. and Swartz, M. (2006). Mental illness in US presidents between 1776 and 1974: A review of biographical sources. *The Journal of Nervous and Mental Disease, 194*(1), 47–51.

Davis. A. S., Maranville, S. J. and Obloj, K. (1997). The paradoxical process of organiza-tional transformation: Propositions and a case study. *Research in Organizational Change and Development, 10*, 275–314.

Davis, K. M. and Gardner, W. L. (2012). Charisma under crisis revisited: Presidential leadership, perceived leader effectiveness, and contextual influences. *The Leadership Quarterly, 23*(5), 918–33.

De Bodt, E., Cousin, J. G. and Roll, R. (2014). *The Hubris Hypothesis: Empirical evidence. Division of the Humanities and Social Sciences, California Institute of Technology, Working Paper 1390*. Pasadena, CA: California Institute of Technology.

De Young, K. (2007). *Soldier: The life of Colin Powell*. New York: Vintage.

Deaves, R., Lüders, E. and Luo, G. Y. (2008). An experimental test of the impact of over-confidence and gender on trading activity. *Review of Finance, 13*(3), 555–75.

Decety, J. and Jackson, P. L. (2004). The functional architecture of human empathy. *Behavioral and Cognitive Neuroscience Reviews, 3*(2), 71–100.

Decety, J. and Michalska, K. J. (2010). Neurodevelopmental changes in the circuits underlying empathy and sympathy from childhood to adulthood. *Developmental Science, 13*(6), 886–99.

Deluga, R. J. (1997). Relationship among American presidential charismatic leadership, narcissism, and rated performance. *The Leadership Quarterly, 8*(1), 49–65.

Dell, M. and Fredman, C. (1999). *Direct from Dell: Strategies that revolutionized an industry*. London: HarperCollins.

Desai, M. (2015). *Hubris: Why economists failed to predict the crisis and how to avoid the next one*. New Haven, CT: Yale University Press.

Dinh, J. E., Lord, R. G., Gardner, W. L., Meuser, J. D., Liden, R. C. and Hu, J. (2014). Leadership theory and research in the new millennium: Current theoretical trends and changing perspectives. *The Leadership Quarterly*, *25*, 36–62.

Dowling, M. and Lucey, B. M. (2014). From hubris to nemesis: Irish banks, behavioural biases and the crisis. *Journal of Risk Management in Financial Institutions*, *7*(2), 122–33.

Dreijmanis, J. (2005). A portrait of the artist as a politician: The case of Adolf Hitler. *The Social Science Journal*, *42*(1), 115–27.

Dulebohn, J. H., Bommer, W. H., Liden, R. C., Brouer, R. L. and Ferris, G. R. (2012). A meta-analysis of antecedents and consequences of leader–member exchange: Integrating the past with an eye toward the future. *Journal of Management*, *38*(6), 1715–59.

Dunn, D. H. (2003). Myths, motivations and 'mis-underestimations': The Bush administration and Iraq. *International Affairs*, *79*, 279–97.

Dutton, J. E. (1993). The making of organizational opportunities: An interpretive pathway to organizational change. *Research in Organizational Behaviour*, *15*, 195–226.

Eason, K. D. (1982). The process of introducing information technology, *Behaviour & Information Technology*, *1*(2), 197–213.

Eccles, B. (2014). Hubris Syndrome and organizational leadership. *Roffey Park Thinking and Opinion*. Available at: www.roffeypark.com/leadership-and-management/hubris-syndrome-and-organisational-leadership (Accessed 10 November 2014).

Ehrlich, P. and Ehrlich, A. (2009). *One with Nineveh: Power, politics and human consumption*. Washington, DC: Island Press.

Eichenberg, R. C., Stoll, R. J. and Lebo, M. (2006). War president: The approval ratings of George W. Bush. *Journal of Conflict Resolution*, *50*, 783–808.

Einarsen, S., Aasland, M. S. and Skogstad, A. (2007). Destructive leadership behaviour: A definition and conceptual model. *The Leadership Quarterly*, *18*(3), 207–16.

Eisenstadt, S. N. (1968). *Max Weber: On charisma and institution building*. Chicago: University of Chicago Press.

Elkind, P., Whitford, D. and Burke, D. (2011). BP: 'An accident waiting to happen'. *Fortune Magazine*, 24 January. Available at: http://fortune.com/2011/01/24/bp-an-accident-waiting-to-happen (Accessed 22 March 2018).

Emerson, R. M. (1976). Social exchange theory. *Annual Review of Sociology*, *2*(1), 335–62.

Engel, J. A. (2005). Hubris is the handmaiden of tragedy: Truman's lesson for Bush. *International Journal*, *60*(2), 531–43.

Epitropaki, O., Martin, R. and Thomas, G. (2018). Relational leadership. In J. Antonakis and D. V. Day (eds) *The nature of leadership*. London: SAGE, pp. 109–37.

Fairweather, J. (2014). *The good war: The battle for Afghanistan 2006–2014*. London: Jonathan Cape.

Feldman, M. S. and Pentland, B. T. (2003). Re-conceptualizing organizational routines as a source of flexibility and change. *Administrative Science Quarterly*, *48*, 94–118.

Ferguson, N. (2012). *The war of the world: Twentieth-century conflict and the descent of the West*. London: Penguin.

Financial Stability Board (FSB) (2017). Artificial Intelligence and Machine Learning in Financial Services: Market developments and financial stability implications. Available at: www.fsb.org/wp-content/uploads/P011117.pdf (Accessed 20 June 2018).

Finkelstein, S., Hambrick, D. C. and Cannella, A. A. (2009). *Strategic leadership: Theory and research on executives, top management teams, and boards*. Oxford: Oxford University Press.

Fisher, N. R. (1976). Hybris and dishonour: I. *Greece & Rome, 23*(2), 177–93.

Fisher, N. (1990). The law of hubris in Athens. In P. Cartledge, P. Millett and S. Todd (eds) *Nomos: Essays in Athenian Law, Politics and Society*. Cambridge: Cambridge University Press, pp. 123–38.

Fiske, S. T. (2009). *Social beings: Core motives in social psychology*. Chichester: John Wiley & Sons.

Fiske, S. T. and Bearns, C. (2014). Stereotyping: Processes and content. In E. Borgida and J. A. Bargh (eds) *APA handbook of personality and social psychology, Vol. 1: Attitudes and social cognition*. Washington, DC: APA, pp. 457–508.

Ford, J. D. and Backoff, R. W. (1988). Organizational change in and out of dualities and paradox. In R. E. Quinn and K. S. Cameron (eds) *Paradox and transformation: Toward a theory of change in organization and management*. New York: Ballinger/Harper & Row, pp. 81–121.

Foucault, M. (1983/1999). *Discourse and truth: The problematization of parrhesia*. Six lectures given by Michel Foucault at the University of California at Berkeley, Oct–Nov. 1983. Available at: http://foucault.info/documents/parrhesia (Accessed 22 June 2009).

Fraher, A. L. (2016). A toxic triangle of destructive leadership at Bristol Royal Infirmary: A study of organizational Munchausen syndrome by proxy. *Leadership, 12*(1), 34–52.

Freedman, L. (2011). Mental states and political decisions: Commentary on … psychiatry and politicians. *The Psychiatrist, 35*(4), 148–50.

Freud, S. (1914). *On narcissism: An introduction*. In J. Strachey et al. (trans.), *The standard edition of the complete psychological works of Sigmund Freud*, Vol. *XIV*. London: Hogarth Press.

Friedrich, R. (1991). The hybris of Odysseus. *The Journal of Hellenic Studies, 111*, 16–28.

Fukuyama, F. (1992). *The end of history and the last man*. New York: Free Press.

Furnham, A. (2010). *The elephant in the boardroom: The psychology of leadership derailment*. Bracknell: Palgrave Macmillan.

Fuxjager, M. J. and Marler, C. A. (2009). How and why the winner effect forms: Influences of contest environment and species differences. *Behavioral Ecology, 21*(1), 37–45.

Gabriel, Y. (2000). *Storytelling in organizations: Facts, fictions, and fantasies*. Oxford: Oxford University Press.

Gabriel, Y. and Connell, N. A. D. (2010). Co-creating stories: Collaborative experiments in storytelling. *Management Learning, 41*(5), 507–23.

Gaglio, C. M. (2004). The role of mental simulations and counterfactual thinking in the opportunity identification process. *Entrepreneurship Theory and Practice, 28*(6), 533–52.

Galasso, A. and Simcoe, T. S. (2011). CEO overconfidence and innovation. *Management Science, 57*(8), 1469–84.

Galinsky, A. D., Magee, J. C., Inesi, M. E. and Gruenfeld, D. H. (2006). Power and perspectives not taken. *Psychological Science, 17*(12), 1068–74.

Garrard, P. (2009). Cognitive archaeology: Uses, methods, and results. *Journal of Neurolinguistics, 22*(3), 250–65.

Garrard, P. (2016). On the linguistics of power (and the power of linguistics). In P. Garrard and G. Robinson (eds) *The intoxication of power: Interdisciplinary perspectives.* Basingstoke: Palgrave Macmillan, pp. 135–54.

Garrard, P. (ed.) (2018). *The leadership hubris epidemic: Biological roots and strategies for prevention.* Basingstoke: Palgrave Macmillan.

Garrard, P. and Robinson, G. (eds) (2016). *The intoxication of power: Interdisciplinary insights.* Basingstoke: Palgrave Macmillan.

Garrard, P., Maloney, L. M., Hodges, J. R. and Patterson, K. (2004). The effects of very early Alzheimer's disease on the characteristics of writing by a renowned author. *Brain, 128*(2), 250–60.

Garrard, P., Rentoumi, V., Lambert, C. and Owen, D. (2014). Linguistic biomarkers of Hubris Syndrome. *Cortex, 55,* 167–81.

Garrett, T. M. (2004). Whither challenger, wither Columbia: Management decision making and the knowledge analytic. *The American Review of Public Administration, 34*(4), 389–402.

Gellman, B. (2008). *Angler: The Cheney Vice Presidency.* New York: Penguin.

Ghaemi, S. N., Liapis, C. and Owen, D. (2016). The psychopathology of power. In P. Garrard and G. Robinson (eds) *The intoxication of power: Interdisciplinary perspectives.* Basingstoke: Palgrave Macmillan, pp. 17–37.

Giddens, A. (1984). *The constitution of society: Outline of the structuration theory.* Cambridge: Polity.

Gilovich, T., Griffin, D. and Kahneman, D. (eds) (2002). *Heuristics and biases: The psychology of intuitive judgment.* Cambridge: Cambridge University Press.

Graen, G. B. and Uhl-Bien, M. (1995). Relationship-based approach to leadership: Development of leader–member exchange (LMX) theory of leadership over 25 years – Applying a multi-level multi-domain perspective. *The Leadership Quarterly, 6*(2), 219–47.

Graf, F. (2006). Myth in Ovid. In P. Hardie (ed.) *Cambridge Companion to Ovid.* Cambridge: Cambridge University Press, pp. 108–21.

Graham, B. (2009). *By his own rules.* New York: Public Affairs.

Gray, D. E. (2007). Facilitating management learning: Developing critical reflection through reflective tools. *Management Learning, 38*(5), 495–517.

Greene, J. and Haidt, J. (2002). How (and where) does moral judgment work? *Trends in Cognitive Sciences, 6*(12), 517–23.

Hackman, R. J. and Oldham, G. R. (1980). *Work redesign*. Reading, MA: Addison-Wesley.

Haleblian, J. and Finkelstein, S. (1999). The influence of organizational acquisition experience on acquisition performance: A behavioral learning perspective. *Administrative Science Quarterly, 44*(1), 29–56.

Hall, E. (2015). *Introducing the Ancient Greeks*. London: Bodley Head.

Halse, C., Honey, A. and Boughtwood, D. (2007). The paradox of virtue: (Re) thinking deviance, anorexia and schooling. *Gender and Education, 19*(2), 219–35.

Ham, C., Seybert, N. and Wang, S. (2018). Narcissism is a bad sign: CEO signature size, investment, and performance. *Review of Accounting Studies, 23*(1), 234–64.

Hambrick, D. C. (2007). Upper echelons theory: An update. *Academy of Management Review, 32*(2), 334–43.

Hambrick, D. C. and Jackson, E. M. (2000). Outside directors with a stake: The linchpin in improving governance. *California Management Review, 42*(4), 108–27.

Hambrick, D. C. and Mason, P. A. (1984). Upper echelons: The organization as a reflection of its top managers. *Academy of Management Review, 9*(2), 193–206.

Hansen, W. F. (2004). *Handbook of classical mythology*. Oxford: Oxford University Press.

Hård, M. and Jamison, A. (2013). *Hubris and hybrids: A cultural history of technology and science*. Abingdon: Routledge.

Hargadon, A. B. and Douglas, Y. (2001). When innovations meet institutions: Edison and the design of the electric light. *Administrative Science Quarterly, 46*(3), 476–501.

Haynes, K. T., Hitt, M. A. and Campbell, J. T. (2015). The dark side of leadership: Towards a mid-range theory of hubris and greed in entrepreneurial contexts. *Journal of Management Studies, 52*(4), 479–505.

Hayward, M. L. A. (2007). *Ego check: Why executive hubris is wrecking companies and careers and how to avoid the trap*. Wokingham: Kaplan Publishing.

Hayward, M. and Hambrick, D. (1997). Explaining the premiums paid for large acquisitions: Evidence of CEO hubris. *Administrative Science Quarterly, 42*, 103–27.

Hayward, M. L., Forster, W. R., Sarasvathy, S. D. and Fredrickson, B. L. (2010). Beyond hubris: How highly confident entrepreneurs rebound to venture again. *Journal of Business Venturing, 25*(6), 569–78.

Hayward, M. L., Rindova, V. P. and Pollock, T. G. (2004). Believing one's own press: The causes and consequences of CEO celebrity. *Strategic Management Journal, 25*(7), 637–53.

Hayward, M. L., Shepherd, D. A. and Griffin, D. (2006). A hubris theory of entrepreneurship. *Management Science, 52*, 160–72.

Heaton, J. B. (2002). Managerial optimism and corporate finance. *Financial Management, 31*(2), 33–45.

Heeger, D. J. and Ress, D. (2002). What does fMRI tell us about neuronal activity? *Nature Reviews Neuroscience, 3*(2), 142–51.

Helin, J., Hernes, T., Hjorth, D. and Holt, R. (eds) (2014). *The Oxford handbook of process philosophy and organization studies.* Oxford: Oxford University Press.

Henderson, D. J., Liden, R. C., Glibkowski, B. C. and Chaudhry, A. (2009). LMX differentiation: A multilevel review and examination of its antecedents and outcomes. *The Leadership Quarterly, 20*(4), 517–34.

Heracleous, L. and Luh Luh, L. (2002). Who wants to be a competent director? An evaluation tool of directors' knowledge of governance principles and legal duties. *Corporate Governance: The International Journal of Business in Society, 2*(4), 17–23.

Hernes, T. (2014). *A process theory of organizations.* Oxford: Oxford University Press.

Highhouse, S. (2001). Judgement and decision making research. In N. Anderson, D. S. Ones, H. K. Sinangil and C. Viswesvaran (eds) *Handbook of industrial, work and organizational psychology, Vol. 2: Organizational psychology.* Thousand Oaks, CA: Sage, pp. 314–31.

Hiller, N. J. and Hambrick, D. C. (2005). Conceptualizing executive hubris: The role of (hyper) core self-evaluations in strategic decision-making. *Strategic Management Journal, 26*(4), 297–319.

Hines, T. (1987). Left brain/right brain mythology and implications for management and training. *Academy of Management Review, 12*(4), 600–6.

Hmieleski, K. M. and Baron, R. A. (2008). When does entrepreneurial self-efficacy enhance versus reduce firm performance? *Strategic Entrepreneurship Journal, 2*(1), 57–72.

Hogan, R. (2009). *Hogan development survey manual.* Tulsa, OK: Hogan Assessment Systems.

Hogan, R. and Hogan, J. (2001). Assessing leadership: A view from the dark side. *International Journal of Selection and Assessment, 9*(1–2), 40–51.

Hogan, R. and Kaiser, R. B. (2005). What we know about leadership. *Review of General Psychology, 9*(2), 169–80.

Hogan, J., Hogan, R. and Kaiser, R. B. (2010). Management derailment. *APA Handbook of Industrial and Organizational Psychology, 3*, 555–75.

Hogeveen, J., Inzlicht, M. and Obhi, S. S. (2014). Power changes how the brain responds to others. *Journal of Experimental Psychology: General, 143*(2), 755–62.

Homans, G. C. (1961). *Social behaviour.* New York: Harcourt Brace Jovanovich.

Hoogenboezem, J. (2007). Brinkmanship and beyond: The political leadership of Franklin D. Roosevelt. *Leadership, 3*(2), 131–48.

Horne, A. (2015). *Hubris: The tragedy of war in the twentieth century.* London: Weidenfeld & Nicholson.

House, R. J. and Howell, J. M. (1992). Personality and charismatic leadership. *The Leadership Quarterly, 3*(2), 81–108.

House, R. J., Spangler, W. D. and Woycke, J. (1991). Personality and charisma in the US presidency: A psychological theory of leader effectiveness. *Administrative Science Quarterly*, *36*, 364–96.

Hoye, R. (2004). Leader–member exchanges and board performance of voluntary sport organizations. *Nonprofit Management and Leadership*, *15*(1), 55–70.

Huff, A. S. (1990). *Mapping strategic thought*. Chichester: John Wiley & Sons.

Iacoboni, M. (2009). Imitation, empathy, and mirror neurons. *Annual Review of Psychology*, *60*, 653–70.

Iacoboni, M., Molnar-Szakacs, I., Gallese, V., Buccino, G., Mazziotta, J. C. and Rizzolatti, G. (2005). Grasping the intentions of others with one's own mirror neuron system. *PLoS Biol*, *3*, e79.

Isikoff, M. and Korn, D. (2006). *Hubris: The inside story of spin, scandal, and the selling of the Iraq War*. New York: Three Rivers Press.

Ismail, A. (2008). Which acquirers gain more, single or multiple? Recent evidence from the USA market. *Global Finance Journal*, *19*(1), 72–84.

Janis, I. L. (1982). *Groupthink* (2nd edn). Boston: Houghton Mifflin.

Janis, I. L. and Mann, L. (1977). *Decision making: A psychological analysis of conflict, choice, and commitment*. New York: Free Press.

Jones, S. and Gosling, J. (2011). *Nelson's way: Leadership lessons from the great commander*. London: Nicholas Brealey Publishing.

Judge, T. A., Erez, A., Bono, J. E. and Thoresen, C. J. (2003). The core self-evaluations scale: Development of a measure. *Personnel Psychology*, *56*(2), 303–31.

Judge, T. A., Locke, E. A., Durham, C. C. and Kluger, A. N. (1998). Dispositional effects on job and life satisfaction: The role of core evaluations. *Journal of Applied Psychology*, *83*(1), 17–34.

Judge, T. A., Piccolo, R. F. and Kosalka, T. (2009). The bright and dark sides of leader traits: A review and theoretical extension of the leader trait paradigm. *The Leadership Quarterly*, *20*(6), 855–75.

Kahneman, D. and Klein, G. (2009). Conditions for intuitive expertise: A failure to disagree. *American Psychologist*, *64*(6), 515–26.

Kahneman, D. and Lovallo, D. (1993). Timid choices and bold forecasts: A cognitive perspective on risk taking. *Management Science*, *39*(1), 17–31.

Kaiser, R. B., Hogan, R. and Craig, S. B. (2008). Leadership and the fate of organizations. *American Psychologist*, *63*(2), 96–110.

Kaye, M. (1995). Organisational myths and storytelling as communication management: A conceptual framework for learning an organisation's culture. *Journal of Management & Organization*, *1*(2), 1–13.

Keltner, D. (2017). *The power paradox: How we gain and lose influence*. London: Penguin.

Keltner, D., Gruenfeld, D., Galinsky, A. and Kraus, M. W. (2010). Paradoxes of power: Dynamics of the acquisition, experience, and social regulation of social power.

In A. Guinote and T. K. Vescio (eds) *The social psychology of power*. New York: Guilford Press, pp. 177–208.

Kershaw, I. (1998). *Hitler 1889–1936: Hubris*. London: Penguin.

Kershaw, I. (2000). *Hitler 1936–1945: Nemesis*. London: Penguin.

Kets de Vries, M. (1990). The organisational fool: Balancing a leader's hubris. *Human Relations*, *43*(8), 751–70.

Kets de Vries, M. (1993). *Leaders, fools, and imposters: Essay on the psychology of leadership*. San Francisco: Jossey-Bass.

Kets de Vries, M. (2003). Doing an Alexander: Lessons on leadership by a master conqueror. *European Management Journal*, *21*(3), 370–5.

Kets de Vries, M. (2016). The Hubris Factor in leadership. In P. Garrard and G. Robinson (eds) *The intoxication of power: Interdisciplinary insights*. Basingstoke: Palgrave Macmillan, pp. 89–99.

Kets de Vries, M. F. K. (2005). *Lessons on leadership by terror: Finding Shaka Zulu in the attic*. Cheltenham: Edward Elgar.

Kets de Vries, M. F. R. and Miller, D. (1997). Narcissism and leadership: An object relations perspective. In R. P. Vecchio (ed.) *Leadership: Understanding the dynamics of power and influence in organizations*. Notre Dame, IN: University of Notre Dame Press, pp. 194–214. (Reprinted from *Human Relations*, *38*(6), 1985, pp. 583–601.)

Keynes, J. M. (1936/2008). *General theory of employment, interest and money*. New Delhi: Atlantic.

Klein, K. J. and House, R. J. (1995). On fire: Charismatic leadership and levels of analysis. *The Leadership Quarterly*, *6*(2), 183–98.

Kramer, R. (2003). The harder they fall. *Harvard Business Review*, *81*(October), 58–66.

Krasikova, D. V., Green, S. G. and LeBreton, J. M. (2013). Destructive leadership: A theoretical review, integration, and future research agenda. *Journal of Management*, *39*(5), 1308–38.

Kroll, M. J., Toombs, L. A. and Wright, P. (2000). Napoleon's tragic march home from Moscow: Lessons in hubris. *The Academy of Management Executive*, *14*(1), 117–28.

Kuhnen, C. M. and Chiao, J. Y. (2009). Genetic determinants of financial risk taking. *PloS one*, *4*(2), e4362.

Kuhnen, C. M. and Knutson, B. (2005). The neural basis of financial risk taking. *Neuron*, *47*(5), 763–70.

Ladd, A. E. (2012). Pandora's well: Hubris, deregulation, fossil fuels, and the BP oil disaster in the Gulf. *American Behavioral Scientist*, *56*, 104–27.

Ladkin, D. (2006). The enchantment of the charismatic leader: Charisma reconsidered as aesthetic encounter. *Leadership*, *2*(2), 165–79.

Langer, E. J. (1975). The illusion of control. *Journal of Personality and Social Psychology*, *32*(2), 311–28.

Langley, A. (1999). Strategies for theorizing from process data. *Academy of Management Review*, *24*(4), 691–710.

Langley, A., Smallman, C., Tsoukas, H. and Van de Ven, A. H. (2013). Process studies of change in organization and management: Unveiling temporality, activity, and flow. *Academy of Management Journal*, *56*, 1–13.

Lansing, J. S. (2003). Complex adaptive systems. *Annual Review of Anthropology*, *32*(1), 183–204.

Lattimore, R. A. (1964). *Story patterns in Greek tragedy* (Vol. *146*). Ann Arbor, MI: University of Michigan Press.

Leavitt, H. J. (1965) Applied organizational change in industry: Structural, technological and humanistic approaches. In J. G. March (ed.) *Handbook of organizations*. Chicago: Rand McNally & Co., pp. 1144–70.

Lee, N., Senior, C. and Butler, M. J. (2012). The domain of organizational cognitive neuroscience: Theoretical and empirical challenges. *Journal of Management*, *38*(4), 921–31.

Levenson H. (1981). Differentiating among internality, powerful others, and chance. In H. M. Lefcourt (ed.) *Research with the locus of control construct*. New York: Academic Press, pp. 15–63.

Leveson, N., Dulac, N., Marais, K. and Carroll, J. (2009). Moving beyond normal accidents and high reliability organizations: A systems approach to safety in complex systems. *Organization Studies*, *30*(2–3), 227–49.

Lewis, M. W. (2000). Exploring paradox: Toward a more comprehensive guide. *Academy of Management Review*, *25*(4), 760–76.

Lewis, M. W. and Smith, W. K. (2014). Paradox as a metatheoretical perspective: Sharpening the focus and widening the scope. *The Journal of Applied Behavioral Science*, *50*(2), 127–49.

Li, J. and Tang, Y. (2010). CEO hubris and firm risk taking in China: The moderating role of managerial discretion. *Academy of Management Journal*, *53*, 45–68.

Liden, R. C., Wayne, S. J. and Stilwell, D. (1993). A longitudinal study on the early development of leader–member exchanges. *Journal of Applied Psychology*, *78*(4), 662–74.

Lieberman, M. D. (2007). Social cognitive neuroscience: A review of core processes. *Annual Review of Psychology*, *58*(1), 259–89.

Lieberman, M. D., Jarcho, J. M. and Satpute, A. B. (2004). Evidence-based and intuition-based self-knowledge: An fMRI study. *Journal of Personality and Social Psychology*, *87*(4), 421–35.

Lin, B. X., Michayluk, D., Oppenheimer, H. R. and Reid, S. F. (2008). Hubris amongst Japanese bidders. *Pacific-Basin Finance Journal*, *16*(1), 121–59.

Lindebaum, D. and Zundel, M. (2013). Not quite a revolution: Scrutinizing organizational neuroscience in leadership studies. *Human Relations*, *66*(6), 857–77.

Lorsch, J. W. (1995). Empowering the Board. *Harvard Business Review*, Jan.–Feb.: 107–17.

Lowenstein, R. (2000). *When genius failed: The rise and fall of Long Term Capital Management.* New York: Random House.

Maccoby, M. (2000). Narcissistic leaders: The incredible pros, the inevitable cons. *Harvard Business Review, 78*(1), 68–78.

McClelland, D. C. and Burnham, D. H. (1976). Power is the great motivator. *Harvard Business Review,* March–April, 100–10.

MacDowell, D. M. (1976). Hybris in Athens. *Greece & Rome, 23*(1), 14–31.

McElroy, T. and Dowd, K. (2007). Susceptibility to anchoring effects: How openness-to-experience influences responses to anchoring cues. *Judgment and Decision Making, 2,* 48–53.

MacIntye, A. (1984). *After virtue: A study in moral theory.* Notre Dame, IN: University of Notre Dame Press.

MacKay, R. B. and Chia, R. (2013). Choice, chance, and unintended consequences in strategic change: A process understanding of the rise and fall of NorthCo Automotive. *Academy of Management Journal, 56,* 208–30.

McKenna, F. P. (1993). It won't happen to me: Unrealistic optimism or illusion of control? *British Journal of Psychology, 84*(1), 39–50.

McLellan, S. (2008). *What happened: Inside the Bush Administration White House and Washington's culture of deception.* New York: Public Affairs.

Majumdar, S. K., Moussawi, R. and Yaylacicegi, U. (2010). Is the efficiency doctrine valid? An evaluation of US local exchange telecommunications company mergers. *Info, 12*(5), 23–41.

Malmendier, U. and Tate, G. (2005a). CEO overconfidence and corporate investment. *The Journal of Finance, 60*(6), 2661–700.

Malmendier, U. and Tate, G. (2005b). Does overconfidence affect corporate investment? CEO overconfidence measures revisited. *European Financial Management, 11,* 649–59.

Malmendier, U. and Tate, G. (2009). Superstar CEOs. *The Quarterly Journal of Economics, 124,* 1593–638.

March, J. G. and Shapira, Z. (1987). Managerial perspectives on risk and risk taking. *Management Science, 33*(11), 1404–18.

Marquand, D. (2007). The pitfalls of pride. *New Statesman,* 3 September, 46–7.

Martin, R., Guillaume, Y., Thomas, G., Lee, A. and Epitropaki, O. (2016). Leader–member exchange (LMX) and performance: A meta-analytic review. *Personnel Psychology, 69*(1), 67–121.

Mason, R. O. (2004). Lessons in organizational ethics from the Columbia disaster: Can a culture be lethal? *Organizational Dynamics, 33*(2), 128–42.

Midgley, M. (2004). *The myths we live by.* Abingdon: Routledge.

Miller, C. C. and Ireland, R. D. (2005). Intuition in strategic decision making: Friend or foe in the fast-paced 21st century? *The Academy of Management Executive, 19,* 19–30.

Miller, D. (1990). *The Icarus paradox: How excellent organizations can bring about their own downfall.* New York: Harper Business.

Miller, D. (1992). The Icarus paradox: How exceptional companies bring about their own downfall. *Business Horizons*, Jan.–Feb., 24–35.

Miller, D. T. and Ross, M. (1975). Self-serving biases in the attribution of causality: Fact or fiction? *Psychological Bulletin, 82*(2), 213–25.

Miller, J. C. (2016). *Ground rules: Words of wisdom from the partnership letters of the world's greatest investor.* New York: HarperCollins.

Minichilli, A., Gabrielsson, J. and Huse, M. (2007). Board evaluations: Making a fit between the purpose and the system. *Corporate Governance: An International Review, 15*(4), 609–22.

Miron-Spektor, E., Ingram, A., Keller, J., Smith, W. and Lewis, M. (2017). Microfoundations of organizational paradox: The problem is how we think about the problem. *Academy of Management Journal, 61*(1), 26–45.

Mishel, L. and Schieder, J. (2017). *CEO pay remains high relative to the pay of typical workers and high-wage earners.* Washington, DC: Economic Policy Institute.

Mitchell, D. and Massoud, T. G. (2009). Anatomy of failure: Bush's decision-making process and the Iraq war. *Foreign Policy Analysis, 5*, 265–86.

Morford, M. P. and Lenardon, R. J. (1999). *Classical mythology.* Oxford: Oxford University Press.

Morgan, M. (2017). *Hubris: 'Intoxicated with power? What, me?'* Cardiff: AcademiWales.

Moses, J. (2007). *Oneness: Great principles shared by all religions* (with an Introduction by the Dalai Lama). New York: Ballantine Books.

Mumford, E. (2006). The story of socio-technical design: Reflections on its successes, failures and potential. *Information Systems Journal, 16*, 317–42.

Myers, D. G. (2002). *Intuition: Its powers and perils.* New Haven, CT: Yale University Press.

Naish, K. R. and Obhi, S. S. (2015). Self-selected conscious strategies do not modulate motor cortical output during action observation. *Journal of Neurophysiology, 114*(4), 2278–84.

Neal, C. S. (2014). *Taking down the lion: The triumphant rise and tragic fall of Tyco's Dennis Kozlowski.* New York: Macmillan.

Nester, W. (2013). Why did Napoleon do it? Hubris, security dilemmas, brinksmanship, and the 1812 Russian campaign. *Diplomacy & Statecraft, 24*(3), 353–64.

Nevicka, B., De Hoogh, A. H., Van Vianen, A. E., Beersma, B. and McIlwain, D. (2011). 'All I need is a stage to shine': Narcissists' leader emergence and performance. *The Leadership Quarterly, 22*(5), 910–25.

Newcombe, M. J. and Ashkanasy, N. M. (2002). The role of affect and affective congruence in perceptions of leaders: An experimental study. *The Leadership Quarterly, 13*(5), 601–14.

Nixon, M. (2016). *Pariahs: Hubris, reputation, and organizational crises.* Faringdon: Libri.

Obhi, S. S., Hogeveen, J. and Pascual-Leone, A. (2011). Resonating with others: The effects of self-construal type on motor cortical output. *Journal of Neuroscience, 31*(41), 14531–5.

O'Connor, E. S. (1995). Paradoxes of participation: Textual analysis and organizational change. *Organization Studies, 16*(5), 769–803.

Offstein, E. H., Madhavan, R. and Gnyawali, D. R. (2006). Pushing the frontier of LMX research: The contribution of triads. In G. B. Graen and J. A. Graen (eds) *Sharing network leadership.* Greenwich, CT: Information Age Publishing, pp. 95–118.

Osnos, E. (2017). Doomsday prep for the super rich. *The New Yorker Magazine,* 30 January.

Otazo, K. (2018) Preventing and using hubris in leaders. In P. Garrard (ed.) *The leadership hubris epidemic: Biological roots and strategies for prevention.* Basingstoke: Palgrave, pp. 193–221.

Otway, L. J. and Vignoles, V. L. (2006). Narcissism and childhood recollections: A quantitative test of psychoanalytic predictions. *Personality and Social Psychology Bulletin, 32,* 104–16.

Ovid (2004). *Metamorphóses: A new verse translation by David Raeburn.* London: Penguin Books.

Owen, D. (2006). Hubris and nemesis in heads of government. *Journal of the Royal Society of Medicine, 99,* 548–51.

Owen, D. (2007). *The Hubris Syndrome: Bush, Blair and the intoxication of power.* Arlington, VA: Politico's Publishing.

Owen, D. (2008). Hubris Syndrome. *Clinical Medicine, 8,* 428–32.

Owen, D. (2011a). *In sickness and in power: Illness in heads of government during the last 100 years.* London: Methuen.

Owen, D. (2011b). Psychiatry and politicians: Afterword. *The Psychiatrist, 35,* 145–8.

Owen, D. (2012). *The Hubris Syndrome: Bush, Blair and the intoxication of power.* New edition. York: Methuen.

Owen, D. (2016). Hubris syndrome. *Enterprise Risk,* Winter, 20–4.

Owen, L. D. (2018). Heads of government, 'toe-holders' and time limits. In P. Garrard (ed.) *The leadership hubris epidemic.* Cham, Switzerland: Palgrave Macmillan, pp. 165–78.

Owen, D. and Davidson, J. (2009). Hubris Syndrome: An acquired personality disorder? A study of US presidents and UK prime ministers over the last 100 years. *Brain, 132*(5), 1396–1406.

Padilla, A., Hogan, R. and Kaiser, R. B. (2007). The toxic triangle: Destructive leaders, susceptible followers, and conducive environments. *The Leadership Quarterly, 18,* 176–94.

Pangarkar, N. and Lie, J. R. (2004). The impact of market cycle on the performance of Singapore acquirers. *Strategic Management Journal, 25*(12), 1209–16.

Papadimitropoulos, L. (2008). Xerxes' 'hubris' and Darius in Aeschylus' 'Persae'. *Mnemosyne, 61*(Fasc. 3), 451–8.

Parliamentary Commission on Banking Standards (2013). *'An accident waiting to happen': The failure of HBOS*. Available at: https://publications.parliament.uk/pa/jt201213/jtselect/jtpcbs/144/144.pdf (Accessed 20 June 2018).

Paulhus, D. L. and Williams, K. M. (2002). The dark triad of personality: Narcissism, Machiavellianism, and psychopathy. *Journal of Research in Personality, 36*(6), 556–63.

Paulhus, D. L., Harms, P. D., Bruce, M. N. and Lysy, D. C. (2003). The over-claiming technique: Measuring self-enhancement independent of ability. *Journal of Personality and Social Psychology, 84*(4), 890–904.

Pavlock, B. (1998). Daedalus in the labyrinth of Ovid's 'Metamorphoses'. *The Classical World, 92*(2): 141–57.

Pennebaker, J. W., Francis, M. E. and Booth, R. J. (2001). *Linguistic inquiry and word count: LIWC 2001*. Mahwah, NJ: Lawrence Erlbaum Associates.

Pennebaker, J. W., Mehl, M. R. and Niederhoffer, K. G. (2003). Psychological aspects of natural language use: Our words, our selves. *Annual Review of Psychology, 54*(1), 547–77.

Pentland, A. (2010). To signal is human: Real-time data mining unmasks the power of imitation, kith and charisma in our face-to-face social networks. *American Scientist, 98*(3), 204–11.

Pentland, A. and Heibeck, T. (2010). *Honest signals: How they shape our world*. Cambridge, MA: MIT Press.

Perman, R. (2013). *Hubris: How HBOS wrecked the best bank in Britain*. Edinburgh: Birlinn.

Perrow, C. (1984). *Normal accidents: Living with high-risk systems*. New York: Basic Books.

Peterson, R. L. (2007). Affect and financial decision-making: How neuroscience can inform market participants. *The Journal of Behavioral Finance, 8*(2), 70–8.

Petit, V. and Bollaert, H. (2012). Flying too close to the sun? Hubris among CEOs and how to prevent it. *Journal of Business Ethics, 108*(3), 265–83.

Pettigrew, A. M. (1997). What is a processual analysis? *Scandinavian Journal of Management, 13*(4), 337–48.

Picone, P. M., Dagnino, G. B. and Mina, A. (2014). The origin of failure: A multidisciplinary appraisal of the Hubris Hypothesis and proposed research agenda. *The Academy of Management Perspectives, 28*(4), 447–68.

Pincus, A. L. and Lukowitsky, M. R. (2010). Pathological narcissism and narcissistic personality disorder. *Annual Review of Clinical Psychology, 6*, 421–46.

Poole, W. (2005). *Milton and the idea of the fall*. Cambridge: Cambridge University Press.

Post, J. M. (1986). Narcissism and the charismatic leader–follower relationship. *Political Psychology, 7*, 675–88.

Post, J. M. (1993). Current concepts of the narcissistic personality: Implications for political psychology. *Political Psychology, 14*, 99–121.

Powell, C. (2012). *It worked for me: In life and leadership*. New York: Harper Perennial.

Puncochar, J. M. and Fox, P. W. (2004). Confidence in individual and group decision making: When 'two heads' are worse than one. *Journal of Educational Psychology, 96*(3), 582–91.

Radice, G. (2010). *Trio: Inside the Blair, Brown, Mandelson project*. London: IB Tauris & Co.

Ranft, A. L. and O'Neill, H. M. (2001). Board composition and high-flying founders: Hints of trouble to come? *The Academy of Management Executive, 15*(1), 126–38.

Rescher, N. (1996). *Process metaphysics: An introduction to process philosophy*. New York: SUNY Press.

Resick, C. J., Whitman, D. S., Weingarden, S. M. and Hiller, N. J. (2009). The bright-side and the dark-side of CEO personality: Examining core self-evaluations, narcissism, transformational leadership, and strategic influence. *Journal of Applied Psychology, 94*, 1365–81.

Reynolds, S. J. (2006). A neurocognitive model of the ethical decision-making process: Implications for study and practice. *Journal of Applied Psychology, 91*(4), 737–48.

Rinaldi, A. (2009). Homo economicus? Neuroeconomics and other disciplines aim to identify the biological traits governing our financial behaviour, but not without accompanying criticism. *EMBO Reports, 10*(8), 823–6.

Roberts, K. H. (1990a). Managing high reliability organizations. *California Management Review, 32*(4): 101–13.

Roberts, K. H. (1990b). Some characteristics of one type of high reliability organization. *Organization Science, 1*(2), 160–76.

Roberts, K. H. and Bea, R. G. (2001). When systems fail. *Organizational Dynamics, 29*(3), 179–91.

Robertson, D. C., Voegtlin, C. and Maak, T. (2017). Business ethics: The promise of neuroscience. *Journal of Business Ethics, 144*, 679–97.

Robertson, I. H. (2012). *The winner effect: How power affects your brain*. London: A&C Black.

Robertson, I. H. (2013). How power affects the brain. *Psychologist, 26*(3), 186–9.

Robinson, G. (2016). Making sense of hubris. In P. Garrard and G. Robinson (eds) *The intoxication of power: Interdisciplinary insights*. Basingstoke: Palgrave, pp. 1–16.

Robinson, J. L. and Topping, D. (2013). The rhetoric of power: A comparison of Hitler and Martin Luther King Jr. *Journal of Management Inquiry, 22*(2), 194–210.

Rock, D. (2008). SCARF: A brain-based model for collaborating with and influencing others. *NeuroLeadership Journal, 1*(1), 44–52.

Roiser, J. P., de Martino, B., Tan, G. C. Y., Kumaran, D., Seymour, B., Wood, N. W., and Dolan, R.J. (2009). A genetically mediated bias in decision making driven by failure of amygdala control. *Journal of Neuroscience, 29*(18), 5985–91.

Roll, R. (1986). The Hubris Hypothesis of corporate takeovers. *Journal of Business, 59*(2), 197–216.

Ronfeldt, D. (1994). *Beware the hubris–nemesis complex: A concept for leadership analysis*. Santa Monica, CA: RAND.

Rosenberg, M. (1965). *Sociey and the adolescent self-image*. Princeton, NJ: Princeton University Press.

Rosenthal, S. A. and Pittinsky, T. L. (2006). Narcissistic leadership. *The Leadership Quarterly*, *17*(6), 617–33.

Rost, K. and Osterloh, M. (2010). Opening the black box of upper echelons: Drivers of poor information processing during the financial crisis. *Corporate Governance: An International Review*, *18*(3), 212–33.

Rowley, H. (2011). *Franklin and Eleanor: An extraordinary marriage*. Melbourne: Melbourne University Publishing.

Russell, B. (1938/2004). *Power: A new social analysis*. London: Routledge.

Russell, B. (1946/2009). *A history of western philosophy*. London: Routledge.

Russell, B. (1956). *Portraits from memory and other essays*. New York: Simon & Schuster.

Russell, G. (2011). Psychiatry and politicians: The 'Hubris Syndrome'. *The Psychiatrist*, *35*(4), 140–5.

Sadler-Smith, E. (2016). Hubris in business and management research: A 30-year review of studies. In P. Garrard and G. Robinson (eds) *The intoxication of power: Interdisciplinary insights*. London: Palgrave Macmillan, pp. 39–74.

Sadler-Smith, E. and Shefy, E. (2004). The intuitive executive: Understanding and applying 'gut feel' in decision-making. *The Academy of Management Executive*, *18*, 76–91.

Sadler-Smith, E., Akstinaite, V., Robinson, G. and Wray, T. C. D. (2016). Hubristic leadership: A review. *Leadership*, *13*(5), 525–48.

Sadler-Smith, E., Robinson, G., Akstinaite, V. and Wray, T. (2019) Hubristic Leadership: Understanding the hazard and mitigating the risks. *Organizational Dynamics*. doi/10.1016/j.orgdyn.2018.05.007.

Saunders, F. C. (2015). Toward high reliability project organizing in safety-critical projects. *Project Management Journal*, *46*(3), 25–35.

Scandura, T. A. and Pellegrini, E. K. (2008). Trust and leader–member exchange: A closer look at relational vulnerability. *Journal of Leadership & Organizational Studies*, *15*(2), 101–10.

Schad, J., Lewis, M. W., Raisch, S. and Smith, W. K. (2016). Paradox research in management science: Looking back to move forward. *The Academy of Management Annals*, *10*(1), 5–64.

Schaubroeck, J. and Lam, S. S. (2002). How similarity to peers and supervisor influences organizational advancement in different cultures. *Academy of Management Journal*, *45*(6), 1120–36.

Schedlitzki, D., Jarvis, C. and MacInnes, J. (2015). Leadership development: A place for storytelling and Greek mythology? *Management Learning*, *46*(4), 412–26.

Schweiger, D. M., Sandberg, W. R. and Rechner, P. L. (1989). Experiential effects of dialectical inquiry, devil's advocacy and consensus approaches to strategic decision making. *Academy of Management Journal*, *32*(4), 745–72.

Schyns, B. and Schilling, J. (2013). How bad are the effects of bad leaders? A meta-analysis of destructive leadership and its outcomes. *The Leadership Quarterly, 24*, 138–58.

Senior, C., Lee, N. and Butler, M. (2011). Perspective–organizational cognitive neuroscience. *Organization Science, 22*(3), 804–15.

Shamir, B. and Howell, J. M. (1999). Organizational and contextual influences on the emergence and effectiveness of charismatic leadership. *The Leadership Quarterly, 10*(2), 257–83.

Shamir, B., House, R. J. and Arthur, M. B. (1993). The motivational effects of charismatic leadership: A self-concept based theory. *Organization Science, 4*(4), 577–94.

Shane, S. and Stuart, T. (2002). Organizational endowments and the performance of university start-ups. *Management Science, 48*(1), 154–70.

Shane, S. and Venkataraman, S. (2000). The promise of entrepreneurship as a field of research. *Academy of Management Review, 25*(1), 217–26.

Sharma, D. S. and Ho, J. (2002). The impact of acquisitions on operating performance: Some Australian evidence. *Journal of Business Finance & Accounting, 29*(1–2), 155–200.

Sheard, A. G., Kakabadse, N. K. and Kakabadse, A. P. (2012). Leadership hubris: Achilles' heel of success. In *Global elites*. Basingstoke: Palgrave Macmillan, pp. 308–31.

Shepherd, D. A. (2004). Educating entrepreneurship students about emotion and learning from failure. *Academy of Management Learning & Education, 3*(3), 274–87.

Shih, Y. C. and Hsu, B. J. (2009). Does stock mis-valuation differentiate the motives for takeovers? *Review of Pacific Basin Financial Markets and Policies, 12*(3), 545–66.

Shimizu, K. and Hitt, M. A. (2004). Strategic flexibility: Organizational preparedness to reverse ineffective strategic decisions. *The Academy of Management Executive, 18*(4), 44–59.

Shipman, A. S. and Mumford, M. D. (2011). When confidence is detrimental: Influence of overconfidence on leadership effectiveness. *The Leadership Quarterly, 22*, 649–65.

Simon, H. A. (1979). Rational decision making in business organizations. *The American Economic Review, 69*(4), 493–513.

Simon, H. A. (1987). Making management decisions: The role of intuition and emotion. *The Academy of Management Executive, 1*(1), 57–64.

Simon, M., Houghton, S. M. and Aquino, K. (2000). Cognitive biases, risk perception, and venture formation: How individuals decide to start companies. *Journal of Business Venturing, 15*(2), 113–34.

Simonton, D. K. (2006). Presidential IQ, openness, intellectual brilliance, and leadership: Estimates and correlations for 42 US chief executives. *Political Psychology, 27*, 511–26.

Simsek, Z., Heavey, C. and Veiga, J. J. F. (2010). The impact of CEO core self-evaluation on the firm's entrepreneurial orientation. *Strategic Management Journal, 31*(1), 110–19.

Sinha, P. N., Inkson, K. and Barker, J. R. (2012). Committed to a failing strategy: Celebrity CEO, intermediaries, media and stakeholders in a co-created drama. *Organization Studies, 33*(2), 223–45.

Sitkin, S. and Bies, R. J. (1993). The legalistic organization: Definitions, dimensions, and dilemmas. *Organization Science, 4,* 345–51.

Smith, J. E. (2016). *Bush.* New York: Simon and Schuster.

Snowden, D. J. and Boone, M. E. (2007). A leader's framework for decision making. *Harvard Business Review, 85*(11), 68–78.

Starbuck, W. H. and Milliken, F. J. (1988). Challenger: Fine-tuning the odds until something breaks. *Journal of Management Studies, 25*(4), 319–40.

Stein, M. (2003). Unbounded irrationality: Risk and organizational narcissism at Long Term Capital Management. *Human Relations, 56*(5), 523–40.

Stiglitz, J. (2008). The $3 trillion war. *New Perspectives Quarterly, 25,* 61–4.

Suedfeld, P. and Leighton, D. C. (2002). Early communications in the war against terrorism: An integrative complexity analysis. *Political Psychology, 23,* 585–99.

Sundaramurthy, C. and Lewis, M. (2003). Control and collaboration: Paradoxes of governance. *Academy of Management Review, 28,* 397–415.

Swap, W., Leonard, D., Shields, M. and Abrams, L. (2001). Using mentoring and storytelling to transfer knowledge in the workplace. *Journal of Management Information Systems, 18*(1), 95–114.

Sylves, R. T. and Comfort, L. K. (2012). The Exxon Valdez and BP Deepwater Horizon oil spills: Reducing risk in socio-technical systems. *American Behavioral Scientist, 56*(1), 76–103.

Taleb, N. N. (2007). *The black swan: The impact of the highly improbable.* London: Random House.

Taleb, N. N., Goldstein, D. G. and Spitznagel, M. W. (2009). The six mistakes executives make in risk management. *Harvard Business Review, 87,* 78–81.

Tang, Y., Li, J. and Yang, H. (2015). What I see, what I do: How executive hubris affects firm innovation. *Journal of Management, 41*(6), 1698–1723.

Tausczik, Y. R. and Pennebaker, J. W. (2010). The psychological meaning of words: LIWC and computerized text analysis methods. *Journal of Language and Social Psychology, 29*(1), 24–54.

Taylor, S. S., Fisher, D. and Dufresne, R. L. (2002). The aesthetics of management storytelling: A key to organizational learning. *Management Learning, 33*(3), 313–30.

Tetlock, P. E. and Boettger, R. (1989). Cognitive and rhetorical styles of traditionalist and reformist Soviet politicians: A content analysis study. *Political Psychology, 10,* 209–32.

Thaler, R. H. (ed.) (2005). *Advances in behavioural finance* (Vol. 2). Princeton, NJ: Princeton University Press.

Thaler, R. H. and Sunstein, C. R. (2008). *Nudge: Improving decisions about health, wealth, and happiness.* New Haven, CT: Yale University Press.

Thibaut, J. W. and Kelley, H. H. (1959). *The social psychology of groups.* New York: Wiley.

Thomaes, S., Bushman, B. J., De Castro, B. O. and Stegge, H. (2009). What makes narcissists bloom? A framework for research on the etiology and development of narcissism. *Development and Psychopathology, 21*(4), 1233–47.

Thompson, S. C., Armstrong, W. and Thomas, C. (1998). Illusions of control, underestimations and accuracy: A control heuristic explanation. *Psychological Bulletin, 123*, 143–61.

Thoroughgood, C. N. and Padilla, A. (2013). Destructive leadership and the Penn State scandal: A toxic triangle perspective. *Industrial and Organizational Psychology, 6*, 144–9.

Toulmin, S. (1990). Medical institutions and their moral constraints. In R. E. Bulger and S. J. Reiser (eds) *Integrity in health care institutions: Humane environments for teaching, inquiry, and healing*. Iowa City, IA: University of Iowa Press, pp. 21–32.

Tourish, D. (2018) Dysfunctional leadership in corporations. In P. Garrard (ed.) *The leadership hubris epidemic: Biological roots and strategies for prevention*. Basingstoke: Palgrave, pp. 137–162.

Tourish, D. (2013). *The dark side of transformational leadership: A critical perspective*. Hove: Routledge.

Tourish, D. and Vatcha, N. (2005). Charismatic leadership and corporate cultism at Enron: The elimination of dissent, the promotion of conformity and organizational collapse. *Leadership, 1*(4), 455–80.

Townsend, D. M., Busenitz, L. W. and Arthurs, J. D. (2010). To start or not to start: Outcome and ability expectations in the decision to start a new venture. *Journal of Business Venturing, 25*(2), 192–202.

Tracy, J. L. and Robins, R. W. (2014). Conceptual and empirical strengths of the authentic/hubristic model of pride. *Emotion, 14*, 33–7.

Trumbull, D. (2010). Hubris: A primal danger. *Psychiatry: Interpersonal and Biological Processes, 73*, 341–51.

Tsoukas, H. and Dooley, K. J. (2011). Introduction to the Special Issue: Towards the Ecological Style. *Organization Studies, 32*, 729–35.

Tversky, A. and Kahneman, D. (1981). The framing of decisions and the psychology of choice. *Science, 211*(4481), 453–8.

Ucbasaran, D., Shepherd, D. A., Lockett, A. and Lyon, S. J. (2013). Life after business failure: The process and consequences of business failure for entrepreneurs. *Journal of Management, 39*(1), 163–202.

Uhl-Bien, M. (2006). Relational leadership theory: Exploring the social processes of leadership and organizing. *The Leadership Quarterly, 17*(6), 654–76.

Valle, M. (1998). Buy high, sell low: Why CEOs kiss toads, and how shareholders get warts. *The Academy of Management Executive, 12*(2), 97–8.

Van den Berghe, L. A. and Levrau, A. (2004). Evaluating boards of directors: What constitutes a good corporate board? *Corporate Governance: An International Review, 12*(4), 461–78.

Van der Heijden, K. (2011). *Scenarios: The art of strategic conversation*. Chichester: John Wiley & Sons.

Vecchio, R. P. (2003). Entrepreneurship and leadership: Common trends and common threads. *Human Resource Management Review, 13*(2), 303–27.

Vega, M. and Ward, J. (2016). The social neuroscience of power and its links with empathy, cooperation and cognition. In P. Garrard and G. Robinson (eds) *The intoxication of power*. London: Palgrave Macmillan, pp. 155–74.

Vince, R. and Broussine, M. (1996). Paradox, defense and attachment: Accessing and working with emotions and relations underlying organizational change. *Organization Studies*, *17*(1), 1–21.

Waldman, D. A., Balthazard, P. A. and Peterson, S. J. (2011). Social cognitive neuroscience and leadership. *The Leadership Quarterly*, *22*(6), 1092–106.

Wales, W. J., Gupta, V. K. and Mousa, F. T. (2013). Empirical research on entrepreneurial orientation: An assessment and suggestions for future research. *International Small Business Journal*, *31*(4), 357–83.

Ward, J. (2012). *The student's guide to social neuroscience*. London: Psychology Press.

Wasserman, N. (2012). *The founder's dilemmas: Anticipating and avoiding the pitfalls that can sink a startup*. Princeton, NJ: Princeton University Press.

Wassermann, F. M. (1953). The speeches of King Archidamus in Thucydides. *The Classical Journal*, *48*(6), 193–200.

Weick, K. E. and Roberts, K. H. (1993). Collective mind in organizations: Heedful interrelating on flight decks. *Administrative Science Quarterly*, *38*, 357–81.

Weinstein, N. D. (1980). Unrealistic optimism about future life events. *Journal of Personality and Social Psychology*, *39*(5), 806–20.

Weinstein, N. D. and Klein, W. M. (1996). Unrealistic optimism: Present and future. *Journal of Social and Clinical Psychology*, *15*(1), 1–8.

Wessely, S. (2006). Commentary: The psychiatry of hubris. *Journal of the Royal Society of Medicine*, *99*(11), 552–3.

Wilson, M. (2003). *The difference between God and Larry Ellison: Inside Oracle Corporation*. New York: Harper Business.

Wise, V. M. (1977). Flight myths in Ovid's 'Metamorphoses': An interpretation of Phaethon and Daedalus. *Ramus*, *6*(1): 44–59.

Wong, E. M., Ormiston, M. E. and Tetlock, P. E. (2011). The effects of top management team integrative complexity and decentralized decision making on corporate social performance. *Academy of Management Journal*, *54*, 1207–28.

Woodward, B. (2002). *Bush at war*. New York: Simon and Schuster.

Woodward, B. (2004). *Plan of attack*. New York: Simon and Schuster.

Yan, H. K. (2009). A paradox of virtue: The Daodejing on virtue and moral philosophy. *Philosophy East and West*, *59*(2), 173–87.

Yukl, G. (1999). An evaluation of conceptual weaknesses in transformational and charismatic leadership theories. *The Leadership Quarterly*, *10*(2), 285–305.

Yukl, G. (2006). *Leadership in organizations*. Upper Saddle River, NJ: Prentice Hall.

INDEX

ABN Amro (bank), 40, 62
'abnormal behaviour' as distinct
    from pathology, 64
abnormal returns to stock, 76
absolute power, 36
abuse of power, 39–40
Achilles, 20, 32
acquisition of firms, 72–3, 76–8
Acton, Lord, 36
Aeschylus, 26–7, 36
Afghanistan invasion (2001), 129
age-related differences in
    people's behaviour, 44
aidos, 24
air travel, 93
Ajax, 32
Alexander I, Tsar of Russia, 28–9
al Qaeda, 129
Alzheimer's disease, 160
ambition in business, 22–3, 81, 83, 87, 92, 138,
    156, 167
American presidents, 10, 51
Amernic, J., 162
amygdala function, 46–7
Anderson, C., 39
Anderson, T.H., 131
'animal spirits', 48
Annan, Kofi, 133
anterior cingulate cortex (ACC), 47
'anticipatory compliance', 122, 125–7
Archidamus, King, 31–3
Aristotle, 25, 143, 172–3
artificial intelligence (AI), 17, 106–7
at-a-distance methods for observing
    hubris, 157–8
Athens and the Athenians, 25, 31–2
attributes of hubristic and charismatic
    leadership, 2–4
autocracy, 67
Avis Car Rental, 141
avoidance approaches, 156–73
'axis of evil' rhetoric, 122, 130

Babiak, P., 53
Bailey, Andrew, 169
balance, lack of, 24
Bank of America, 146

Bank of England, 165–8
banking sector, 62, 82–3, 102–3, 164–8
Barnard, J.W., 51–2
baseball organizations, 79
Bea, Robert, 97
'bear' markets, 44
Beaverbrook, Lord, 116
behavioural approach to hubristic
    leadership, 70–88
Behavioural Insights Team (BIT), 70
behavioural science, 70–1
'belonging paradoxes', 137, 141
Berglas, S., 13
Bergson, Henri, 144
Bernanke, Ben, xiii
Bezos, Jeff, 74
the Bible, 1, 33
'big data', 162
bin Laden, Osama, 128–9
bipolar disorder, 51–2, 57
Black-Scholes formula, 98, 101
'black swan blindness', 101–2
Blair, Tony, 6, 34, 51, 58–61,
    67, 114, 121, 130, 160–1
Blau, P.M., 111
Blix, Hans, 129
blowout preventer (BOP) system, 94, 97
board members: responsibilities of, 170;
    vigilance on the part of, 77–8, 88; see
    also insider directors; outside directors
Boeing (company), 153
Bonaparte, Napoleon, 19, 28–30
bookmakers, 45
'both/and' mindset, 136
bounce-backs, entrepreneurial, 86
bounded rationality, 72, 82
bovine spongiform
    encephalopathy (BSE), 107–8
Bristol Royal Infirmary, 119
British Petroleum (BP), 63, 93–7, 101,
    106, 108, 137, 162
Browne, John (Lord), 63, 95–6, 162
'bubbles', financial, 44
Buffett, Warren, 24
'bull' markets, 44
Burns, T.R., 108
Bush, George H.W., 124, 127–8

Bush, George W., 7, 34, 58–60,
    95–6, 120–30, 133
'Bush Doctrine', 128–9

cabinet government, 62, 67
Callaghan, James, 114
Cameron, David, 70
Campbell, Alastair, 114
Campbell, W.K., 10
capitulation to irrelevance or death
    by hubristic leaders, 148, 151
Carillion (company), 1
casinos, 45
Castro, Fidel, 34, 58, 119
'cautious restrainers', 124–7
celebrity status (CEO), 74–5, 95, 171
Challenger space-shuttle
    disaster (1986), 16, 82, 103
Chamberlain, Neville, 58
charisma and charismatic leadership,
    1–8, 14, 17, 28, 31; dark and bright
    sides of, 4–5, 7–8
charm and manipulation, leaders
    succeeding by means of, 142
Chemical Safety Board, US, 96
Cheney, Richard ('Dick'), 67, 96,
    123, 125, 127
chief executive officers (CEOs), 74–80; chairing
    boards, 77–8; loneliness and isolation of,
    51; remuneration of, 77, 171; suffering
    from depression, 52; superstar status of,
    74–5, 95, 171
Chilcot Inquiry, 34
CIA, 34
Churchill, Winston (and Churchillian
    tone), 51–2, 57, 60
classical economics, 72
climate change, 108
'clinging on' by hubristic leaders, 147–8, 171–2
Clinton, Bill, 124
Clinton, Hillary, 162
Clymene, 22
Coates, J., 38, *43*, 44
cognitive neuroscience, 37
Coles, A.J., 52
Collins, J., 146–8, 151–4
'colluders', 122–4, 127, 131
Columbia space-shuttle disaster
    (2003), 16, 82, 103, 137
Comfort, L.K., 97
Compaq (company), 153
complex adaptive systems, 106
'complexification' (Rescher), 153
complicity in the hubristic leadership
    process, 65

conducive context / environments (toxic
    triangle), 7, 15, 67, 119, 120, 127, 128,
    130, 133
confidence, advantages of 83;
    see also overconfidence
'conformers', 122, 127
Confucianism, 33
Conger, Jay, 2–3
contagion, financial, 98
Continental Baking, 141
'Cookie Monster study', 39
core self-evaluation (CSE), 79–80
corruption, 36–7
cortisol, 44
'cosmic order', 23
Craig, R., 162
Craig, S.B., 14
Crosby, Sir James, 165
cultural change, 170
cumulative abnormal returns, 76

Daedalus, 19, 22–24, 107, 139
Daimler (company), 7
Davidson, Jonathan, 51, 54–5, 57,
    65–6, 116, 121
decision-making processes and styles,
    12, 14, 43–9, 72, 82, 120, 131
'decoupling' trajectories (Miller), 140
Deepwater Horizon oil spillage, xiv, 16,
    63–4, 93–7, 103–8, 137, 154, 162–3
defensive behaviour, 137
Dell, Michael, 87, 114, 117
Delphic Oracle, 32
democratic governance, 67
denial of risk and peril, 147, 150
depressive disorders, 52, 57
'derailment' of leaders, 53–5, 61–2, 142
Desai, Meghnad (Lord), 99
destructive leaders (toxic triangle), 7, 55, *118*
destructive leadership, 2, 3, 7, 11, 14–17,
    118–120, 122, 137
destructive outcomes, 2–3, 7, 11, 14–17,
    122, 131–3, 136–9, 145, 153–4, 156
Dewey, John, 144
*Diagnostic and Statistical Manual
    of* Mental *Disorders* (APA), 9,
    11–12, 55, 64, 66
dictatorship, 67
DICTION text analysis program, 159
Digital Equipment Corporation, 153
Disney (company), 153
dopamine, 45–6
Dryden, John, 51
dyadic linkages, 112, 115–18
Dyson, James (Sir), 86

early warning signs of hubris, 53, 134,
143–4, 158, 161
economic behaviour,
determinants of 72
Economic Policy Institute
(Washington DC), 171
Eden, Anthony, 58
Edison, Thomas, 86
Ehrlich, Paul and Anne, 108
Eisenhower, Dwight, 51
Elkind, P., 96
Ellison, Larry, 10
emotional responses, 47
emotionally-charged narrative, 20
empathy, reduction in, 40–2
ENRON (company), 5
entrepreneurship, 80, 83–7
equilibrium, disturbance of, 24
escalation, pursuit of, 146–7
excess, going to, 138, 143, 173
'exchange rules', 111
executive education, 179
executive (CEO) remuneration,
156, *157*, 171
expectations, inflation of, 85
extreme events, 102–7

failure of businesses, 83–8; amongst
start-ups, 83; benefits from, 86–8
Falklands War (1982), 67–8, 161
Federal Reserve and Federal Reserve
Bank, 98, 100
Ferguson, N., 30
Financial Conduct Authority (FCA) and
Financial Services Authority (FSA), UK,
165–6, 169
Financial Security Board and Financial
Stability Board, US, 17, 106
Finkelstein, S., 4
Fiorina, Carly, 10
First World War, 117
'focusing' trajectories (Miller), 140
followers, 111, 114
Foucault, Michel, 65
founding of businesses, 85
Fox, P.W., 81
framing tasks and effects, 46–7
Frances, Allen, 11
'Frankenstein effect', 108
Franklin, Benjamin, 156
Freedman, L., 67
Freud, Sigmund (and Freudian
theory), 9, 34, 51, 158
Frisinger, Håkan, 117
Fukuyama, F., 128

Fuld, Richard J., xii–xiv, 7, 16
functional magnetic
resonance imaging (fMRI), 37–8

gambling, 45–6
Garrard, P., 71, 158, 160
Gasparino, Charlie, xiii
gender differences, 44, 167
Geneen, Harold S., 141
genetic factors, 46–8
Gerson, Michael, 130
global financial crisis, 62, 164
God, 121–2
Goldman Sachs, xii–xiv
Goodwin, Fred, 40, 62
governance, 13, 75, 78, 92, 136, 156, *157*,
164–169
Graham, Billy, 121
'grandstanding', 60
'grasping for salvation', 151
Greece, ancient, 144; *see also*
Athens and the Athenians
Greek myth and Greek tragedy,
8, 19–21, 24–5, 32–3
Greenspan, Alan, 100
'groupthink' effect, 81–2, 122,
127, 136–7, 147, 169
Gulf War (1990–91), 127
Gyllenhammar, Pehr, 117

Haghani, Victor, 98
Haliburton (company), 94, 97, 137
Halifax Bank of Scotland (HBOS), xiv,
102–3, 164–8
Hambrick, Donald, 73, 76, 82
Hansard, 158
hard-to-access groups, 157–8
Hare, R.D., 53
Harley Davidson (company), 150
Hassel, Karl, 148
Hayward, M., 73, 76, 84–5
Hayward, Tony, 94, 96
heads of government, physical
or mental illness of, 58–9
Hector, 20
hedge funds, 97
Hegel, G.W.F., 144
Heraclitus, 144
Herodotus, 26
Hewlett Packard (company), 153
high reliability organizations (HRO)
theory, 93, 163–4
Hilibrand, Lawrence, 98, 100
Hinduism, 33
Hitler, Adolf, 30–1

Hogan, J., 53, 142
Hogan, R., 50–3, 142
Homan, G.C., 111
'honest signals', 158
Hopkins, Harry, 118
hormones, 38, 43
Hornby, Andy, 165
Horne, Sir Alastair, 32
Howe, Sir Geoffrey, 60–1
Howe, Louis, 112, 117–18
hubris, xi, xiv–xv; collective, 63; dark side
    of, 4–8; definition of, 13; as a hazard for
    entrepreneurs, 84–5; in history, 26–32;
    immunity factors for, 62–3; measuring
    of, 79–81; and narcissistic leadership,
    1–2, 8–14; organizational, 97, 104–5,
    165, 168–70; paradox perspective on,
    135–43; process perspective on, 135,
    143–53; seen as an accident waiting
    to happen, 92–3, 105; in strategic
    management research, 76–8
Hubris Factor, 76–8, 171
Hubris Hypothesis, 12, 71–6;
    core features of, 73
'hubris–nemesis complex', 23
Hubris Syndrome, 6, 24, 50, 54–68, 111,
    121, 160–2; among business leaders,
    61–4; among political leaders, 58–61;
    antecedents of, 57; characteristics of,
    55–8; criticisms of the concept, 64–8;
    symptoms of, 55–7, 64
Huffington, Arianna, 86
Hughes, Ted, 22
humility, 24, 34, 138
Hussein, Saddam, 14, 52, 123–31
hybris, 20, 25, 44–5

Icarus, 20–4, 33
Icarus paradox, 139–41
illusion of control, 73–6, 88, 106
'in-groups' and 'out-groups',
    81–2, 112–14, 127
insider directors, 77–8
instinct, 134
integrating and building alliances,
    leaders succeeding by, 142
integrative complexity, 121–2
integrity, xii
intelligent restraint, 32, *33*, 72,
    124, 127, 129, 168
intentionality, 16
interconnectedness between systems, 102, 134
interdisciplinarity, 48
International Statistical Classification
    of Diseases (ICD), 64

intoxication with power, 5, 7, 16–17,
    38–42, 49–51, 55, 65, 112, 117, 172
intuition, 120–1, 127
'inventing' trajectories (Miller), 140
Iraq invasion (2003), xiv, 6–7, 34,
    59–60, 67, 119–33; conducive
    context for, 130
irrational exuberance, 37, 39, 44,
    72, 134, 167, 169
ISIS (organization), 120
ITT (company), 141, 154

James, William, 144
Janis, I.L., 122
Japanese manufacturers, 150–1
Jobs, Steve, 10, 74, 86
John Paul II, Pope, 133
Johnson, Lyndon B., 57
Jungian theory, 34

Kaiser, R.B., 14, 50–1
Kalanick, Travis, 1
Kanungo, R.N., 3
Kelley, H.H., 111
Kennedy, John F., 58
Kershaw, I., 30
Kets de Vries, M., 31
Khosrowshahi, Dara, 1
Kissinger, Henry, 51, 123
Kosovo War (1999), 6, 59, 161
Kozlowski, Denis, 36–7
Kristol, Irving, 128

Langley, A., 145–6
language, study of, 158–60
Law, Andrew Bonar, 113–17
Lay, Kenneth, 5
leader–member exchange (LMX) theory,
    111–12
leadership: dark side of, 2–5, 17; strengths
    and corresponding weaknesses of, 138–9;
    see also charismatic leadership; narcissistic
    leadership
'leadership trap', 141
'learning paradoxes', 137
Le Hand, Marguerite, 118
Lehman Brothers, xii–xiv
Leibniz, Gottfried, 144
LG (company), 148, 151
Libby, I. Lewis ('Scooter'), 123
Lincoln, Abraham, 51
Linguistic Inquiry and Word
    Count (LIWC) software, 159
linguistic markers, 157–62
Lloyd George, David, 58, 113–17

Lloyds Bank, 164–5
lock-in, 10, 148
Long Term Capital Management (LTCM),
    xiv, 16, 93, 97–108, 154, 163; human
    and technological resources at, 101
loss-avoidance system, 45
lotteries, 70–1
Lowenstein, R., 100
luck, xii, 84

MacDonald, Eugene F., 148–50
Machado, N., 108
Machiavellianism, 9
machine learning, 17, 106–7, 162
MacIntyre, Alasdair, 172
mad cow disease *see* bovine
    spongiform encephalopathy
Major, John, 160–1
Malinowski, Bronislaw, 111
malleability of charisma and hubris, 6
mania and manic behaviour, 45–6
Mao Zedong, 52
Mason, R.O., 82
Massoud, T.G., 122
mathematical finance, 93, 98, 163
Matthews, Ralph H.G., 148
Mattis, James, 11
mental illness, 51–4, 58
Meriwether, John, 98–9
Merton, Robert C., 98, 101–2
Midgley, Mary, 35, 107–8
military action, 130, 161
Miller, D., 139–41, 153–4
Milosevic, Slobodan, 34
mirror neurons, 40–1
mistakes, learning from, 87
Mitchell, D., 122
Mitterrand, François, 58
'money men', 172
motor-evoked potentials, 41
motor resonance, 41–2
Motorola (company), 146, 151
Murdoch, Iris, 160
Mussolini, Benito, 52
myth *see* Greek myth

Napoleon *see* Bonaparte
narcissism, 8–14, 40, 51, 65; dark side
    of, 9; definition of, 8, 13; 'grandiose'
    and 'vulnerable', 13; link with power,
    12–13; organizational, 99–101; and
    over-confidence, 12
narcissistic leadership, 1–2, 8–14, 17; strengths
    and weaknesses of, 10
narcissistic management, 76

narcissistic personality disorder
    (NPD), 9–13, 65
'nasty surprises', 16–17, 106–107
NatWest (bank), 62
National Aeronautics and Space
    Administration (NASA), US, 16, 82, 103–4
Nelson, Horatio, 19
nemesis, 6, 19, 27–34, 55, 60–2;
    in classical mythology, 31–2
Némesis, 33–4
neoconservatism, 7, 127–8
Nester, W., 29
neural pathways, 45
neural substrates, 37, 40–1
'neuromania', 38
neuroscience, 37–8, 46–9, 160
Nietzsche, Friedrich, 86
Nixon, Richard M., 51, 58
'normal accidents theory', 93
Northern Rock (bank), 164
'nudge' concept, 70

Obama, Barack, 95–6
Odysseus, 32
oil spills, 93–7; *see also Deepwater
    Horizon* oil spillage
onset of hubris, 161
'opaque' models, 17
Operation Barbarossa, 30
oppositional tendencies, 136
optimism, 74
organizational approach to hubris, 90–108;
    role of organizational
    sub-systems in, 92
organizational cognitive neuroscience
    (OCN), 37
organizational culture, 63, 94, 103, 154,
    164–71
outside directors, 167
over-claiming, 12
over-confidence, 12, 17, 22–5, 44–5, 48,
    53, 60, 63, 68, 71–4, 81–8, 92, 97–100,
    107, 111, 131, 133, 137–9, 147, 167–72;
    lessons to be learnt from, 85–7
Ovid, 8, 19–23
Owen, David (Lord), 54–8, 62–6,
    112, 116, 121, 162

Padilla, A., 7, 118
Page, Larry, 10
paradox: definition, 136; organizational, 137
paradox of hubristic leadership, 138–43, 173;
    at leader level, 142–3; at the organization
    level, 139–41
paradox perspective on hubris, 135–43, 153

Parliamentary Commission on
    Banking Standards (PCBS), 165–6
parrhesia, 65
Paulson, Hank, xiv
Paulus, Delroy L., 159
Peirce, Charles Sanders, 144
Peloponesian War, 31–2
Penn State scandal, 119
Pennebaker, J.W., 159
Pentland, A., 158
Perle, Richard, 128
Perrow, Charles, 92–3, 162–3
personality disorders, 9, 50–2, 57, 64–5
personality traits, 64; the 'Big Five', 9
personalization, 5, 7, 17
Pettigrew, A.M., 145
Phaethon, 20–3, 33
Phoebus, 22, 23
phronesis, 143
Plato, 135
polarized thinking, 137–8
political leaders, 158
positive attitude, xii
Powell, Colin, 123–31
power: disorders of the possession
    of, 57; motivation of need for, 13
practical wisdom, 172–3
premiums paid in acquiring
    other firms, 72–3, 76–8
pride, 'hubristic' and 'authentic', 81
process, definition of, 145
process ontology, strong, 144
process ontology, weak, 144
process perspective on hubristic
    leadership, 135, 143–53
process philosophy, 144–6
processes, owned, 144
processes, unowned, 144, 145, 153
processual analysis,
    research strategies for, 145–6
prudent leaders, 172
Prudential Regulation Authority, 165–6
psychological constructs, 79
psychopathy, 9, 53
Puncochar, J.M., 81
Putin, Vladimir, 133

The Queen, xi, 71

RAND Corporation, 34
rationality, 72
Reagan, Ronald, 124, 162
recklessness, 7–8, 36, 44, 67–8,
    77, 111, 139, 165, 167
relational approach to hubrism, 110–34

Rescher, N., 144, 145, 153
resilience in the face of business failure, 86
reward systems, xii, 45
Rice, Condoleezza, 67, 123–7
risk aversion, 47–8, 52
risky behaviours, 36, 45–8, 63–4, 76, 78,
    88, 94–5, 102, 106, 163, 166–7
Roberts, K.H., 163
Robinson, G., 68
Rodchenkov, Grigory, 65
Roll, Richard, 71–3, 76, 83
Roosevelt, Franklin D., 112, 117–18
Roosevelt, Theodore, 57
Royal Bank of Scotland (RBS), xiv,
    40, 62, 154, 164
Rubbermaid (company), 146
Rumsfeld, Donald, 123–4, 127–31
Russell, Bertrand, xi, 39, 50, 55
Russell, G., 64, 66
Russia, 28–30, 65

'scaling the heights', 148
scapegoating, 137
Scholes, Myron, 98–102
Schrempp, Jürgen, 7
self-aggrandizing, 146
self-confidence, 81
self-efficacy, 87
self-obsession, 8–9, 51
September 11th 2001 (9/11) attacks,
    7, 60, 122, 127–33
serotonin, 46
servant leadership style, 35
Shah of Iran, 58
Shakespeare, William, 70, 110
shareholder value, 5
Shelley, Mary, 108
Sheraton Hotels, 141
Sierra Leone, 161
Simon, Herbert, 72
situational nature of charisma
    and of hubristic leadership, 7
Skilling, Jeffrey, 5
Smith, J.E., 120, 125–6
social cognitive neuroscience (SCN), 37
social exchange theory (SET), 111
social intuition, 126
social media, 8
socialized leadership, 5
sociotechnical systems (STS),
    90–2, 97, 101–5; subsystems of, 91
sophrosyne, 24, 32, 173
Soros, George, 10
Sorrell, Martin, 171
Spartans, 31–33

stages of degeneration, 146
Stein, M., 101
stereotyping, 42
Stevenson, Lord, 165
Stiglitz, Joseph, 119
stories, use of, 20
strategic management research, 76–80
strengths-into-weakness
      paradox, 138–43, 153–4
successes and failures, repetition of, 82
survival rates for new businesses, 84
susceptible followers (toxic triangle),
      3, 15, 74, *92, 118*, 119, 120, 122
Sylves, R.T., 97
systems thinking, 132

takeovers, 72–3
Taleb, Nasim Nicholas, 101–2
Taliban regime, 129
teamwork, xii
Tenet, George, 128
tensions, *positive* and *negative*, 136
testosterone, 43–4
Thaler, Richard H., 70, 72
Thatcher, Margaret, 58, 60–1,
      67–8, 114, 160–1
Thibaut, J.W., 111
'thinking big', 20, 25
Three Mile Island accident (1979), 92
Thucydides, 27, 33
Tierney, Dominic, 11
'time-bomb' trajectories (Miller), 140
'toe-holding' relationships, 110–18, 122–6, 133
Tolstoy, Leo, 28
top management teams (TMTs), 83
Topfer, Mort, 114, 117
'toxic triangle', 7, 15, 118–19, 131–3
Tracy, Jessica, 81
trade wars, 150
trading, financial, 43–4, 48
transcranial magnetic stimulation, 41
transformational leadership, 4, 79
transitory nature of hubris, 6
Transocean (company), 94, 97, 137
Trumbull, D., 33
Trump, Donald, President, 1, 11, 65,
      81, 150, 157–62
trust, 112, 114

Twitter, 161
Tyco International, 36

Uber (company), 1
unintended consequences, 16–17,
      23–4, 67, 91, 102, 106, 108,
      118, 134, 137, 145, 153–4, 156, 163, 172
United Nations, 127–30
'unreal' nature of senior
      leaders' jobs, 51
upper echelons theory (UET), 82–3

Valle, M., 73
Value at Risk (VaR) calculations, 98, 101
variant Creutzfeld-Jakob disease, 107
Vecchio, R.P., 87
venturing in business, 85–7
'venturing' trajectories (Miller), 140–1
vision, 10
volition, 16
Volvo (company), 117

'war on terror', 7, 129
Wassermann, F.M., 31
weapons of mass destruction, 124
Weber, Max, 3
Welch, Jack, 10, 74
'We-to-I' ratio, 161
'whistle-blowing', 65
Whitehead, Alfred North, 144
Whitelaw, William, 114
Wilson, Harold, 160
Wilson, Woodrow, 51
'winner effect', 42–3
Wolfe, Tom, 37
Wolfowitz, Paul, 67, 123–8
Woodward, Bob, 122–3, 128–9
WPP (advertising group), 171
Wright, Joseph S., 150

Xerxes, 19, 26–9

Yukl, G., 6

Zenith Radio Corporation, 148–54;
      process flowchart for the rise
      and fall of, 151–2
Zeus, 22